IF IT WAS RAINING PALACES I'D GET HIT BY THE DUNNY DOOR

IF IT WAS RAINING PALACES I'D GET HIT BY THE DUNNY DOOR

The Ashes travails of a whingeing Pom

NIGEL HENDERSON

IF IT WAS RAINING PALACES I'D GET HIT BY THE DUNNY DOOR
The Ashes Travails of a Whinging Pom

© 2007 Nigel Henderson
Nigel Henderson has asserted his rights in accordance with the Copyright, Designs and Patents Act 1988 to be identified as the author of this work.

Published By Pitch Publishing (Brighton) Ltd A2 Yeoman Gate Yeoman Way Worthing West Sussex BN13 3QZ
Email: info@pitchpublishing.co.uk Web: www.pitchpublishing.co.uk

First published 2007

A catalogue record for this book is available from the British Library.
10-digit ISBN: 1-9054110-8-1 13-digit ISBN: 978-1-9054110-8-5

Printed and bound in Great Britain by Cromwell Press
Cover design and layout by Swallow Company

For KP Henderson (1917-1985)

ACKNOWLEDGEMENTS

I am indebted to Sue Corbett, for trying to learn to understand cricket and tolerate it, if not falling head-over-heels in love with it; to Irene Henderson, for initial reading of the text and suggestions; to Robert Henderson, for staying up half the night to help me book tickets, creating the website and sundry technical advice; and, keeping it in the family, to Fiona Henderson, for driving us to the airport. Thanks are also extended to Patrick Kidd, for his enthusiasm in publishing excerpts that are contained in the book on his excellent creation, The Times's blog Line and Length, David Townsend for miscellaneous ticket brokering and good company in Melbourne and Sydney, Walter Gammie for the same and John McNamara, for helping me into a Paddington taxi after an evening on the tiles. I'm also grateful to Paul at Pitch for continuing to believe my books are worth publishing; Bill Swallow for designing the cover, twice over because of unforeseen circumstances, Jan Swallow for editing; and Graham Morris for the cover photograph.

Contents

You little humdinger, you

SYDNEY, 11 FEBRUARY 2007

PAUL Nixon threw himself into the crowd. Well, the tiny group of England spectators who, as the match had sped to its unlikely conclusion, had increasingly made themselves heard from the concourse in front of the Bill O'Reilly Stand; Andrew Flintoff performed a bow of "I'm not worthy-ness" in front of the same fans; and England, who had proved worthy only in the last ten days of their Ashes tour, and their followers, watered down to a sprinkling from the tidal wave who had travelled to see the country's defence of the urn, larked around in the latest downpour from the snarling Sydney skies that had threatened even at this late stage to ensure a third, and deciding, meeting with Australia in the Commonwealth Bank one-day series finals, at Adelaide. That was a place Flintoff and his men had good reason to want to avoid.

I knew all this only from the pictures in the Australian newspapers the following morning. Almost as soon as the clouds started to empty for the final time we turned from our seats five rows back in Bay 26 and scarpered for the cover of the overhanging Churchill Stand, eschewing celebration for shelter. I would have been happy to remain singing in the rain, revelling in the Australian spectators' unfamiliar experience of the shock of defeat – a feeling I had encountered more than once too often in the previous three months - but Sue, my cricket-phobe girlfriend, who, to her credit and my chauvinistic shame and surprise, was emerging from her aversion with a speed wholly unanticipated, had suffered one soaking too many on this day of changeable weather and changing fortunes. Having had the intricacies of the Duckworth/Lewis method explained – it was not a new form of contraception, I reassured her – she was ready for a warm bus, a dry white wine and the comfort of the sheets of even a two-star King's Cross hotel.

The photographs left me feeling a little peeved: had these supporters who frolicked so promiscuously with the "inadequate" Nixon, as one Australian journalist curiously referred to the veteran wicketkeeper, put in the hard yards? Had they been there in Canberra for the first day of the tour, when a combined Australian second and third team under the guise of the Prime Minister's XI dispatched England's tin-pot bowling to all parts of the Manuka Oval and raised the spectre that this touring team was not all it had been cracked up to be? In Brisbane, when Steve Harmison sent his first ball of the Ashes series to second slip, unfortunately not by way of an Australian bat? In Adelaide on the final day – I'm sorry, I can't bring myself to think about that just yet - or at the back-to-back Tests in Melbourne and Sydney, the jewels in the crown of the Antipodean sporting summer, which fell as good as four days short of their allotted running time?

I doubted it: the main contingent of the Barmy Army, particularly their ubiquitous trumpeter Billy Cooper, were reported to have been stood down from duty after the Twenty20 international on January 9 and though I thought I caught a glimpse of Vic Flowers, their cheerleader, waving his flag and gearing up for another chorus of

Everywhere We Go as I watched the first CB final from Melbourne on television, many, I was convinced, were Johnny-come-latelys, backpackers out for a day of fun before returning to a back-breaking week on the strawberry farm, or expats and would-be émigrés touched only peripherally by 90-odd days of cricket failure.

But I knew someone who had. Me. I had flown 15,000 miles, driven several thousand more and eaten more chicken parmigiana than was probably healthy for one man as England's ineptitude went from bad to terminal. I had sat upright on trains that traversed whole deserts in the time it took Australia to wrap up a Test match, watching diverse characters such as a Kiwi surfer-dude who tried to engage his fellow passengers in bouts of arm wrestling, including one who turned him down on the grounds that he had cerebral palsy. Shame. That might have been some spectator sport.

I had spent more than £5,000 of my own money, £5,000 of Sue's and slept in 26 separate beds that I shared with her and, quite often, a species of bug that left us both looking like refugees from a smallpox outbreak. I had watched bemused as the world-beaters of the Greatest Ashes Series In History (trademark: English newspapers, September 2005) became pale imitations of their illustrious selves in the Most Anticipated Ashes Series of All Time (copyright: the Australian media, November 2007).

On top of that fostered by my cricket team's failings on the field, I had invited scorn and ridicule, fighting verbal battles with Australian cousins that, in the face of mounting evidence and a hatstand of intimidating green and gold sombreros, could not be won; worse, my love of cricket, that delight in the game for its skills, techniques, aesthetic qualities, reversals of fortune and subplots, that outweighs any concerns about a result, had showed significant indications of being on the wane; worst of all, I had discovered that I really *was* a whingeing Pom.

Surely, if Flintoff was to going to prostrate himself before anyone, it should have been me.

She'll be right

THE WARM UPS

THIRTY minutes out from Sydney early on the morning of Saturday November 4, the captain of Emirates Flight 412 from Dubai informed us that the weather at Kingsford Smith airport was fine and clear. It hadn't occurred to me that it would be anything but. For this was Australia, land of sand, sea, sun and some awesomely talented cricketers whose abilities, it was often argued, could be directly traced to the nourishing quality of the outdoor lives that they led. Twenty-five minutes later, as we descended through mist and light drizzle, I peered anxiously for the runway on the screen on the back of the seat in front of me that relayed images from a camera on the nose of the plane. Before I had found it we had hit Tarmac, safely if bumpily, but it was perhaps the earliest sign that England's attempts to retain the Ashes they had secured 14 months earlier for the first time in 16 years were to be subject to a degree of turbulence not reckoned on.

On the first leg of the journey, the seven-hour haul from Gatwick to Dubai, I had indulged myself by watching an hour-long highlights package of the 2005 series on the in-flight entertainment system. It was perhaps a foolish move, for I had avoided doing so in the intervening period, the realist in me aware that cricket's fates are fickle and had they changed sides for the briefest of moments – particularly had Glenn McGrath avoided turning his ankle on a wayward ball in the warm-up for the second Test at Edgbaston – England could have been looking down the barrel of a 3-0 defeat or more, rather than a 2-1 triumph. The open-top bus would have stayed in the garage, the Queen would have been forced to bestow honours on rather more deserving candidates than Paul Collingwood, whose reward for his contribution of 17 runs to the victory so riled Shane Warne, and the Freeman of Preston's mother-of-all-benders would not have passed into popular mythology.

So it was that my copy of *The Ashes: the greatest series*, all ten hours and one minute of it, had remained securely on the shelf at Woolies. Now, though, it seemed inappropriate to deprive myself further. If I was expecting the players to get psyched up, I must do the same myself. Besides which, it was something to take my mind off my ingrained fear of flying, a phobia that returned at the same rate as the molecules of Johnnie Walker, with which I had fortified myself for the journey, evaporated from my pores.

I experienced a couple of JFK moments as the footage rolled past me: the anxious phone calls I had made to Sue from my bed – there must have been at least half-a-dozen of them – on the decisive Sunday morning when Shane Warne, Brett Lee and Michael Kasprowicz were threatening to render England's attacking efforts at Edgbaston in vain; the strange afternoon we spent as almost the only customers in a Windsor pub, wolfing down a plateful of roast potatoes left over from Sunday lunch, as Australia lost careless wickets in the follow-on at Trent Bridge and England threatened to implode on their way to a modest total. (The dénouement, with Ashley Giles and Matthew Hoggard guiding England home was played out in our sparsely occupied bar, while in the adjacent one, Manchester United and Newcastle supporters stood shoulder to shoulder watching as the teams contested an early-season Premiership fixture on Sky. Who said the Ashes captured the imagination of the country?)

But more than those, I enjoyed reliving images that had remained in my mind but that were not necessarily crucial to the outcome of the series: I'm thinking of Glenn McGrath's removal of Michael Vaughan in the first innings at Lord's in a spell that left England almost in ruins at 21 for five, the captain's stumps uprooted as he stooped desperately to dig out a delivery that fizzed through low with the acceleration of a Catherine wheel. As an opening statement, McGrath had made one of the most potent – but I allowed myself a smug smile in the knowledge of what was to come after that demoralising defeat. I'm thinking also of Andrew Strauss flying horizontally from second slip to clutch Adam Gilchrist's edge out of Nottingham's thin air in his outstretched left hand – surely the best catch ever to be caught on a still camera. But most of all, I'm thinking of Steve Harmison's slower ball that did for the fluent Michael Clarke just before the close on the Saturday at Edgbaston. It was that above all which confirmed that England were playing with a cricketing intelligence as equally unfamiliar as their aggressive approach.

It was heart-tugging stuff that brought a tear or two to the eyes and I might have stood up and placed my hand patriotically on my chest - had I not had four courses of airline food crammed on to the tray on my lap.

We spent three days adjusting to the new time zone in the Sydney suburb of Glebe before we got back into travelling mode for the trip to Canberra, four hours or so in the hire car, for the opening game. It was on my mind, not to mention a cricket fan's duty, to make a brief detour from the South Western Freeway to the pleasant Southern Highland town of Bowral, where Sir Don Bradman had grown up and, largely, learned his cricket. I had been before, in 1994, to watch England play a one-day match on the charming Bradman Oval but had been disappointed that the museum, built on the same site, had not been open that day.

This was a chance to rectify that, and although the museum's founding director, Richard Mulvaney, had recently resigned amid falling visitor numbers, which were being blamed on its failure to move with the times, I, for one, was not left lamenting the lack of an interactive battle with Brett Lee. Why should I have been when there was British Movietone News to provide rare footage of Bradman bowling – a flick of the wrist suggesting he might have had some form as a leg-spinner – documents claiming that a proposed match between England and France in 1789 had been cancelled because of that most frustrating of impediments to play – revolution, in this case the French – and accounts of the extra-curricular activities of the Aboriginal team that had had a ten-year start on the white settlers when they toured England in 1868? (They played 47 games between May and October, drawing big crowds to their post-match displays of native sports, the most popular among them the 100 yards race backwards and the art of Dodging the Cricket Ball as performed by a man called Dick-a-Dick. Who wouldn't pay to see that?)

I was only lured away from the displays by the knowledge that I had left Sue stewing over a cup of tea in Stumps, the obligatory cricket-themed café downstairs, for rather too long. Lunch was in full swing when I found her and she had all but been forced from her table by what appeared to be a party of Saga customers. While real men might not eat quiche, elderly ladies evidently did, a coachload of them tucking greedily into The French Cut, massive wedges of the stuff. As sustenance for the coming journey to Australia's seat of government we opted for sandwiches and although the Bodyline foccacia was tempting, we paid homage to the better things in the game, me with a suitably rustic Village Green (a huge doorstep of beetroot, cucumber, tomato and grated carrot) and Sue with a Sir Don itself (a subtle mix of oven-roasted turkey and brie with cranberry sauce). Mmm.

We pressed on to Australia's capital, leaving the town by a route over which a banner was slung that advertised an upcoming cricket festival. But this was no ordinary cricket festival. It was one without cricket. In fact, that was how it was being promoted. "The world's only two-day cricket event where no cricket is played," the banner announced. Now that might be the kind of cricket event Sue could get into, I thought.

"South Africa were here last year, mate," came one shout.

"You're the worst of the lot, you actually wanted to be a Pom," came another.

"Nice ass," came a third.

Kevin Pietersen was taking a bit of a barracking as he strutted, hands on hips, on the boundary edge.

Out of the blue, as one of Cameron White's huge swipes went soaring over Pietersen's head at deep mid-wicket and our position on the grassy bank of the picturesque Manuka Oval, Sue asked: "Do players actually *like* fielding?" It was an innocent question but also a pertinent one in light of the amount of leather-chasing the English were enduring at the hands of the Prime Minister's XI on their first day of action. I rummaged around for a satisfactory answer as another missile fired by the Victoria captain homed in on us. I tried to explain that, to some extent, it was an often dull task, but always a crucial one; that the time when the least seems to be happening is when the greatest concentration is necessary; that the best fielders excel in such situations because of simple pride in their skills, but complexities such as these were not going to be easily grasped by a viewer still coming to terms with the rudiments - and still a long way from the conviction that she really wanted to.

I had tried hard to educate – should that be indoctrinate? – Sue over the previous few years of our relationship, seemingly with little success. Hours of television exposure had procured little response, apart from pained questioning – "do we really have to watch this?" – or beseechments to see what was on the other side.

In May 2002, I took her to her first live game – the first day of the England v Sri Lanka Test at Lord's. Surely she would not be able to resist the spectacular twin sights of the historic pavilion and the space age media centre in one of world sport's most stunning arenas. If she did, I might at least expect the sensual aesthetic of watching fit, young men parade around in tight white clothing to provide a certain frisson, although that might have been offset by a glimpse of Andrew Caddick's ears flapping in the breeze as he strode in from the Nursery End (for years she would continue to confuse him with Marcus Trescothick). And if that didn't spark at least a measure of curiosity, a thought that this might be a game worth getting to know more intimately, I knew something that would: the sun. Yes, in England, in May. I had deliberately booked a seat in the uncovered section of the new Grandstand, so that if nothing else, she could top up her tan should the chance arise; unfortunately, while the golden orb in the sky did its part, forcing its way through the cloud early in the day, the box office team failed to do theirs and we watched with some despondency as its rays stopped stubbornly on the very row in front of ours.

I at least had the saving grace of hundreds by Marvan Atapattu and Mahela Jayawardene to absorb me.

A year later, I tried again when, for my fortieth birthday, we went to Barbados. With extraordinary but marvellous timing, Australia were playing the third match of their four-Test series at Kensington Oval during our stay. I managed to persuade Sue to vacate her position by the hotel pool to join me for the third day: the side-on view from the Mitchie Hewitt stand, before it was redeveloped for the 2007 World Cup, provided a remarkably intimate perspective on proceedings. But, despite her proximity to two of the most exciting Test cricketers of our generation in Adam Gilchrist and Brian Lara, she remained unmoved, only really perking up at lunchtime when we sneaked outside and bought beer and home-made goat curry from a stall in a nearby front garden. (Ah, cricket as it was before the ugly appearance of signature sponsors and ambush marketing.)

Thinking that, rather like trying to teach a child to read by sticking a copy of *War and Peace* in front of them, I was making her run before she could walk, I did what any bloke would do: I went to the other extreme. I dragged her along to the inaugural evening of Twenty20 cricket, the Surrey/Middlesex derby at The Oval. The glorious evening sunshine, and the prospect of a game of cricket crammed into three hours straight after work meant more than 10,000 were similarly inspired but of more concern to Sue was the long queue at the pavilion bar. By the time she had returned with a wine and beer Mark Ramprakash was ready to strike the winning runs against his former county.

So, as the trip to Australia approached, I could see disaster, of the relationship if not the cricketing sort, lurking on the horizon: if Sue did not embrace the game to at least some extent, it could be a very long three and half months. Perhaps some literature would help. I went to Waterstones and picked up a copy of *What is a googly: the mysteries of cricket explained*, a book, first published in 1992, that had begun to enjoy a new lease of life towards the end of the 2005 series as mystified women – and while trying not to be sexist about this, it probably was mainly women – tried to work out what the blokes in their office were getting so worked up about. And whether they wanted to be part of it.

The Times reviewer quoted on the back cover seemed to imply success was inevitable. "The ideal gift book for cricket lovers to bestow upon the uninitiated," he promised, but when I waved the thin volume in front of her, her eyes glazed over, before she whacked me for getting in the way of a crucial plot development in *Emmerdale*.

To be fair, she would have had to read through 109 pages before reaching the chapter which would signal whether she was ready to attend a match. It was time to go subliminal. Our working hours were so wildly divergent – Sue had to get up at 5am, while my shifts at *The Times* meant that I thought about going to bed only a couple of hours before that – that I took to sneaking into the bedroom shortly after midnight, switching on the small lamp on my side of the bed and reading short passages quietly over her gently snoozing body. I couldn't be sure that any salient facts were permeating her dream life, although I did detect her breathing deepen and some more agitated moans than usual when I got stuck into the lbw law.

Back at the finest stadium in the Australian Capital Territory, the agitated moans were coming mostly from me. Phil Jaques, the New South Wales left-hander, had smashed a run-a-ball century before taking leave of proceedings, allowing a little over ten overs for his team-mates to really rub it in: Adam Voges, who would make the Test squad before the end of the summer, hit 39 off 32 balls, Travis Birt nabbed 40 off 45, White's brutality raised 30 from 14 and Shaun Marsh, left-handed but straighter and more stylish than Jaques, smacked an unbeaten 78 off 56. A total of 112 was added in those last overs as the Prime Minister's XI racked up a record 347 for five from their allotted 50.

The England bowlers had received what should have been a salutary lesson. Sajid Mahmood had gone for a mind-boggling 97 from nine overs, including six no-balls and four wides, and James

Anderson, obviously believing that the long-hop was a worthwhile skill to be mastered, fared little better. As an Australian nearby me observed at a volume that should have reached the hapless pair in the middle: "If White can do this, what do you think Ponting's going to do to you?" It was a prospect I thought best not to dwell on.

The one ray of light had come early in proceedings, before the chill in the morning air had completely dissipated, when Flintoff had cut one back, forcing an inside edge from Tim Paine and Geraint Jones had tumbled athletically to his left to pluck the chance inches from the turf. Well, at least that had proved one thing, I thought: Duncan Fletcher's faith in the Kent wicketkeeper had not been misplaced after all. Such a catch could only enhance the confidence of the Papua New Guinea-born, Brisbane-raised, Welsh-heritaged Englishman. He was clearly destined for a tour that would silence his critics, of which there were many, including me. Half an hour later, though, Jaques dabbed at a ball outside the off stump, edged the ball at a comfortable height close to Jones's left shoulder and watched in wonderment as the wicketkeeper parried it in the direction of third man. He was on 21 at the time, on his way to the first of two centuries in three days against the tourists and the question marks were once more hovering above Jones's head.

Such form was timely for Jaques, for his name was being mentioned in the media as a possible opening partner for Matthew Hayden for the first Test. Questions had been raised about whether Justin Langer's head was in the right place, perhaps literally as well as figuratively, having retired hurt from his previous international seven months earlier after taking a fearsome blow on it from a Makhaya Ntini delivery. It was one way to celebrate his 100th Test match and enough to make him seriously consider whether he wanted to play a 101st.

If England's bowling had proved inadequate, their batsmen were determined not to show them up. While Andrew Strauss looked in exquisite form, his team-mates appeared to be stuck in a time warp, the button jammed in Ashes 2005 "attack mode". This was not necessarily advisable against the pace of Shaun Tait, who was unrecognisable from the change bowler that had made little impact in his debut Tests in that series. The slinging action, and the collapse of the legs that provided the suspension to enable it, was still in place, but the ball seemed to be propelled from his hand at a rate a couple of yards faster than before. It certainly took Marcus Trescothick by surprise and he soon edged to second slip. Alastair Cook and Kevin Pietersen were victims of over-ambitious cross-bat shots, giving the wicketkeeper steepling catches off Ben Hilfenhaus, and Strauss fell to Tait, albeit for an attractive run-a-ball 67, when he joined the band of unhappy hookers, and looped a catch to mid-on.

Tait, a South Australian, was vying for a first Test place with Stuart Clark, the New South Welshman whom England would cross swords with in their second warm-up match in Sydney. Glenn McGrath and Brett Lee, who'd also forced himself into international calculations with a blistering performance for the Prime Minister's XI against the Indians in 1999, were certain to spearhead the pace attack in Brisbane but there was a vacancy for the role previously held by the likes of Michael Kaprowicz. (Jason Gillespie, after his poor return in England, had disappeared off the selectors' radar altogether, to the point that late in the summer he let fly with a verbal assault in which he claimed that although he was still one of the best bowlers in the country, they thought he was too old. Four-letter words were used.)

Clark had impressed in South Africa, where he had replaced a McGrath who had chosen to stay in Australia to nurse his sick wife, but was already 31, Tait's elder by more than seven years. Besides, he was seen as a McGrath clone and the Australian media seemed to think it was unlikely that the selectors would go for two bowlers so similar. Personally, I couldn't agree with the reasoning – two

McGraths and one Warne would usually be sufficient to trouble England – but that was obviously mitigating against him.

So, though, was Tait, who broke my train of thought by steaming in and claiming a third wicket by scattering Andrew Flintoff's stumps to the wind third ball. He followed up with the most beseeching, but unsuccessful, of lbw appeals against the nonplussed Ashley Giles. The selection, to me at least, seemed a no-brainer. Tait scared *me* and I was 70 yards away.

After he had made his point, however, the match rather petered out. With the conclusion inevitable and the sun beginning to sink behind the first of several Sir Donald Bradman Stands we would see on our trip, the Australians around us began to get restless. They rose from their miniature folding deckchairs, gathered together their rugs and eskies and tramped their way through the detritus of liquid lunches – and a few liquid breakfasts and afternoon teas, too – towards the exits. This much-lauded England team were obviously not doing it for them, at least not so they'd want to watch to the bitter end, but for us there was no choice. It was our duty to observe the last rites and as the sandalled feet on stocky legs, and some smoother naturally-tanned ones, scrunched past our two bodies on the bank, the sole ACT representative, Adam Ritchard, duly performed priestly duties. His medium pacers were the side of medium that makes Ian Bell's occasionals look decidedly rapid, but he was smart enough to nip out Jimmy Anderson and Monty Panesar and confirm a 166-run mauling.

Back at the hostel, I tried to construct some arguments in England's defence: I noted with a trace of satisfaction that Matthew Hoggard and Steve Harmison, Mr Swing and Mr Bounce themselves, would return for the serious stuff. And this, after all, was meaningless fare, a chance just to stretch stiff muscles and awaken sluggish reflexes after a debilitating flight. Besides, hadn't Australia, to much amusement, lost to Somerset and Bangladesh before the first Test in England? But my mental jury was not convinced. There would have to be a retrial – and that would start in 36 hours at the SCG.

With the final session of the first day of the match between the New South Wales XIV (otherwise known as the SpeedBlitz Blues) and an England XIV going on almost unnoticed in front of them, an advance platoon of the Barmy Army engaged their Australian counterparts in the first significant skirmish of the winter – a singing duel at three paces.

Losing interest in events on the field after Jaques and Simon Katich had carried on where the Prime Minister's XI had left off, they decided to try out some of the songs which would later form the centrepiece of the Army's vocal routine. There was no doubting the wit of some of the lyrics, while others of a more personal nature were a bit near the mark, but what became quickly apparent was that if you wanted to truly offend a native supporter, the best way was to question his economic viability. While the Australian troops good-naturedly accepted barbs about their convict history and the sexual activities that might be sought out by a lonely farmhand at an isolated ranch in the Outback, they only really got riled when the Poms turned their sights on their exchange rate.

To the tune of *He's Got The Whole World in His Hands*, they belted out the observation that we were getting "Three Dollars to The Pound." Truth was it was nearer Aus$2.4, but that wouldn't have scanned. However, it was enough to enrage one local, who infiltrated the unused corporate hospitality boxes above the Barmies' position and hurled a large jug of beer over the insulting hordes. Such was the state of inebriation of some of them they didn't notice.

Earlier, I had rushed Sue to the ground, convinced that the English team would be such a draw in their first proper tour game that the whole of New South Wales, locals and tourists alike, would stop what they were doing, and get on down to the SCG. The Opera House would stand silent, shops in the ugly but ever-crowded Darling Harbour would bring down their shutters and Bondi Beach would offer up surf that no one would ride. Hunter Valley wines would go untasted, the Blue Mountains could turn purple and no one would notice and the Harbour Bridge would be left unscaled. Thousands would travel in from Wagga Wagga and Wollongong and other places beginning with W and with lots of syllables.

I was wrong.

The ground was less than a quarter full. There had been no need to queue at the ticket windows as I had envisaged and niggles in the back of my mind that we might get locked out proved an almost hilarious miscalculation. Official figures later put the attendance at a little over 11,000 in a stadium that can house nearer 45,000 but it had taken a while to build up. Yet that seems the way in Australia. Being on time for the start of the day's play appears to be on a par with a social gaffe like being the earliest to arrive at a party.

We climbed up to the top tier of the Monty Noble Stand, but after the race to get there, for what should have been the first serious business of the tour, I felt a strong sense of anti-climax. The weather was fine – hazy, with high, speckly cloud – but the atmosphere, far from being possible to cut with a knife, could not have been disturbed by being pummelled with a blunt instrument. The England team, having lost the toss, trotted on to the field with a similar air of detachment, the encouraging noises of those trying to whip their team-mates up into some sort of readiness rising above the sounds of the few hands clapping in the Members' Pavilion.

It was as if the spectators knew in their hearts that this was a contest – a 14-a-side one, no less – that was flawed as a concept, like the attempt to introduce substitutes to one-day internationals. There was a sense of unease, that the involvement that the committed cricket follower seeks to draw from a game, was missing. While there were plenty of claims to be staked, issues to be decided, on both sides – Steve Harmison and Matthew Hoggard, for two, needed tidy starts, if not to peak too early – the competitive element that could bring out the best in the players, would test them in pressure situations that were bound to present themselves in the course of the series, was absent.

Peter Roebuck, writing in the *Sydney Morning Herald* the following morning, decried it as a bogus match watched by a bewildered crowd, and while Roebuck's opinions are ones that I regularly disparage, that was probably about right. He went on to suggest that had the West Indies or India requested such a game against one of the strongest state sides they would have received short shrift. But I found it hard to believe that Cricket Australia had simply bowed down and tipped their hats in deference to the Mother Country.

There is, however, one kind of pleasure that can be taken from these sort of occasions: the freedom to roam. I have always been fascinated by the variety of shapes a game can take on simply by moving seat. Behind the bowler's arm will give you privileged information about swing and seam deviation, side-on gives you more of a perspective on speed and length, deceptions in flight and the opportunity to abuse whoever's fielding on the boundary edge.

Of course, if you're a seasoned cricket watcher, you already know this. But this was the explanation I was giving to Sue as I dragged her from the Monty Noble Stand to the Ladies' Pavilion, to the Churchill Stand to Yabba's Hill. I would have liked to call out something in honour of the legendary barracker, real name

Stephen Gascoigne, who between the wars was an ever-present on the famous expanse of grass, now concreted over, but nothing witty sprang immediately to mind. In the event, one of his most famous observations could have been directed at the wayward Steve Harmison: "Your length's lousy but you bowl a good width," he once said.

By mid-afternoon we had completed a full circuit. This was rare fun because at Test stadia, this movement is rarely, if at all, possible these days. At a well-attended match you are usually herded into your seat, your knees pressed up hard against the one in front and by the time you've opened your newspaper to soak up the overnight opinion on pitch conditions, the platitudes of the captains and selection speculations, you're being forced to scramble to your feet again to let someone else past. When you've done this for about the third time, the advertising inserts and loose pages in your paper have floated to the ground, the rest of it has folded into a configuration that would need an origami expert to unravel and you have no alternative but to throw it down and angrily jump up and down on it, leaving the wise words of a CMJ or a Gideon Haigh largely unread. Still, it prevents you developing deep-vein thrombosis.

It is not so different now in domestic cricket, especially at the major grounds, where gates into many stands are routinely boarded up, presumably to save cash on stewarding in this era of risible health and safety regulations and ludicrous lawsuits. Though, as a boy visiting the Oval, and taking up sole occupation of the Vauxhall Stand, where I could practise my nascent commentary skills without being disturbed by a man in a fluorescent yellow jacket, I never came to any harm.

What's more, to take a walk round a cricket ground is to step back and forth through history. Take the SCG, since that's where we are at the moment. The Monty Noble, our starting point, was erected in 1936 in honour of an all-rounder some have judged to be the greatest Australia has produced – and one of their best captains. To my shame, I had never heard of him – a black mark on my cricketing street-cred I grant you - but the salient facts I think you should absorb from my subsequent research are that he was named a Wisden Cricketer of the Year in 1900, was nicknamed Mary Ann after his Christian and middle names, Montague and Alfie, and went on to be a dentist and author. There's nothing like living a full life.

Moving anti-clockwise you step into the Members' Pavilion, one of the two stands with a distinctive green roof – the other is the Ladies' Stand – that give the ground most of its character and provide such a stunning profile, particularly when the sun begins to drop behind them on a day/night game. First built in 1878, rebuilt in 1886, and extended in 1903, the eyes and ears that have occupied its seats must have experienced some sights and sounds over the years. Look diagonally across from there and you see the Doug Walters Stand. It's due to be demolished. I wonder what Doug makes of that.

We settled, finally, in the bays in front of the Brewongle, a more modern construction of 1980, where a disparate group of Poms were slowly merging into the Barmy Army unit mentioned above as the England performance continued to fail to capture the imagination. The interest that had at first focused on Harmison and Hoggard had waned as neither managed to convince that their absence in Canberra was a compelling argument for England's wretched display. And as Jaques, Simon Katich, and Michael Clarke, the latter most stylishly, pushed the New South Wales total to within touching range of 250, beer was tossed down throats at a similar rate to which provocative banter emerged from them. Kevin Pietersen re-engaged attention for a few moments with a quite remarkable catch, taken running back over his head a step from the fence, to remove Katich and give Ashley Giles his second wicket.

Giles had seemed a step ahead of fellow left-arm spinner Monty Panesar when he got eight overs to his rival's three at Canberra, but for those looking for further confirmation that the Warwickshire player had usurped him in the battle for the slow bowling berth in Brisbane the situation was confused when neither took to the field at the start. And, after 14 overs, the picture misted over even more when Flintoff relayed a message to Steve Harmison, patrolling the long leg boundary in front of the Members' Stand, that a spinner was required. Which one would it be? We waited for a moment, breathing paused, before Harmison turned to the dressing-room behind him and put us out of our misery – by stroking an imaginary long beard. The cult Sikh gambolled excitedly on to the field and Giles wasn't far behind. By the end of the day Panesar at least had the wicket of Clarke, caught at slip for 50, for his toils before the close came on 325 for five.

It wasn't a disaster but it wasn't the lift we were looking for after Canberra. The doubts were already beginning to creep in and they weren't about to be made any better. The next two days began with Sue wiping small fragments of croissant off her face, the consequence of my spluttering over my breakfast newspaper.

First it was Botham. Ian bloody Terrance Botham. Then it was Marcus bloomin' Edward Trescothick. Two stories: one stupid, one sad.

Botham had complemented his television earnings with an "outspoken" – is he ever anything else – column in the *News of the World* back home, making me groan and Sue push back her chair and take refuge behind a serviette.

"What does he want to go and say that for," I sighed.

"Who?" Sue replied, slightly irritably. She never liked discord at breakfast.

"Bloody Botham. He's such a prat. Great all-rounder I grant you, but still a prat. He's just asking for us to get a thrashing."

"What's he done?"

"Just listen to this."

I started to read aloud:

'ASHES great Ian Botham has mocked Australia's ageing warriors, whom he feels may crack and fail to last the distance this summer. Shane Warne, Glenn McGrath, Adam Gilchrist, Matthew Hayden and Justin Langer were yesterday dubbed "Dad's Army" in Britain's News of the World after the famous British comedy series set during World War II.

Australia may begin the first Ashes Test in Brisbane next week with its oldest Test side in 80 years, prompting Botham to attack Ricky Ponting's bunch of "colonial geriatrics".

"The Aussies are a year and a half older than when the teams clashed last time and they were creaking then - especially in the bowling department," he said.

"If they go into a Test with Shane Warne, Glenn McGrath, Adam Gilchrist, Matthew Hayden, Justin Langer, Stuart MacGill and Damien Martyn, the Aussies will have seven players aged 35 and over.

"I can't imagine there has ever been a team that old in international cricket.

"There are some great cricketers in that list, but when Father Time starts to call, it can all fall apart very quickly."

While Botham is a noted pot-stirrer, his claims have substance this time because there is a feeling that the more youthful England's chances of retaining the urn improve with each day the series is "alive".'

"Substance my arse," I said, folding up the paper and planting it down on the table with such force that the froth on the top of my cappucino separated from the rest of the drink, floated upwards and plopped down onto my trousers. "Substances, maybe.

Botham's always been fond of his substances. Well, if the Aussies weren't fired up enough already, that'll do it."

"He's just being positive," reasoned Sue.

"He's just being repetitive," I countered, something buried in the back of my mind slowly coming to the forefront of consciousness. Botham, I recalled, had been this way before, about five years ago, but then his ageist attack had been against England.

In 2002, just before the start of the series against Sri Lanka, itself a forerunner to the 2003 Ashes in Australia, he had described England's decision to play three cricketers over 30 – Alec Stewart, John Crawley and Dominic Cork - as a giant backward step. He suggested that Stewart would be the only one to make the trip Down Under, and that England should instead have eased Ian Bell into their thinking.

Even David Graveney, the England chairman of selectors, had been bowled over by this outburst. "You can't call players over 30 Dad's Army," he had bristled.

Not that the Aussies were bothered by Botham's attack, even if they had known it was a habitual one; it took more than that to pierce their mental armour. Indeed the confidence of Justin Langer, always considered one of the most sensitive Australians, partly because of his reaction to jibes about his height, partly for taking issue with the Barmy Army's tendency to consistently "no-ball" Brett Lee from the sidelines, was barely dented. "I say to people who reckon I'm past my best that I've just made my highest first-class score (he had, 342 for Somerset against Surrey, and not even at Taunton)," he responded, looking forward to blowing out the 36 candles on his birthday cake the following week. Ricky Ponting, meanwhile, sized up Botham's bouncer in a split second, depositing it one bounce to his favoured point on the boundary fence just in front of square leg. "These guys are the best players in Australia, regardless of age," he wrote in his column in *The Australian*. "They have seen every situation you can be confronted with and know how to fight their way out of tough positions and get in front from there."

It was 1-0 to Australia in the verbal Ashes.

Equally disturbing, but in an altogether different way, was the news that greeted us the following morning. Marcus Trescothick was going home. Only a week after informing the Australian media he was stress-free, he had had a reoccurrence of the psychological problems that had afflicted him in India months previously. Reports suggested he'd been found sobbing in the dressing-room and needed to be consoled for two hours. At heart a homebody who found the pressures of the touring schedule at odds with his emotional needs, it was thought prudent to put him on the first flight back to Heathrow. But it got me thinking: only two days earlier, the Australian press had dished out critical treatment to Trescothick and his team-mates for attending a U2 concert in the wake of the Canberra debacle. Did this bring home to him the full extent of the media glare the series was to be played under and send him retreating back into a lonely shell?

My first concern was, however, fearful and purely selfish – what would we do without a second opening batsman after the injury problems of Michael Vaughan? – my second more pragmatic: Alistair Cook had proved himself an opener of some ability and would slip into that role with comfort. I felt sorry for Trescothick, sorry that we wouldn't see the   effortless cover drives that called for minimal footwork, the unfussy leave outside the off stump that he had more or less patented and was the antithesis of the description "shouldering arms". Less sorry was Jeff Thomson, the feared Australian paceman of the 1970s, who suggested that he'd be happy to see the whole of the England team returning home with depression in January.

Not that there hadn't been any interesting cricket going on on these two days. England had swiftly rounded up the New South Wales innings despite a morning downpour which silenced the

5,000 schoolchildren bussed in for the day - and then batted quite well themselves, despite Trescothick's early departure to Brett Lee.

Kevin Pietersen had announced himself properly with a supreme hundred, and marked it with an audacious reverse sweep for four off Nathan Hauritz, the off spinner. Andrew Strauss had seemed untroubled on the way to his second fifty of the tour until Stuart Clark, who had yet to make his case to be selected ahead of Shaun Tait in Brisbane, suddenly did so, snapping up, one-handed, an amazing return catch from the Middlesex man before getting Ian Bell to nibble his second ball behind.

Flintoff, batting in a serious – I hesitate to say competitive – game for the first time in a long while, picked up a fifty, but it was a shaky one, the occasional lusty blow failing to compensate for a tentative defensive technique that would be scrutinised more fully over the coming weeks. The Lancastrian picked up most of his boundaries from Hauritz and Beau Casson, whose name suggests more a Hollywood film star than the rather innocuous chinaman bowler that he turned out to be. Stuart MacGill would have provided a rather sterner test for the England captain but remained in the dressing-room, officially nursing a minor injury but more likely at the request of the Australian authorities, anxious that the tourists should not be given a sighting of serious wrist spin ahead of the first Test. Simon Katich, the New South Wales captain, was probably acting under instructions but any time that he had to field the ball in front of the sightscreen at the Paddington End he copped a fearful earful from some sozzled locals for not bowling him. Like me, they were ignorant of MacGill's injury, and they felt quite justified in launching a barrage of abuse at Katich that was not particularly humorous or original. When one ran out of things to shout, another took up the baton of vitriol. It was as if they were operating a barrackers' relay event.

Another lone barracker decided to take his ire out on James

Anderson in a bizarre post-tea session but was silenced when the Lancashire pace bowler, enjoying one of the genuinely impressive spells that he produced throughout the tour, if too infrequently, dismissed two New South Wales batsmen in two balls. When Anderson then removed Moises Henriques and Giles bowled Michael Clarke, Katich might have been regretting retiring at the interval on 55. It meant his side were effectively 165 for seven and with a lead of only six from the first innings I found myself indulging in an unlikely dream – and wondering if I was the only one in the ground to do so. Wrap up the tail, and we could chase about 180 in 25 overs and start the tour proper with an improbable win. We could inject some competitiveness into this game of counterfeit cricket that was dying on its feet. And what better way to inform Australia of our attacking intent. What might that do for confidence?

We'll never know: Hauritz and Casson happily added an untroubled 29 and Flintoff called a halt in the evening sunshine at the earliest opportunity. But the position of the match was so neatly poised that had there been a fourth day available – as there ought to have been – the crowd would have been treated to some truly interesting cricket.

Still, while England may not have gained much from the match, I felt I had. Despite initial resistance Sue had allowed me to impart to her some of my wealth of knowledge of the game. And the signs were that she was actually banking some of it. As we walked back to our hotel from an unappetising pasta meal in King's Cross, she admitted that understanding a little about it had made it more interesting for her. There was, however, something ambiguous about her statement: "Now, when I ask how long's left and you say six overs, I know that it's only 36 balls." It made me think she was just waiting for it to be over.

I tested her in my best kindergarten teacher voice. "So what do we call a run that hasn't come off the bat."

"An extra," she shot back.

"Or, over here, it's sometimes known as a sundry," I added. "And what's it mean if an umpire lifts his leg and pats it."

A momentary silence. "It's a leg bye," she replied.

"Not that he's in the Masons, then?"

We parted company with the England side for the one and only time the next day, as they flew down to Adelaide for their other game before the first Test. It would mean I'd miss another sighting of Shaun Tait, of South Australia, who would be fired up going into the game after being named in the Australia XIII along with Stuart Clark, whose three for 50 at a pace only a few clicks faster than amiable at the SCG had not convinced me. Mitchell Johnson, a left-armer with a swift, slightly stiff action, who was much favoured by Dennis Lillee, was the third member of a trio of quicks certain of securing only one place in the team. Shane Watson, a batting all-rounder had been preferred, wrongly in my opinion, to Michael Clarke, a class act if ever there was one. But Watson's misfortune – he pulled a hammy during Queensland's one-day match with Western Australia later in the week – allowed Clarke to step back into the middle order. I liked the Cricinfo description of Watson's injury: "Picked to bat at number six against England, he mouthed 'ow' after feeling the pain in his delivery stride and walked back to the end of his run-up and began rubbing the back of his right leg." Ow? An English bowler would have been stretchered off and flown back to the UK.

We, meanwhile would use the eight days or so to amble up the east coast to Brisbane. If we liked the sound of somewhere on the map, we would turn off the beaten track – in this case the 966 kilometres of Pacific Highway between the two cities – to investigate. It was a small compromise on my part, but in a cricket-free week I could still keep an ear on Ashes developments on the car radio.

In truth, I had been looking forward to this part of the trip ever since it had begun to take shape in my mind. I imagined myself in some sort of sporty number, roof peeled back to let the sun and wind ruddy my face, an endless red landscape ahead, a constant view of the sea to my right; instead, I found myself in a claustrophobic Hyundai, knees forced up under the steering wheel, admiring not the ocean and rocks turned a deep crimson by the passage of time, but field after field of livestock. In different company, there were sheep jokes aplenty to be had. If it wasn't paddock after paddock, it was creek after creek and national park after national park. I began to think Australia was one big national park, which I decided would make quite a good slogan for the nation's tourist board. It was better than "Where the bloody hell are you?" anyway.

Where the bloody hell were we anyway? An intersection had brought us tantalisingly within reach of a place called Tea Gardens. Neither Sue nor I needed much of an excuse to stop for a cuppa and besides, it was that time of the afternoon. We nodded at each other, confirming that we both assented to the manoeuvre, and turned right. After a few kilometres, we cruised – as much as anyone can cruise in a cramped Hyundai – into a small, quaintish town, population 850, although none of them seemed to be about. We drove until we could go no further, past small motels, B&Bs and houseboats on the adjacent Myall River, one of which looked welcomingly like a restaurant. Taking seats outside in strong sunshine but a muscular wind, we watched the feathers of a group of wading birds flutter as they went about their wading duties, and a woman and child saying their goodbyes to a husband and father, who broke an agreeable silence by hopping onto a jetski, revving her up and shooting up river. Then, contrarily, we ordered a couple of milkshakes.

That turned out to be a good choice, because Tea Gardens, ironically, was not known for its tea. It should have been, but when the Australian Agricultural Company moved to the area in 1826, they couldn't get it to grow. Still, the name stuck.

The temptation to stop for the night was undeniable but we wanted to push on to Port Macquarie, once a penal settlement but now a holiday resort and a place so desirable to live, we were told, that 14 families a week were moving to the area. It was 31 degrees outside according to the digital thermometer on the dashboard, but some very strange things were happening not that far behind us. An unpleasant weather system, we heard, had dropped sleet on Melbourne, disrupting a high-scoring domestic game between Victoria and Tasmania, and snow on outlying Victoria, while firefighters in the Blue Mountains, close to Sydney, were contending with bush fires, despite similarly wet conditions there, an incongruity I found hard to reconcile with my limited understanding of the environment. Surely the rain would put out the fires?

We arrived in Port Macquarie still in bright sunshine and immediately knew we wanted to stay there. The drive down to the middle of town took us past a vista of dramatic beaches: softly-sanded and with the surf up, they looked a picture. The avenues grew wider, giving a sense of space we had hardly yet experienced, and I clocked a small cricket oval off to our left, encircled by the obligatory picket fence and the ubiquitous Norfolk Island pine trees (helpful in limiting beach erosion, apparently). It didn't take long for us to decide we wanted to kick back and relax for a few days before heading further north.

No sooner had we made that decision and booked three days in a spacious hotel apartment with a sea view and large balcony – at about the same cost of a night in Sydney – than the weather caught up with us: the sun disappeared, the wind picked up and the temperature plummeted. The hail followed and we spent the next day not luxuriating on the balcony, exposing our pasty English epidermi to the heat of the sub-tropics, but under cover in the café of a wildlife park, sipping hot chocolate and occasionally venturing out to feed recalcitrant wallabies some nibbles.

By Saturday, after the weather had warmed up again, we wandered up to the Oxley oval, the one I had spotted on the drive into town and I got my live cricket fix, a hard-fought derby, at least I assumed it was a derby, between the Port Panthers and the Macquarie Hotel. What this club match lacked in quality it made up for in sweat and toil. It was the Australian attitude to sport made flesh. No chase between ball and man was a foregone conclusion and a bowler of only medium pace seemed to strain every muscle in his body as he galloped in with an intensity most Englishmen would be embarrassed to show. It was as if each delivery had heart and soul in it.

Oh, that England should be showing such dedication in Adelaide. It wasn't easy to find out. When I tuned to *Grandstand*, the weekend sports show on ABC radio, via Sue's mobile phone, I found most attention extended to the Australian Open golf in Sydney. Fortunately, patience paid off and before long I was listening attentively to an Ashes debate featuring Jonathan Agnew, Jim Maxwell and Glenn Mitchell, while Ian Bell and Paul Collingwood were compiling a stand of 178 in the background.

Could England retain the Ashes away from home, Mitchell, the host, wanted to know. Agnew was definite. Of course they could. They'd beaten them at home and gained more experience since. The pressure was on Australia, whose public demanded that they win them back and they'd wake up to a distinctly disenchanted media if they didn't get off to a good start in Brisbane, a ground where they had a particularly good record – they hadn't lost a Test there in 18 years.

If England's new-ball bowlers could get it right, it would be a very finely tuned Test, opined Maxwell, but Agnew was not confident on that score, Steve Harmison having dropped out of the South Australia match with a side strain. The paceman had not worked hard enough, he said, bowling only five of 51 overs in the New South Wales second innings. Maxwell alluded to Australia's ageing squad but felt, even so, that they would get 20 wickets quicker than England. Then there was the Monty Panesar/Ashley Giles conundrum – Panesar had been preferred to Giles in Adelaide, which surely made him favourite for Brisbane. Just when it seemed none of the commentators could decide on a winner – there were too many variables, said Maxwell – the Australian pair opted for their own side. Mitchell submitted a 3-1 scoreline but then admitted he couldn't see where England's single victory would come. "Pietersen will have to bat for long periods," he said, "and I can't see a draw in anything that isn't rain-affected." Maxwell went for 3-0. "England's bowling just isn't good enough – unless one of ours treads on the ball," he said.

On the Monday, three days before the start of the Test, we left Port Macquarie with some sadness; there's always a sense of regret when you haven't made the most of a place – and we hadn't. Apart from the visit to the koala park; we had preferred relaxation to the tourist imperative to do things. Thus the Historical Society Museum, said to have some terrifying baby dolls and an award-winning collection of Victorian frocks – or maybe it was the other way round – had been left off our itinerary. "Next time," I said as we rolled along the Oxley Highway to rejoin the Pacific Highway. "Yes, next time," confirmed Sue, knowing we would almost certainly never be back this way in our lives, although she didn't seem to be entirely joking when she suggested that I leave her and pick her up on the way back after the Test.

We were still a good 500 kilometres from our destination, probably too much for me, as the only driver, to do in one day so we set off with no particular port of call in mind, but options to stop at Coffs Harbour or Byron Bay.

I had some desire to see the latter – and not only for the reason that our guide book described it as a "hedonistic pleasure park", a place where you could "indulge your wildest instincts". I wanted to see it to cleanse myself of a cowardly act I had yielded to during a similar, solo, trip during the 1994-5 Ashes tour.

I had found myself in Newcastle, an industrial city north of Sydney, and not a place I would have had reason to visit had England not been playing a four-day game against New South Wales at the romantically-named Number One Sports Ground. But, in an era when four-day warm-up games, and several of them, were thought necessary preparation for a Test series – and the cricket authorities were keen to take them outside the state capitals – I had been forced to take the three-hour train journey to get there. Fortunately I had booked a reasonably comfortable youth hostel, secured my own room and was content to walk the 45-minute circuitous route to the ground for each day's play. Unfortunately, I had quickly made the acquaintance of Barry, my next-door neighbour in the hostel.

Barry was not there for the cricket. He was there for love. Of the unrequited kind. A short, bespectacled and generally unprepossessing bus driver from Bootle, he was surprised when one of his passengers, a nurse from Australia, took a shine to him. She had, he told me blinking from behind lenses thick enough to serve a British Army helicopter pilot on a night raid in Basra, turned his life upside down, swept him off his rather small feet and taught him there was more to existence than the public transport system of urban Liverpool. Then she had disappeared. Without a word and with barely a trace. And that bare trace had led him to a hospital near Newcastle, where he had tracked her down, confronted her, and been told, amid the angry clattering of bedpans, to get lost. This story would not have been so sad, or tragic, if Barry had not, in a moment of passionate madness, taken all five weeks of his annual holiday in one go before flying halfway round the world to try to reclaim her. I listened sympathetically to his upsetting tale, advised him against returning to the hospital for another try – these days I'd have no doubt warned him he was straying dangerously into stalker territory. But now he was at a loose end, thousands of miles from home, with four weeks to spare and nothing with which to fill them.

As a lone traveller it is often nice to team up, especially if you have similar interests or are heading the same way. But Barry and I did not have similar interests; and he quickly grew worryingly dependant. I would creep out of my hostel room, turn the lock while steeling myself for it not to click too loudly, only to wheel round and find Barry's face peering up at me. He seemed to have a sixth sense regarding my movements and, against my better judgement and despite the fact that he had never been near a cricket ground in his life, I let him join me for a day at the match. But the crunch came at the end of the contest – which England, for the record, lost by four wickets after Steve Rhodes, the reserve wicketkeeper, curiously opened the batting in both innings – when Barry came up with a solution to his dilemma.

"Why don't I come with you to Brisbane for the Test match?" he said, as if it was the answer to all his problems.

I should have been flattered that somebody was prepared to share my company for several days, but, let's face it, I was a poor substitute for an Australian nurse. And I couldn't be sure that, without his glasses, and in the middle of the night on a dark train, he wouldn't mistake me for one. My mind reeled in panic and I desperately searched its deepest recesses for why this would not be such a good idea. Then it went into overdrive.

"Na, I don't think you'd enjoy it that much," I countered. "I mean it's like what you saw today, only five times as bad."

"I quite enjoyed it," he said.

"But you didn't understand anything that was going on," I pointed out, hoping that the desperation in my voice wasn't too obvious.

Barry looked like he was going to sulk. "Well, what else am I going to do," he sniffed.

Fearing responsibility for a hostel suicide, I blurted out the first thing that came into my head. "Byron Bay," I said.

"What?"

"Byron Bay," I repeated. "It's supposed to be great. Thousands of backpackers go up there. There are beaches, the nightlife's mad, apparently. You'll meet loads of people, have a great time, maybe find a new girlfriend."

He didn't look convinced but I unrolled a giant map from my backpack and outlined with my index finger the route up the coast. By midnight I had practically booked his bus ticket for him. The next morning I skipped down to Newcastle station before it was light. When I turned the lock and swung round in the dark I half expected him to be perched there, shining a torch accusingly into my eyes. But he wasn't and I never saw him again. Perhaps he did go to Byron Bay, had met another Australian nurse and opened a bar. I was sure I would recognise him from his glasses and my guilt would make me his best patron. Or maybe he had gone back to Bootle a beaten man, and I was to blame.

In the end, we didn't stop in Byron Bay, nor Coffs Harbour, but somewhere in between. Sue liked the sound of the quiet seaside town of Yamba but first we explored – without getting out of the car – the inland community of Maclean. Its original inhabitants, if you disregard the Aborigines – and you shouldn't because the Gumbaingirr and Yaygir peoples were a particularly inventive bunch – were mainly colonising Scots. Mainly, it should be noted, farmers who swapped the Highlands for, quite literally, the lowlands: lying on the Clarence River, the town is only six metres above sea level. The Celtic connection was one the tourist board in the area was keen to encourage, marking telegraph poles with tartan patterns and street signs bilingually in English and Gaelic. We didn't stay long enough to taste the local speciality – haggis – and continued the 20 kilometres to Yamba, named after the aboriginal for headland. We found a spacious motel on what appeared to be part of the headland and walked into town for a beer at a pub overlooking a lovely beach and with a paunchy Staffordshire bull terrier, which seemed unable to find a comfortable resting place in the sun, for a pet.

The build up continued unabated. As we had an al fresco breakfast at a deserted café the next morning 50 yards' walk from the motel, Shane Warne was laying into Geraint Jones in print – more precisely the pages of the tabloid *Sydney Daily Telegraph*, which had headed each page of its pre-series coverage with the words 'ASHES REVENGE'. Jones, who had been dropped in favour of Chris Read as wicketkeeper for the last two Tests of the preceding English summer, had done little to justify his return, but Duncan Fletcher, whose memory was so selective that it judged Jones' one top quality innings for his country – in partnership with Flintoff at Trent Bridge in the 2005 Ashes – above all others, was certain to reinstate him. Indeed, it transpired that he had been told before the warm-up games that he would definitely be in the team for Brisbane – a decision which surprised Jones himself, who somehow, it later emerged, had inveigled his way on to the tour selection panel. Two fifties in 19 innings since Trent Bridge didn't really support Fletcher's case that the Kent player was much the superior batsman to Read, even if an inferior gloveman, but on the basis that turkeys don't vote for Christmas, Jones wasn't going to put his hand up in favour of his rival.

But Warne's criticism, far from being the sensational put-down that the newspaper headline suggested, was as precisely directed as one of his flippers – and as potentially injurious. And it didn't stop at Jones. He also professed bewilderment at the possibility that Ashley Giles, injured for the best part of a year, might be favoured over Monty Panesar, who had 32 wickets in ten Tests since making his debut against India in the preceding March.

"They're trying to strengthen the batting, when they're losing two of the most important arts – 'keeping and spin bowling," Warne said. Few English fans would have disagreed with that, but the use of Panesar ahead of Giles in Adelaide implied that the Sikh of Tweak, as he would later be immortalised on a banner, was a shoo-in for the Gabba. Perhaps Fletcher took Warne's words as a double bluff and believed that Jones and Giles were the players they most feared. Or maybe not.

Still, it was something to think about as we set out on the last stage of the journey, which would take us to Brisbane after a brief detour to take some snaps of Surfer's Paradise.

Prime Minister's XI v England XI

Played at Manuka Oval, Canberra, on 10 November 2006 (50-over match)
Result Prime Minister's XI won by 166 runs

Prime Minister's XI innings (50 overs maximum)		R	M	B	SR
PA Jaques	c Cook b Collingwood	112	166	110	101.81
✝TD Paine	c ✝Jones b Flintoff	6	22	16	37.50
MJ Cosgrove	c Strauss b Giles	24	54	34	70.58
TR Birt	b Mahmood	40	53	45	88.88
SE Marsh	not out	78	96	56	139.28
AC Voges	c Pietersen b Anderson	39	43	32	121.87
✳ CL White	not out	30	17	14	214.28
Extras	(b 1, lb 1, w 9, nb 7)	18			
Total	**(5 wickets; 50 overs; 228 mins)**	**347 (6.94 runs per over)**			

Did not bat BR Dorey, AM Ritchard, SW Tait, BW Hilfenhaus
Fall of wickets 1-15 (Paine, 5.3 ov), 2-75 (Cosgrove, 16.4 ov), 3-162 (Birt, 29.1 ov), 4-214 (Jaques, 36.4 ov), 5-292 (Voges, 46.2 ov)

Bowling	O	M	R	W	Econ	
JM Anderson	10	1	65	1	6.50	(2w)
A Flintoff	10	0	55	1	5.50	(1nb, 1w)
SI Mahmood	9	0	97	1	10.77	(6nb, 4w)
MS Panesar	3	0	17	0	5.66	
AF Giles	8	0	53	1	6.62	(2w)
PD Collingwood	10	0	58	1	5.80	

England XI innings target: 348 runs from 50 overs)		R	M	B	SR
ME Trescothick	c White b Tait	2	3	6	33.33
AJ Strauss	c Hilfenhaus b Tait	67	92	67	100.00
AN Cook	c ✝Paine b Hilfenhaus	4	24	14	28.57
PD Collingwood	c Jaques b White	35	53	41	85.36
KP Pietersen	c ✝Paine b Hilfenhaus	7	15	10	70.00
✳ A Flintoff	b Tait	1	9	3	33.33
✝GO Jones	not out	13	70	41	31.70
AF Giles	run out (White/ ✝Paine)	13	30	19	68.42
SI Mahmood	st ✝Paine b White	22	22	22	100.00
JM Anderson	lbw b Ritchard	0	4	4	0.00
MS Panesar	c White b Ritchard	1	6	9	11.11
Extras	(lb 3, w 9, nb 4)	16			
Total	**(all out; 38.4 overs; 169 mins)**	**181 (4.68 runs per over)**			

Fall of wickets 1-3 (Trescothick, 0.6 ov), 2-24 (Cook, 6.6 ov), 3-107 (Collingwood, 19.6 ov), 4-119 (Strauss, 21.5 ov), 5-123 (Pietersen, 22.5 ov), 6-124 (Flintoff, 23.1 ov), 7-146 (Giles, 30.5 ov), 8-177 (Mahmood, 35.4 ov), 9-178 (Anderson, 36.4 ov), 10-181 (Panesar, 38.4 ov)

Bowling	O	M	R	W	Econ	
SW Tait	8	2	21	3	2.62	(1nb, 3w)
BW Hilfenhaus	8	1	49	2	6.12	(3nb, 3w)
BR Dorey	5	0	27	0	5.40	
AM Ritchard	4.4	0	24	2	5.14	
CL White	7	0	32	2	4.57	(3w)
AC Voges	2	0	13	0	6.50	
MJ Cosgrove	4	0	12	0	3.00	

New South Wales v England XI

Played at Sydney Cricket Ground on 12,13,14 November 2006 (3-day match)
Result Match drawn

New South Wales 1st innings (50 overs maximum)		R	M	B	SR
PA Jaques	c Harmison b Giles	107	194	157	68.15
EJM Cowan	b Harmison	26	38	28	92.85
✹ SM Katich	c Pietersen b Giles	68	194	120	56.66
MJ Clarke	c Trescothick b Panesar	50	132	87	57.47
AW O'Brien	c Trescothick b Anderson	6	22	22	27.27
D Smith	c ✥Jones b Harmison	45	158	113	39.82
MC Henriques	lbw b Harmison	29	65	57	50.87
NM Hauritz	c Giles b Hoggard	5	20	8	62.50
B Casson	not out	3	20	4	75.00
NW Bracken	c Trescothick b Anderson	8	15	15	53.33
Extras	(lb 1, w 3, nb 4)	8			
Total	**(9 wickets dec; 101.1 overs)**	**355 (3.50 runs per over)**			

Did not bat B Lee, SR Clark, SCG MacGill, GD McGrath
Fall of wickets 1-38 (Cowan, 9.4 ov), 2-193 (Jaques, 45.5 ov), 3-216 (Katich, 54.2 ov), 4-224 (O'Brien, 59.4 ov), 5-289 (Clarke, 76.6 ov), 6-334 (Henriques, 93.6 ov), 7-343 (Smith, 97.5 ov), 8-343 (Hauritz, 98.1 ov), 9-355 (Bracken, 101.1 ov)

Bowling	O	M	R	W	Econ	
MJ Hoggard	17	5	58	1	3.41	
SJ Harmison	20	1	95	3	4.75	(1nb, 3w)
JM Anderson	15.1	3	45	2	2.96	
A Flintoff	15	4	52	0	3.46	(3nb)
MS Panesar	19	2	58	1	3.05	
AF Giles	15	3	46	2	3.06	

England XI 1st innings (120 overs maximum)		R	M	B	SR
ME Trescothick	b Lee	8	15	14	57.14
AJ Strauss	c & b Clark	50	88	57	87.71
AN Cook	lbw b McGrath	59	158	96	61.45
IR Bell	c ✥Smith b Clark	0	6	2	0.00
KP Pietersen	c Lee b Bracken	122	258	171	71.34
✹ A Flintoff	b Clark	62	105	102	60.78
PD Collingwood	c Jaques b Hauritz	5	15	17	29.41
✥GO Jones	b McGrath	13	42	35	37.14
AF Giles	b Lee	9	43	32	28.12
MJ Hoggard	not out	7	38	19	36.84
SJ Harmison	b Bracken	2	7	6	33.33
Extras	(b 1, lb 3, w 1, nb 7)	12			
Total	**(all out; 90.4 overs)**	**349 (3.84 runs per over)**			

Did not bat JM Anderson, SI Mahmood, MS Panesar
Fall of wickets 1-9 (Trescothick, 3.5 ov), 2-95 (Strauss, 19.5 ov), 3-95 (Bell, 21.1 ov), 4-166 (Cook, 37.4 ov), 5-282 (Flintoff, 65.1 ov), 6-289 (Collingwood, 68.6 ov), 7-330 (Jones, 79.3 ov), 8-332 (Pietersen, 82.6 ov), 9-346 (Giles, 89.2 ov), 10-349 (Harmison, 90.4 ov)

Bowling	O	M	R	W	Econ	
GD McGrath	18	2	63	2	3.50	(1nb)
B Lee	13	2	57	2	4.38	(5nb)
SR Clark	17	1	50	3	2.94	(1nb, 1w)
NW Bracken	14.4	1	51	2	3.47	
MC Henriques	3	0	24	0	8.00	
B Casson	11	1	50	0	4.54	
NM Hauritz	14	2	50	1	3.57	

New South Wales 2nd innings

		R	M	B	SR
PA Jaques	run out (Mahmood)	4	6	4	00.00
EJM Cowan	c ✠ Jones b Hoggard	8	18	12	66.66
✱ SM Katich	retired hurt	55	130	90	61.11
MJ Clarke	b Giles	68	169	105	64.76
AW O'Brien	c Strauss b Anderson	2	18	20	10.00
✠ D Smith	b Anderson	0	2	1	0.00
MC Henriques	lbw b Anderson	12	29	22	54.54
NM Hauritz	not out	20	35	32	62.50
B Casson	not out	12	25	22	54.54
Extras	(b 6, lb 5, nb 2)	13			
Total	**(6 wickets; 51 overs)**	**194 (3.80 runs per over)**			

Did not bat NW Bracken, B Lee, SR Clark, SCG MacGill, GD McGrath
Fall of wickets 1-4 (Jaques, 0.4 ov), 2-18 (Cowan, 4.2 ov), 2-118* (Katich, retired not out), 3-132 (O'Brien, 35.2 ov), 4-132 (Smith, 35.3 ov), 5-156 (Henriques, 41.5 ov), 6-165 (Clarke, 43.1 ov)

Bowling	O	M	R	W	Econ	
MJ Hoggard	7	2	24	1	3.42	
SJ Harmison	5	0	27	0	5.40	
MS Panesar	13	2	38	0	2.92	
JM Anderson	10	1	40	3	4.00	
AF Giles	8	0	32	1	4.00	
A Flintoff	4	1	11	0	2.75	(2nb)
PD Collingwood	4	1	11	0	2.75	

Players per side 14 (11 batting, 11 fielding)

Done like a dinner

THE TESTS

Happy as a bastard on Father's Day

BRISBANE

"WELCOME to hostel-land," I trumpeted, throwing open the door to our room, a grand gesture that almost forced it off its hinges. A stunned silence ensued. The tropical environs of the outside had seemed to force itself inside. The fridge was germinating a new experiment in horticulture, the bed looked as if it might host a multitude of microbes waiting to work their magic on unsuspecting human flesh and the shower and toilet, hidden behind a sliding door, were best left hidden. This was not the indulgent en-suite double our *Lonely Planet* guide had promised us, but it was Somewhere to Stay – literally: you couldn't argue that a hostel with that name didn't do what it said on the tin.

I was aware that this was make-or-break time. "It's perfectly clean," I protested unconvincingly as Sue's face crumpled into the shape of a bedsheet discarded by a man enduring a particularly disturbed passage of sleep. To be fair, this was not fair. This was not a girl who did rough: four stars and an Egon Ronay recommendation were usually the minimum requirements.

"You'll get used to it," I murmured, as we lugged our colossal, matching black hold-alls over the threshold and sought space for them in the tight confines either side of the bed. In truth, there was barely room to swing a cat – and you could have tried because a giant ginger tom was splayed contentedly across the reception counter when we checked in.

However, my guilt was not entirely assuaged by the fact that I had explained well before we had bought the plane tickets that financial considerations meant that some economies on comfort would have to be made. That, of course, was after I had cannily compressed Sue's desire for a year-long round-the-world trip into a three and half month Australian adventure that would, by pure coincidence, tally with England's Ashes tour, and spent Aus$174 on a single ticket to the third day at Adelaide on Ebay (face value nearer $40).

We had arrived in the city late in the afternoon on "tight-arse Tuesday", 36 hours before the start of the first Test, when the aptly-named Pavilion Bar, in the equally appropriate Boundary Street, a lengthy thoroughfare that careered towards the Brisbane River and the Central Business District from our trendy enclave of West End, was serving pizza at a knockdown Aus$10 a go. But we weren't so easily bought and, after a beer outside in the evening sun, sought out the other culinary options, which were plentiful and varied. On one side of the street was a plush eatery offering "advanced Australian fare", which was as good a pun on a national anthem that I'd heard, but the prospect of swallowing seared baby wallaby on a marinated crust of freshwater crocodile snout, or some other such native concoction, got my oesophageal juices flowing in utterly the wrong direction. That said, so did the vegan restaurant opposite, where the clientele - mainly students and butch lesbians - stooped over their plates dangling facial jewellery and hair extensions into their soup.

We settled on Satchmo's, a jazz-themed café, and after I rattled through my first chicken parmigiana of the trip, we strolled back to the hostel, where Sue checked the bed for scorpions and quaffed two-thirds of a bottle of wine to deaden the effect of her surroundings and I sat up watching a fascinating documentary about the second tied Test in history. Australia's game against India in Madras in 1986 was played in such stifling heat that Dean Jones kept throwing up by the side of the pitch before completing a double century and being rushed to a city hospital to be connected to an intravenous drip.

Jones recalled that deserving cases from rickshaw accidents and industrial disasters were wheeled out into the corridors and ignored while a bed was found for the "important Australian Test cricketer", while Allan Border, his captain, revealed that his response to Jones's whingeing about the conditions had been to tell the Victorian middle-order batsman that if he didn't shape up, he'd get a Queenslander – in other words, someone with the requisite toughness – to come out and finish the job.

If the programme was designed to heighten patriotic feelings ahead of the Ashes – not to mention make the Australian players realise the level of commitment that was required – events at Brisbane were to prove that it succeeded.

The opening day of a Test series is always special, but I knew this one was going to be more special than most as soon as I rose from my hostel bed at 6.30am and stepped outside to feed my coffee habit from the machine on the communal verandah. There, on the steps that separated our original, mainly wooden structure from the more modern building I saw a man in a Barmy Army T-shirt being interviewed by an Australian television crew. (It could be a dangerous thing wearing a Barmy Army T-shirt: you could never be sure when a media representative would leap out of the bushes and demand you be a spokesman for the nation.)

I caught a snippet of the conversation, smiling inwardly at his answer to a query about how he could afford to take the winter off to follow England round another country: he simply grinned and swept his arm around in an arc, inviting the cameraman to take some shots that would prove to the audience the paucity of the accommodation he was obliged to occupy.

Caffeine-reinvigorated, I passed the interviewee again, hoping against hope that he hadn't forecast a wildly optimistic outcome to the Test series, and roused an initially unresponsive Sue. By 7.40, we were on the road – a long, straight one called Vulture Street – to the ground. As we walked, we were joined by people with the same goal, spilling from side streets and *en masse* from South Bank Station, down a ramp to our left. It felt as if we were extras in a meticulously choreographed number from a well-known musical or part of a protest group marching on a parliament with a genuine grievance and the conviction of right on our side: in fact, we were just cricket fans desperate to get to the Gabba early enough to circumvent the promised heavy security in time for the start.

The first ball of an Ashes series is not one you want to miss.

It is not so much that the opening delivery sets the tone for what is to follow – although there are those who adamantly maintain that it does – but more that it provides an outlet for all the hopes, the expectations, and the anticipations of the months that have preceded it. It is like a great outpouring of breath that has been held too long, the type that might be expelled by a Buddhist who's been over-zealous in his meditation practice.

We took our seats, two from the end of a row in Bay 43, although it could have been Bay 34 or 76 such was the appearance of uniformity the Gabba had taken on since it had been rebuilt in the past 13 years, when I was there last. There were no stands as such. Its mainly yellow seats were still interspersed in no discernible pattern with others in turquoise and maroon, but to all extents and purposes they were now enclosed inside a compact concrete bowl. Stray too far from home in search of a decent sandwich in the morning session and it could take you until after tea to find your way back.

In those halcyon days of 1994, I stood next to the pitch after England's inevitable defeat and an acquaintance kindly took a photo. There would be no such memento this time: crowds in the intervening years, as far as the authorities were concerned, had become a necessary evil, to be restrained and restricted at all times, and now any form of entry on to the outfield would be punished with a severe fine. Of course, the notion that a few footsteps treading on the hallowed turf at the end of the game would cause irreversible damage was absurd: on the first day itself, before play got underway, there were shoals of people perusing the pitch and the square. Who were they all – the privileged besuited and booted? Several recognisable faces identified them as television and radio pundits, gofers and groundsmen, marketing men and women – here's Nasser, there's Bumble and there's that girl with the headphones and clipboard who's always busying herself on the periphery – all trailing marks of the right to be there, their superiority to the masses converging in the stands.

There was joking and friendly banter in the rows in front of us as a couple of Australians, with the ruddy complexions, facial hair and hands the size of wheelbarrows that suggested workers of the land, perhaps farmers, had to get out of their seats to allow in a mixed-sex group of Poms and found that they were hedged in by the old enemy; a further bunch of England fans – all of them male, squeezed in behind us – tying their flags to the railings or laying them across seats where there was space.

Our immediate neighbour moved in at the end of the row: "Are you Dave's mate?" he asked, leaning across Sue.

"Yes," I said. "Are you Paul?"

"Darren," he said, proffering his hand.

Who was Paul, then, I thought. I was sure Dave Townsend, my work colleague and perennial ghost writer for Mike Gatting from whom Darren had also bartered tickets for the Test, had mentioned I'd be sitting next to a Paul.

Darren was a tallish, thickset disc jockey from Blackpool, affable, with the gift of the gab, not surprisingly, and a penchant for disappearing at various points throughout the afternoon to the bay diagonally opposite, where he would find members of the Barmy Army, dispersed by Cricket Australia's ticket policy, to enjoy a beer with. Some of those exposed to the sun all day had taken to watching the game in the pub, he later told us.

Paul, I surmised, was the guy who squeezed in unnoticed between Darren and Sue at some point during the Australians' opening partnership. More quietly-spoken, he was an electrician who'd been working his way around much of south-east Asia and was now doing his darnedest to follow the Ashes. He seemed to know my name but for the reason that we never formally introduced ourselves, I came to refer to him simply as The Man Who Isn't Called Darren.

This pair, along with Sue, were to be my companions in the endurance of failure over the next four and half days, although as the dignatories assembled for the opening ceremony – since when did a cricket series need an opening ceremony; weren't these the preserve of Olympic Games and football World Cups? – I took a moment to myself, a kind of meditation reflecting on the fact that this was *it*, this was what all the waiting, the planning, the talking and the travelling had been about. Before us lay 25 days, brimful of hope, expectation, but mostly, potential. But I was jolted out of my attempted reverie by a sight and sound not normally experienced within the confines of a Test venue – apart from at

Twenty20 matches. It was the wailing of The Young Divas, an Australian girl group unknown to me but hugely popular in their homeland, whose rendition of their national anthem was such that I thought it was being reinterpreted as a Lionel Richie love song. As the schmaltzy performance continued, flags of the combatant countries were slowly raised up two parallel white poles. Oh deary, deary me.

I remember the first ball at the Gabba in 1994 with some dismay. In my mind's eye I see Martin McCague, the hefty opening bowler raised in Australia, delivering with his heavy stride a ball wide of off stump: Michael Slater, a fellow Australian, perhaps outraged to see his former compatriot in opposition, picks the width and length instantaneously, leans on to the back foot and crashes it through cover point for a boundary. It is a stroke of instant disrespect and the bowler – who had played for Western Australia before opting for a county career with Kent and jumping ship straight into England's weaker pace attack by virtue of being born in Northern Ireland – seems ruined from then on. He concedes 80 runs from 14 erratic overs on the first day and only fractionally atones with the wickets of tailenders Craig McDermott and Glenn McGrath on the second. Come the second innings he is sidelined with a stomach complaint and can't bowl and never plays for his – adopted – country again.

Except, of course, the memory plays tricks. Slater's shot to the cover boundary was not from the bowling of McCague but that of Phillip De Freitas, as liable as almost anyone to open his spell with what was always termed, unforgivably, as a "loosener". Like an Australian of any recent vintage would bowl one of those. It is unlikely that 12 years down the line, however, in the Ashes series of 2018-19, that anyone who was there for the first ball of the 2006-7 series will mistake what they saw.

Justin Langer has run on to the field to a rousing cheer a little ahead of Matthew Hayden, his opening partner, a gesture that signals Australian intent: body language that says to England, 'we're off and running; can you keep up with us'. You'd like to think that Steve Harmison, measuring his run-up at the Stanley Street End, is having similar thoughts, answering, if you like, in the affirmative. In his imagination, what is he seeing? In his body, what is he feeling? In his mind, what is he thinking? I know what I'm thinking, feeling and seeing in my imagination. I'm not seeing a wicked bouncing delivery that rears up unexpectedly to the splice of Langer's bat and lobs gently into the slips where the arc of three men and a gully have time to casually discuss among themselves who should go for it before Paul Collingwood pushes his team-mates out of the way and accepts responsibility – although that would be nice.

No, what I'm anticipating is a ball on a good length, just outside the off stump, with good carry, and which Geraint Jones, side-steeping just a fraction towards first slip, takes cleanly. What I'm also seeing is Langer making a slight movement forward, studying the ball watchfully, undecided whether to commit himself fully to the front foot or back and at the last minute withdrawing his bat – or, perhaps, having a little nibble.

What I'm not anticipating is Steve Harmison racing in, skipping through his delivery stride and spraying the ball, at some pace, wide of a bemused Langer, wide of the return crease outside his off stump, wide of the wicketkeeper, wide of first slip and straight into the hands of Andrew Flintoff, the second man in the cordon. But this *is* what I'm seeing. It's not immediately apparent to us up high behind long leg where the ball has ended up – but not, we are sure, in the gloves of Geraint Jones, who is partially obscuring our view.

PART TWO

I turn to Sue for confirmation, but see in her eyes that she's not sure that this isn't what's meant to happen.

"Has that… that's gone to first slip," I half state, half ask Darren.

"Second," he says. " Yes, Flintoff's got it."

"I don't believe it," I say, but by then we're laughing. "Nooo!"

The crowd is cheering as well. Or jeering. Whatever, it's a remarkable start to a Test series and, for sheer drama, beats the living daylights out of a vicious square cut for four. For sheer *implausibility* it beats the living daylights out of a square cut for four. The reaction, for hours, days and even months later, is like a an A-level exam question: Steve Harmison delivers the first ball of the most anticipated sporting event in Australian history directly into second slip's hands: it is two years to the day that he was ranked the best bowler in the world. Discuss.

The murmurings continue all around us but three balls later Langer is brought to his knees by a yorker which he digs out; in fact, he does more than dig it out, he gets enough bat on it to send it skirting backward of square on the leg side, too square for the man at long leg to get round in time to stop it. Moments later, he flashes at one outside the off stump and, although at catchable height, it careers through the gap between slips and gully and away to the boundary at third man, unguarded as is strangely customary these days. In the second over Matthew Hayden plays and misses as he aims a hugely expansive drive at Matthew Hoggard, and then gets an outside edge just wide of gully playing the same shot. In such small margins are the distinctions between success and failure recorded.

We have to wait until almost an hour and half of the first session is up until England land their first blow, when Hayden, forced on to the back foot, edges to second slip. I am out of my seat yelling in delight, not something I am prone to do but it is Australia and each wicket against them seems worth three of anyone else's. And symbolically it is Flintoff who strikes. Our leader, as I mistakenly think is signalled by the black armband around his bicep – it is actually a tribute to his wife's grandfather, who has recently died. But equally symbolically, it is Ponting, the man who has carried a heavy can for the Ashes defeat in 2005, who hits back, greeting a quick but short ball from Harmison, who had bloodied him at Lord's in the corresponding Test in England, to the fence in front of square. A stroke of complete control.

Shortly after lunch we are, as England fans, resigned to Langer completing his hundred, a remarkable comeback full of cuts, punchy drives and pulls. The second half of Langer's career has brought a remarkable change in batting character. He's the ugly duckling turned into the swan, the chrysalis that's become the butterfly. From a dabber and nudger, impossible to remove, he's become the handsome strokemaker, still impossible to remove. There probably never was a more immoveable Australian.

But just as he's advanced, untroubled, from his lunchtime score of 68 to 83 he shapes to play another withering cut; the blade of his bat scythes it with the contempt of Freddy Krueger garrotting another hapless teenage victim, and it seers away into the off side with the velocity of a missile fired low enough to avoid enemy radar. But Kevin Pietersen, the sole border guard patrolling the covers, is roused from his perennial self-absorption and a split second later the ball slams into the centre of his hands as he stoops to his right. It's a great shot and it's just as good a catch and I have a perfect view of it. I've now seen Pietersen snaffle two stunning efforts in the field on this tour, not bad for a man who looked like his hands had been surgically swapped over during the Ashes of 2005. Was it five chances he dropped, or seven? I can't remember, but it was a good few. He was probably owed the sitter that Warnie put down on the last day at the Oval.

Damien Martyn helps Ponting to add a more watchful 57, but when he cuts Ashley Giles carelessly to slip, the Australians are 198 for three and there is a chink of light. Giles attempts to pull back the curtains the full way when, from round the wicket, he draws Ponting forward, and hits him plumb in front. Billy Bowden, the umpire, begins to raise his crooked index finger but as the Barmy Army and the rest of the English in the ground get ready to celebrate, the digit seems to hover in mid-air for a moment and instead of continuing its trajectory to about a foot in front of his face and straightening, the customary and conventional method of signalling a batsman's demise, it reverses its orbit and makes landfall on the side of his nose, which he proceeds to scratch with some vigour. The cheer in the collective English throat is momentarily trapped in the trachea, the fear in the communal Aussie larynx fleetingly glued to the gullet before both are freed in one almighty sigh of disappointment or relief.

Bowden, when I see the replay later on a bar television, is as guilty as Basil Fawlty in the episode about the Germans when he confides to Polly: "I mentioned the war once but I think I got away with it." But he hides it well. This man could be flown secretly to a neutral country, kept awake for a week and interrogated at intervals by three intimidating CIA officers and he would still come up with the same response: "Not out."

It's not just the crooked finger that's to blame in my opinion. Bowden maintains that he is physiologically unable to straighten it in the orthodox manner because of arthritis, but I wonder whether, more poignantly, he is psychologically able to come to terms with a poll of Australian Test cricketers that has voted him the second-worst umpire in the world. This vote, revealed after a series against the West Indies that contained a number of contentious decisions, is not as straightforward as it might appear. Being considered the second-worst umpire on the ten-strong elite panel appointed by the International Cricket Council is not so bad: in the bigger scheme of things, it makes you the ninth best umpire on the planet.

I'm not saying he's biased; I'm not saying he's a cheat; that would be ridiculous. All I'm saying is that that might have been playing on his mind when he had to rule on an exceptionally close lbw decision against the captain of Australia, the symbolic head of that voting panel, on the first day of the most anticipated Ashes series of all time.

Or I could be quite wrong. The meeting of the ball and pad in front of the stumps may, by some unknown form of quantum physics, have resulted in the almost instantaneous itch on Bowden's proboscis.

As it is Ponting goes on from 72 at the time of his fortuitous escape to be 138 not out by the end of the day. With Michael Hussey, a player so hungry you feel as if he must have been held in an underground dungeon and fed only scraps in the years that he was unable to force his way into the Australian middle order – in truth he was honing his skills on England's county grounds, where he made a habit of scoring triple-centuries – he has added an unbroken 148 in 42.4 overs. For almost half the day's play, England have gone wicketless. The curtains have been well and truly drawn closed again.

It is the time when late afternoon merges into evening, 5.4 overs into the England reply on day two, and Darren, The Man Who Isn't Called Darren and I all have our heads in our hands. If we were to look up and around us we would see hundreds of England supporters adopting a similar pose. There is an empty seat beside me: Sue is somewhere deep in the bowels of the stand, vomiting. It is not the result of over-consumption of alcohol, more the consequence of the heat, the walk to the ground and the hours we have spent travelling, but it is the most pertinent comment on the difficulty England find themselves in. Facing the prospect of scoring 403 to save the follow-on, we have started quite well, which is a pleasant surprise because after Australia's declaration, Brett Lee and Glenn McGrath are aware that they can give it full throttle in the 17-over session to come. But then it has gone horribly, horribly wrong.

The noise must have been apparent to the England openers as they strapped on their thigh pads, aligned their chest guards and psyched themselves up in the dressing-room for the initiation they were about to receive. You wouldn't have blamed either of them for stripping off all of their equipment just before they were due to go out and making a swift excursion – or two - to the gents. You understand why Trescothick has cut and run. What would this have done to his already tender mental state? The sound is building to a crescendo, spreading out from all parts and meeting in the middle of an arena that is so enclosed that it would have no means of escape except to head upwards, rising fountain-like through and over where any roof would be. But, instead it seems to remain static, suspended over the centre of the pitch where Andrew Strauss and Alastair Cook are taking guard. Lee is scratching a mark at the end of his run-up like a bull pawing the earth before making a charge.

I look for positives amid the cacophony. Strauss is now an experienced international opener, 31 Tests in his locker, and a seemingly phlegmatic character; Cook has only played nine, but a double-century he scored for Essex against the tourists in a game the weekend ahead of the fifth Test of the 2005 Ashes, earned him plenty of Australian respect. And he has responded expertly to the pressures as they have been piled upon him in his fledgeling career. Pulled out of an England A tour to the Caribbean in March 2006, he scored 60 in his first Test innings in India and an unbeaten century in the second. His chief asset is reckoned to be an ice-cool temperament.

But the pair of them can hardly have experienced anything like this before: on their shoulders rests the burden of giving England a start, drawing the sting of a fired-up Australian attack. Second ball, though, they, and the whole of England are given a moment of respite. Lee, operating at a ferocious pace, swings the ball down the leg side, it evades Adam Gilchrist's dive, although he gets both hands to it and, my, it looks so good to see a ball race to the fence with England batsmen at the crease, even if no one's hit it. Strauss glances another boundary, drives one squarer perhaps than he intended and Cook punches wristily through the covers. I wouldn't say I was beginning to relax, but I do notice that not every muscle in my body is rigid almost to the point of rigor mortis. As we romp along at around five an over, those around me are cheering up as well, imitating the umpires as they signal a four, waving their flags. Two inflatable kangaroos, maybe forced from the hands of their original owners, have been refitted in T-shirts bearing the cross of St George, and are being brandished above a couple of English heads.

Suddenly, though, it all changes, with two wickets in two balls. Strauss pulls an innocuous ball from Glenn McGrath, but in having to drag it from too far outside off stump he has got it on the lower part of the bat and lifted it. The ball swirls high into the air behind square leg before re-entering the earth's atmosphere and plummeting towards splashdown in an area 30 yards forward of long leg. The opportunity interests Michael Hussey at mid-wicket and Brett Lee, racing in from the latter position on the fence. We can see the potential for a collision, but as the men close in on each other, they are not thinking of that and have eyes only for the shiny red leather orb dropping rapidly from the sky. A wicked thought occurs to me as I will the ball to land between them: it involves two Australian cricketers, an ambulance on the outfield, and a paramedic radioing an A&E department with an estimated time of arrival. At this moment, Strauss, running hopefully but with his concentration more anxiously focused on the two as they converge, is probably thinking something similar. Perhaps he's even considering the possibility of taking out two birds with one stone. That would be a result.

There are two cases of Australian fielding misadventure that I'm familiar with and now I'm gambling everything on there being a third. On Christmas Eve, 1976, Jeff Thomson smashed into Alan Turner, advancing from mid-wicket, as he tried to take a return catch off a bouncer to Zaheer Abbas that the Pakistani had lobbed up on the leg side. Thomson went headlong for it but in mid-dive caught sight of Turner also coming in for the catch. Turner landed on top of the quick bowler's right arm while he was still in the air and the pair crashed to the turf as the chance went begging. Thomson got up, in a fury, ready to give Turner, who was lying still on the ground, a good kicking – until he realised that his arm was dangling uselessly from its shoulder, all the ligaments torn or damaged. After surgery, he spent Christmas Day in a sling in an Adelaide hospital crazy from pain that only hourly shots of morphine would ameliorate. When he got home to Brisbane, he was in such agony that he started throwing glasses at the wall – presumably with his good arm. He missed the Centenary Test against England – it didn't matter; Dennis Lillee took 11 wickets and we lost by 45 runs – but, despite fears that he would not be the same bowler he had been before, he recovered well enough to take 23 wickets in the Ashes in England later that year.

More well known, probably because it is of more recent vintage, is the incident involving Steve Waugh and Jason Gillespie in a Test against Sri Lanka in Kandy in 1999. Waugh had been running back, also in the square leg region, to take a catch when he lost sight of the ball in the sun, not to mention the sight of Gillespie loping in from the boundary with a similar intention. When the two came together, they threw up a cloud of dust the like of which you normally only see when a couple of characters in a children's cartoon are in a pile-up; no doubt both of them saw a group of birdies circling them after the dust had cleared. Gillespie, it was apparent, had a broken leg, Waugh a face like a bulldog chewing a wasp and being stung at the same time. They were helicoptered off to Colombo like a couple of American soldiers wounded in a raid on a Vietnamese village.

But our hopes of something similar are extinguished as Hussey gets there a split second ahead of Lee, grasping the ball and reeling away in triumph, initially unaware that he has dug his studs into the fast bowler's leg in the process. Lee is on the floor, inspecting his kneecap through an enormous hole that Hussey's spikes have torn in his trousers there, the catcher himself is being assailed by joyous team-mates and Strauss is trooping off, a second dismissal of the tour to one of his favourite strokes, but unforgivable when there are two men placed there for it.

The batsmen have crossed, bringing Cook down to face McGrath, who switches to round the wicket to the left-hander. This tactic worked well for England – and especially for Flintoff – during the 2005 Ashes and Adam Gilchrist, denied the room to unfurl his expansive drives through the covers, was made to look mortal. I suspect, though, that McGrath's decision is based more on his dismissal of Cook in Sydney – and discredits the theory that warm-up games have no real bearing on what comes later.

Cook had looked in no danger in that innings, on the way to an impressive 59, but when McGrath had gone round the wicket, he had trapped him lbw. That, I felt, was more the outcome of a tall batsman being unable to jam down on a ball keeping low, not the strategy itself. If there is a fault in Cook's defensive technique it is that he doesn't bend his knee enough and get over his front leg in playing forward. It is the action of a batsman who half expects the ball to spit at him without warning – a fault that may only cost him dearly against the best of bowling but one that few of the established pundits have picked up in their rush to be first to label him as the next great thing, a future England captain, a batsman with a wonderful future in front of him.

I wonder if I am imagining this, until, finally, Mark Taylor, the former Australia captain, pipes up about it on the Channel 9 commentary during Cook's back-to-the-wall hundred in the second innings of the third Test in Perth. In the meantime, I'm just whistling against the wind. Because it is not leg-before that brings about Cook's downfall. Instead, the lanky Australian metronome puts the ball on that awkward length that makes a batsman uncertain whether to go forward or go back and in his confusion, Cook is turned chest on to the delivery and edges the easiest of catches to Warne at first slip.

McGrath has two in two balls and the place is in uproar: the man written off by Ian Botham, the second eldest of the Dad's Army platoon – Sergeant Wilson to Shane Warne's Private Godfrey – is on a hat-trick. Mr Mainwaring may not be panicking, but I imagine Andrew Flintoff is pacing up and down in the dressing-room, wondering how to repel this figurative German invasion.

Paul Collingwood is the man sent out to face the crisis and to add a little more to the already high level of pressure, Ponting sticks a man in at silly mid-off, right in the Durham man's eye line.

Collingwood survives but before the end edges behind to give Stuart Clark, a revelation in accuracy and almost indiscernible movement, his first Ashes wicket. You can tell the English because they are the ones sitting down, hidden by the thousands of Australians up on their feet, their fingers raised just in case the umpire is in any doubt.

My mind is swimming as I walk away from the Gabba: a sickly Sue has already returned to the hostel. I have plenty of time to cast my thoughts back over the day's play, one in which chances have come and gone for England. Ponting had charged on to 196 in the morning and early afternoon sessions, which, by my reckoning, means Bowden's failure to give him out on the first day has cost us 124 runs – not to mention those that his partners accrued while he was at the crease, among them Hussey, bat as broad as a moat and solid as a castle door, until the heroic Flintoff musketeered a way through. Just when we thought that we were landing significant blows, with Ponting, furious to miss out on a double century, and Adam Gilchrist, another dangerman, dismissed by Hoggard in a single over (two lbw appeals miraculously upheld by Steve Bucknor), Michael Clarke and a swishing tail of Warne, Lee, and particularly Stuart Clark, pummelling sixes with an air that mixed insolence and insouciance, dumped us back on our arses and barely able to last the count.

A frustrated Steve Harmison, who had followed his first day precedent by starting with a wide on the second day as well, showed the aggression that was lacking in his bowling when Shane Warne poked a ball back down the pitch, picking up the ball and hurling down the unguarded wicket. "He's hit the stumps at last," crowed Channel 9 commentator Bill Lawry, whose comments I have heard through the $15 earpiece that, at the flick of a switch, provides coverage from either the television network or ABC radio. "He's a better thrower than he is a bowler." A few months later Lawry was voted Australia's third best commentator, but, having previously found him a man who likes nothing more than the type of dig at the Poms that would be anathema to Richie Benaud, I can't say he does much for me. Thankfully, Benaud, of course, topped the poll of 15,641 respondents. Less understandably, Kerry O'Keefe, the Australian leg-break bowler of the early Seventies, claimed second place, despite a style that focuses less on the cricket and more on his after-dinner speaking engagements or his behaviour at a barbecue the previous night. He feigns self-deprecation but seems to find his antics strangely hilarious. I thought he was the only one, but the figures suggest I'm in the minority. Unfortunately his fellow commentators are too willing to indulge his vanity.

Sue was not the happiest of sights when I returned to the hostel. But, despite her sickness, which had left her flat on her back on the bed, she had at least discovered the air conditioning, hidden high up behind the curtains. Food was the last thing on her list of needs, so I stepped out into Brisbane's nightlife alone. Not being in the mood to sit sadly on my own in Satchmo's or Tukka's, I instead decided to sit sadly on my own outside Slice, an informal but welcoming pizza takeaway. At the counter, the operator, on hearing my accent, told me that he had been forced to take on extra staff to help meet the unending demand for his products among English supporters holed up in the hotels and backpackers' resorts around the city. Their enormous 36-slicer had proved the most popular for delivery. He showed me one just out of the oven and explained that they were too big to be conveyed by motorbike – well one without an enormous sidecar anyway. As if to illustrate the point, a man drew up in a small car, stuffed it precariously on his back seat and chauffeured it away to be savoured and devoured by some hungry – or greedy – mouths in another part of town.

It was while flicking through a copy of the *Brisbane Courier & Mail*, the local daily paper, while I waited to be served my more modest six slicer – I think that's a ten-incher in old money – that I came upon an advert offering a service that could well be needed by England supporters as the despondency over the team's performance increased by the day. Cleo's, based only 200 metres from the Gabba, was targeting customers from the cricket with a brazenness you definitely wouldn't find in the classifieds at *The Times*. For Cleo's was a brothel. I thought that in the interests of research I should find out more – for example, did the Barmy Army or their Aussie counterparts The Fanatics make the better bed partners? Did cricket success have any influence on that?

Scientific studies had shown that football fans in the throes of victory enjoyed huge rises in testosterone; maybe I could get anecdotal evidence from the workers of a similar effect in cricket – but I was too nervous just to get on the phone there and then. I'd never spoken to a madam before and thought that an Australian one might be more than a bit scary so, instead, after finishing my Hawaiian, I stopped off at an internet café on the way back to the hostel and popped the name into the search engine.

Disappointingly, Cleo's, which turned out to be a member of the legally-recognised Queensland Adult Business Association, had no website, but another licensed bordello, also close to the cricket ground, did have. The QABA's code of ethics stated that its brothels were committed to safe sex. What did that mean in a cricket context? That you had to keep your pads on? This was dangerous territory, but curiosity got the better of me and I pressed on, taking a 360 degree virtual tour of one of the establishments, totally unaware that I was about to be revealed as a raving pervert in front of a roomful of web-surfers. It was when I clicked the link for a view of the clients' private suites that things took a turn for the embarrassing. Suddenly, a seductive, refined female Australian voice simpered from the computer in front of me, promising, at a volume that turned heads in an instant, to take me on "an erotic ride" I'd never forget. As I frenziedly sought a button that would silence the saccharine siren, she informed me that "passionate décor will heighten your every experience". Unlike Somewhere to Stay, I would have thought, but was too chastened to do so. And, besides, before I could react, someone calling herself Lilly offered to make my fantasies come true – and it didn't involve us retaining the Ashes. I wanted a crack the size of those developing on the Gabba pitch to open up and swallow me, but it didn't, so in desperation I thumped a series of buttons until the screen eventually went blank, pushed back my seat while studiously trying to avoid eye-contact with anyone, and slipped a two dollar coin next to the till as I made my exit as hastily as I could.

"You were a long time," said Sue when I arrived back at the hostel, sweating profusely and breathing heavily.

"Er, yes," I replied. "I just stopped off to check some emails. Pizza was good though."

⁂

A daily public-address announcement at the Gabba ordered people not to "offend, insult, disparage, humiliate (and any number of other synonyms for upset) persons of another race. Obviously, Cricket Australia had failed to pass the message on to their cricketers, who on the third day did all of those things – to their English counterparts.

In McGrath's first over, on a pitch displaying cracks that Geoffrey Boycott could get his car keys, house keys and his auntie's pinny down without disturbing the surface, a ball lands on one and moves away from Kevin Pietersen almost as much as a Shane Warne leg-spinner, but a darned sight quicker. The wicket presents such a disturbing sight when it is pictured on the giant replay screen that you feel as if the Australian drought – the worst apparently in 1,000 years, although who's been keeping records that long I don't know – has been visited on this one strip of baked earth. The only surprise is that there isn't the skull of a camel or kangaroo lying on a length.

We're 53-3 at the start and this is not what we want to see. Ian Bell, who impressed me the previous night, is also beaten, although his technique continues to look sound. Sounder, at least, than that of Pietersen, who has clearly decided to fight fire with fire, even if that means throwing away the batting textbook. Fortune favours the brave initially as he aims an ugly pull at a ball from Lee that is on him too quickly and spirals up just beyond mid-on, where Stuart Clark, unsure whether to backpedal or turn and run and take it over his shoulder, eventually opts for the latter and makes a complete hash of it. Clark, whose happy-go-lucky expression doesn't seem to change whether he is taking wickets or dropping catches, wears an inscrutable look as he ambles amiably back to mid-on. Perhaps he knows the chances will come at regular enough intervals.

He is right.

McGrath shoots one back off a crack and Pietersen, deciding to leave the ball, is rapped on the back pad. This time Billy Bowden's finger is up in an instant and although slow-motion replays suggest that the ball would have missed by a margin later ascertained to be 6.9cm, you can't blame him for the decision. At full speed, Pietersen looks as doomed as an impala wandering into a lions' enclosure.

If Flintoff has been pacing up and down in the dressing-room, by the time he gets to the middle, he is drained of nervous energy; he appears horribly static at the crease, afraid to attack and wary of moving his feet and, not surprisingly, does not last long – three balls to be exact. His limp defensive stroke outside the off stump is the shot of a man in denial. At 79 for five, I'd like to join him in that frame of mind. Geraint Jones and Bell provide some resistance, adding 47 in a little over 20 overs, which are not without their moments of entertainment, supplied mainly by the much-maligned wicketkeeper.

First he meets a Clark half-volley on middle and off with the full face of the bat and sends it streaking across the surface through mid-on for four. Then he almost leaves Billy Bowden, umpiring at square leg, in need of a hip replacement operation with a bone-shuddering sweep off Shane Warne that knocks him off his feet, though Bowden, to his credit, doesn't milk it, springing back up, alert with knees bent, turning this way and that as if worried the sniper will unleash a second, decisive shot from another angle. Jones is not best pleased because Bowden, now checking his hat for a player's sunglasses that are perched there, and his radio to the third umpire, which may have cushioned the blow, has prevented a certain four. But his pleasure with his earlier drive off Clark was so evident that he held the follow-through long enough for a skilled sculptor to have cast him in bronze and produced a statue by the end of the day.

The Bowden incident, rib-tickling as it is, temporarily releases the pressure on English spectators - if not their batsmen - but it is soon back to reality as Jones's resistance is ended by McGrath nipping one back, allegedly off the cracks, and catching him in front. Ashley Giles, in his guise as extra batsman, scythes, skews and miscues his way into the twenties; these would be important runs in a closely-fought match, but in this context, one in which England are being massacred, they are little more than a distracting irrelevance. Especially as the impressive Bell is undone flashing at a widish ball from Clark shortly after he has completed a well deserved fifty. Having occupied the crease for 12 minutes short of four hours and faced 162 balls, you can't help feeling that he's not been rewarded with the score he deserves. His effort would be worth double against many another attack.

The end is not long in coming: Steve Harmison, Matthew Hoggard and James Anderson do not detain the scorers unduly and we have to endure three displays of Glenn McGrath's annoyingly blokey acknowledgement of the crowd's appreciation. First, when he takes his fifth wicket, he raises the ball above his head and turns to various sections of the ground to greet the applause; then, when he disappears to the deep, where a sizeable group of Australian fans are bowing in respect for his Messiah-like qualities, he gives them the simple thumbs-up; it's the Aussie version of the tip of the cap. And finally, having finished with figures of six for 50, he leads the team off to rollicking cheers and shows the ball once more to his admiring disciples. He even feigns a slight limp in a sly response to the Botham sledges.

Grudgingly I'll admit it's a fine comeback for a man who's not seen Test action for ten months, and fearfully, I'll grant you, he might be a handful when he really hits form. Trouble is, I don't feel as if he's had to bowl that well to achieve it.

Attention now, in my corner of the ground – and probably most others and certainly on the television and radio commentaries – turns to the question of the follow-on. It is a no-brainer: England are 445 runs behind and Australia's bowlers have only delivered 62 overs. They could probably put England back in twice and they'd still fail to pass Australia's first innings total. But the sight of Matthew Hayden jogging off suggests he is going to get his pads on, a decision that leaves Ian Chappell, the man at the microphone on Channel 9, in a state somewhere on the outskirts of the hinterland of incredulous. "If they are going to bat again I just can't believe it," he says, although I can't help feeling the strine version, "starve the lizards", would have been a more eloquent way of expressing his astonishment.

Amid the general disbelief, however, the counter-arguments are raised: the opinion that McGrath, Lee and Clark have borne the brunt of a four-man attack – Warne, who has gone curiously wicketless, has delivered only nine overs – and need a rest, and the suggestion that the Test in Calcutta in April 2001, when they sent the hosts back in and lost, has left an indelible mark on the Australian psyche. Maybe, fancying that England can hardly bat more badly than they have in their first innings, they are cautious of having to chase a small total – something that has been a bit of an Achilles' heel despite their general dominance of the international game in recent years – on a pitch with cracks potentially widening by the minute.

Ah yes, the cracks. When Australia bat again, it is as if a large curtain has been drawn around the square while one of the groundsmen has sneaked on with a wheelbarrow full of earth and filled them all in. James Anderson, entrusted with opening the bowling in place of the wayward Harmison despite conceding 18 more runs from one fewer over than the Durham man in the first innings, finds not the spiteful areas of the pitch, but the malevolent meat of Hayden's bat. The ball goes screaming to the fence on so many occasions that by the close Australia have increased their lead by 181. To add insult to injury, the wickets column of the six-strong English attack is unadorned. One man, Hayden, is out, but that can be put down to over-confidence in his running. Anderson proves too quick for him, tearing in from long leg and returning smartly to Jones for the wicketkeeper to whip off the bails with the Queenslander inches short. It is the hollowest of victories and only brings in Ponting, determined to grind Pommie noses into the dust. It is as close to meaningless cricket as you'll get and I can't believe that any but the most psychopathic Australian is really enjoying it. Yet, as the landmarks pass – Ponting reaches 9,000 Test runs – it seems as if the personality disorders are in plentiful supply. And even if the majority of Australian spectators have grown weary of the slaughter, there's still Bill Lawry to revel in English pain: when a frustrated Paul Collingwood shies at the stumps at the non-striker's end from gully and the ball careers off for four overthrows, the commentator is beside himself with joy. "The wheels have fallen off the England bandwagon," he gloats, presumably before being dragged off to the asylum, enraging me enough to switch straight back to the radio broadcast.

It was a heavy-legged troop back to the hostel that night.

The question the following morning is how long Australia will bat on for: they are 626 runs to the good already and to a large extent, the game is on hold until England have to bat again. That feeling, the sense that the crucial action comes only when England are batting, is one that seeps into my being more the longer the tour goes on.

Langer, on 88 overnight, advances, tucking a single into the leg side to complete his 23rd Test century. He celebrates in the modern way, arms aloft, punching the air, removing his helmet and receiving the firm grip of his captain in congratulation. It's pure showbiz; one of the most predictable hundreds of his career is marked as if he has just won the Nobel Prize for batting. It's Australian triumphalism at its finest and the acclaim intensifies as Ponting immediately leads his partner off the field. The declaration has been made.

I look at Darren and the Man Who Isn't Called Darren and raise my eyebrows. No words are necessary but I say some anyway. "Here we go then."

"Yep," replies Darren.

"Oh shit," says the Man Who Isn't Called Darren.

Someone with a very dubious sense of humour is in charge of the musical entertainment between innings and sessions at the Gabba. England fans have already endured the dubious talents of the acoustic-guitar wielding Greg Champion and his sidekick, David Brooks, and their reworking of the Tight Fit UK number one *The Lion Sleeps Tonight*. The new lyrics, which replaced "wimoweh/wimoweh/wimoweh, itself a misheard version of the original song's chorus of "uyimbube' ("you're a lion" in Zulu apparently) with the repeated rendition "They whinge away/they whinge away/they whinge away", have not proved universally popular with the Barmy Army who, I have read, have threatened to boycott the rest of the tour. This is a glorious case of Barmy hypocrisy, of course, seeing as it comes from a group of supporters that have not tired of reminding their hosts that their ancestors arrived in Australia in ball and chains and, by their emphasis, in their regular warblings of the national anthem, that "God Save *Your* Queen". Now, as Strauss and Cook strap on their abdominal protectors and Freddie no doubt gives an inspirational Churchillian speech, Coldplay's hit song *(I will try to) Fix You* is transmitted over the public address system. Is this some discreet message from the Australian authorities offering extra coaching to Steve Harmison and his hapless band of fast bowlers or, in light of Chris Martin's plaintive, high-pitched tone, a desperate plea for a more competitive series?

A strong sense of déjà vu begins to overtake me as England's openers make a start equally as comfortable as that of their first innings; Andrew Strauss clips Brett Lee off his pads for four, Alastair Cook hooks the same bowler emphatically from in front of his face, but we are on 29, only one run ahead of the score on which we lost our first two wickets first time around, when Strauss is lured into a mistake, a fatal mistake which has striking and infuriating similarities to one he made earlier. Stuart Clark pitches short and Strauss reacts obligingly instinctively, a manoeuvre that involves a swivel of the hips and feet and enough bottom hand to help the ball into the long leg region.

If you could have zoomed into my face at that moment you would have seen it go through rapid transformations that can probably only otherwise be achieved by a series of Botox injections. From a scowl of concentration possibly as intense as those of the batsmen, the muscles in my forehead lift and expand as Strauss connects pleasingly enough; when I realise that the ball is heading low and fast to Ryan Broad, the substitute fielder, positioned right in front of me, my eyes widen and pupils dilate like a man anticipating the gruesome fate of a character in a horror movie. And as Broad swoops in the few yards he needs to in order to pouch the chance in his lap, my mouth, too, is opening in dismay. By the time the cosmetic surgeon has finished with me I have formed an expression in my vocal chords which will accompany me around the continent from this day on. "For fuck's sake, Strauss," I shout.

Shortly afterwards, Bell, the hero of the first innings – although mainstay might be a better word – gives Shane Warne his first wicket of the match when he pushes forward to the leg-spinner's 'slider', a ball that goes more or less straight on instead of turning, and hits the front pad microseconds before coming nicely out of the middle of his bat. Warne, as usual, doesn't hold back in his appeal but with the combined sound of bat and pad, as well as the reasonable stride the batsman has taken down the pitch, I don't think it can be out. The trouble with Steve Bucknor as an umpire, though – and this must be as maddening for a batsman as it is for those watching – is the length of time he takes to make a decision. Some umpires are instinctive, go with their gut feeling, use a bit of intuition. Not Bucknor. He is like a clunky and unwieldy 1970s computer, the kind that takes up a whole room or more, that has to run all the information backwards and forwards through numerous slightly smaller processors, calculating and recalculating before whirring the answer back to the master machine. WiFi broadband he is not. So, finally, just when we think Bell, who has yet to score, is safe, Bucknor receives his print-out, studies it intently, and slowly, almost apologetically, reveals its conclusion. It is more bad news for England.

Our hopes of a better showing in the second innings are fast fading. Warne is now in his element, coming round the wicket and turning the ball from the footmarks into the left-handed Cook. There are two short legs stationed for any slight error, one squarish, one straighter and a little deeper. It is the squarer one who is called into action as Cook pushes out in front of his pad, gets a thick inside edge and Hussey takes the catch, a comfortable one. Paul

Collingwood, at the other end, looks so far out his depth against the movement of Clark that you half expect a group of bronzed men in skimpy trunks from the Surf Lifesaving Queensland to run on and haul him to safety.

But Collingwood is at least not one to panic in these situations: he's read the notices on the beach and knows that rather than fighting against a riptide, you should let it carry you where it will, then swim parallel to the shore to escape it. Back on dry land he begins to flourish – on one occasion helping a Brett Lee bouncer over first slip and into the hands of the sightscreen attendant, who nonchalantly gets up from his shaded position, takes a couple of steps to his left and takes the catch. What a country.

At 91 for three, Collingwood is joined by Kevin Pietersen and thus begins the partnership that restores some English pride, if it has no significance, ultimately, on the result. It is the most enjoyable of afternoons. At last, we feel as if this is what we're here for: sitting in strong Queensland sunshine, watching England batsmen dish out some punishment to the Aussies. Collingwood punches fours off the back foot and pulls strongly, while Pietersen sets out to antagonise Warne, moving his feet superbly to flip him through the on-side against the spin. He hits it so cleanly, places it so well, that mid-on is passed in an instant and deep mid-wicket can't get around to cut it off. Perhaps Pietersen is having flashbacks to the Oval 2005. Some of his shots are risky, but they were then, and they came off. Pietersen is a man who toys with the devil.

There is a noteworthy moment in the relationship between these 'best mates' and it comes as Pietersen gets off the mark, with a single to mid-on. As soon as he gets up the other end he wants to take guard in the crease at the non-striker's end but Warne is standing in his way: the batsman gives him a little nudge, provoking him to move, but there is a little reluctance. Finally he does, but there is no acknowledgement of his presence from Warne.

I think too much has been made of this Hampshire alliance. To me it is like a marriage of two A-list celebrities whose individual fame does still not totally satisfy them and who seek even more attention in their coming together. They are like the Posh and Becks of international cricket. Which one is which I'll leave you to decide but as Pietersen begins to get on top, Warne, picking up a defensive return from the batsman, hurls it back towards the wicketkeeper in an act of petulance. It never reaches Adam Gilchrist's gloves because Pietersen, whose bat is hanging back over his shoulder, neatly adjusts and redirects it with a clever upper cut. Then the staring begins, the egos expanding and chests billowing with every moment that passes. The press will make a lot of it the next day, but I'm sure it's just part of the act and what they want; Warne even looks as if he's suppressing a smile.

The fours are now flowing – and most of them from Warne's bowling. Full tosses and flippers, they are all coming the same to Collingwood and Pietersen, who unleash the full repertoire from inside-out drives over extra cover to the slog sweep and the loft over mid-on. Fifties are reached and even when McGrath is brought back, the pair are nicely in the groove. It is a time to forget the bigger scheme of things – the score, for example – and just enjoy the moment.

Of course, it cannot last. Collingwood gets nervy in the 90s and lofts a shot just short of long-on. His impetuosity hinted at, it is finally fully revealed as he attempts the one big hit that will take him to a first century against Australia in only his second Test against them. He keeps his head down and relies on his fast hands to serve him as he advances down the pitch but the shot is so premeditated that Warne maybe spots him coming - I'm sure at least that's what he'd like us to think – perhaps drops it a little shorter and manifestly turns it sharply. As the ball rips past Collingwood's outside edge – a fair way wide of his outside edge in all honesty - Gilchrist is not tested in completing one of the simplest stumping chances of his career. He's out by a mile, but as the Australians rush to Warne and congregate around him, Collingwood is turning back, pointlessly placing his bat back in the crease, perhaps gathering his thoughts as he comes to terms with what he has done. It's a huge blow to the travelling England faithful, who have been starting, against their better natures, to allow a drop of belief to return to their hearts.

Collingwood gets a standing ovation, but it's admiration mixed with disappointment for us and another reminder that while British sportsmen and women are experts at the plucky defeat, the brave rearguard action is rarely carried through to a satisfactory conclusion.

If Collingwood's dismissal is suicide, Flintoff's, eight overs or so before the close, is death by misadventure. Warne bowls a shortish one outside off stump, Flintoff, three elegant fours and one streaky one in his 16, steps back to pull, but the spin disrupts his projections and he miscues horribly down the ground to long-on, where Langer takes the easiest of catches. In fact, the little bugger is celebrating, I'm sure of it, before it's in his hands. He's punching both fists and a smile is breaking out on his face down below us just before he pouches it. Flintoff has turned away in shame and disgust as soon as he's connected with it. It's not a shot you'd associate with an England captain; in fact it's a shot you'd be ashamed to associate with a club No 8 on an average Saturday afternoon. Warne has four for 108.

We needed the BASTARDS. And we needed them now. The Brisbane Anarchists Spanking The Arse of Representative Democracy, that was. I knew about their existence only from their anarchical (naturally) approach to advertising. The scribbled recruiting forms glued to every third lamp-post on the road from my hostel to the Gabba showed that they would have no truck with the crass capitalist world of marketing – but they seemed just the sort of people who would be willing to disrupt an Ashes Test match, George Davis circa 1974-style, with the most crucial three sessions to come. England, five wickets down and facing a day-long fight to avoid defeat in the first match of their defence of the urn, would otherwise have to rely on the contrasting talents of Kevin Pietersen (he had it in spades) and Geraint Jones (he had it in trowels); a splash of oil, or something worse, on a length at both ends would surely be a more foolproof way of frustrating Australia's ambitions of laying down a marker for the series and going to Adelaide one-up.

Further investigation, however, proved discouraging: the BASTARDS' favourite activity was entitled Anarchy in the Afternoon. That was no good – we could be all out before lunch. But I suppose that's the point of such lawlessness: by definition anarchists reserve the right not to be morning people.

I'd have to look for salvation elsewhere, then, maybe in the form of prayer. The Brisbane International Christian Centre, which seemingly welcomed anyone and everyone, at any time, was also on my route, so too the Serbian Orthodox Church, a quaintly beautiful building which I don't have the architectural language to adequately describe. But believe me, it was nice.

Or maybe Darren's idea would come off. Darren had flown into Brisbane the night before the match started, and was jetting out pretty much as soon as it finished. Not for him the hope of a series-equalling win at Adelaide, a morale-boosting triumph in Perth, a hard-fought draw in Melbourne and a Monty Panesar-inspired clincher at the Sydney Cricket Ground. Noticing, as the fourth evening drew to a close, the encouraging build-up of clouds behind the back of Bay 72 of the Gabba structure, he hit upon a meteorologically-satisfying solution that proved he had, if nothing else, paid attention in geography lessons. He theorised that if enough England supporters could be persuaded to enjoy a post-cricket mug of tea or two, the kettles utilised would release sufficient steam into the atmosphere to make a game-curtailing storm a near-certainty. Detailed to spread the word around the Barmy Army at their hangout, he had them all singing "Brew Up for England" by chucking out time.

Unfortunately, somewhere along the line, he must have got the science wrong: the fifth day dawns, like the four before it, warm and bright, and within four balls, Pietersen, on 92 overnight, has slapped Brett Lee straight to mid-wicket. The innings lasts less than an hour and half longer.

The Ashes - 1st Test

Australia v England

Played at Brisbane Cricket Ground, Woolloongabba, Brisbane, on 23,24,25,26,27 November 2006 (5-day match)
Result Australia won by 277 runs

Australia 1st innings		R	M	B	4s
JL Langer	c Pietersen b Flintoff	82	136	98	83.67
ML Hayden	c Collingwood b Flintoff	21	88	47	44.68
✱ RT Ponting	lbw b Hoggard	196	464	319	61.44
DR Martyn	c Collingwood b Giles	29	79	62	46.77
MEK Hussey	b Flintoff	86	257	187	45.98
MJ Clarke	c Strauss b Anderson	56	153	94	59.57
✟ AC Gilchrist	lbw b Hoggard	0	3	3	0.00
SK Warne	c ✟ Jones b Harmison	17	42	26	65.38
B Lee	not out	43	90	61	70.49
SR Clark	b Flintoff	39	34	23	169.56
GD McGrath	not out	8	26	17	47.05
Extras	(b 2, lb 8, w 8, nb 7)	25			
Total	**(9 wickets dec; 155 overs; 690 mins)**	**602**	**(3.88 runs per over)**		

Fall of wickets 1-79 (Hayden, 18.3 ov), 2-141 (Langer, 28.5 ov), 3-198 (Martyn, 47.2 ov), 4-407 (Hussey, 108.4 ov), 5-467 (Ponting, 126.3 ov), 6-467 (Gilchrist, 126.6 ov), 7-500 (Warne, 135.3 ov), 8-528 (Clarke, 141.3 ov), 9-578 (Clark, 149.1 ov)

Bowling	O	M	R	W	Econ	
SJ Harmison	30	4	123	1	4.10	(1nb, 6w)
MJ Hoggard	31	5	98	2	3.16	(1nb)
JM Anderson	29	6	141	1	4.86	(1w)
A Flintoff	30	4	99	4	3.30	(3nb, 1w)
AF Giles	25	2	91	1	3.64	
IR Bell	1	0	12	0	12.00	(2nb)
KP Pietersen	9	1	28	0	3.11	

England 1st innings		R	M	B	SR
AJ Strauss	c Hussey b McGrath	12	25	21	57.14
AN Cook	c Warne b McGrath	11	27	15	73.33
IR Bell	c Ponting b Clark	50	228	162	30.86
PD Collingwood	c ✟ Gilchrist b Clark	5	24	13	38.46
KP Pietersen	lbw b McGrath	16	72	44	36.36
✱ A Flintoff	c ✟ Gilchrist b Lee	0	4	3	0.00
✟ GO Jones	lbw b McGrath	19	90	57	33.33
AF Giles	c Hayden b McGrath	24	61	39	61.53
MJ Hoggard	c ✟ Gilchrist b Clark	0	12	6	0.00
SJ Harmison	c ✟ Gilchrist b McGrath	0	5	5	0.00
JM Anderson	not out	2	9	8	25.00
Extras	(b 2, lb 8, w 2, nb 6)	18			
Total	**(all out; 61.1 overs; 283 mins)**	**157**	**(2.56 runs per over)**		

Fall of wickets 1-28 (Strauss, 5.4 ov), 2-28 (Cook, 5.5 ov), 3-42 (Collingwood, 10.6 ov), 4-78 (Pietersen, 27.4 ov), 5-79 (Flintoff, 28.3 ov), 6-126 (Jones, 49.2 ov), 7-149 (Bell, 56.2 ov), 8-153 (Hoggard, 58.2 ov), 9-154 (Harmison, 59.2 ov), 10-157 (Giles, 61.1 ov)

Bowling	O	M	R	W	Econ	
B Lee	15	3	51	1	3.40	(5nb, 2w)
GD McGrath	23.1	8	50	6	2.15	(1nb)
SR Clark	14	5	21	3	1.50	
SK Warne	9	0	25	0	2.77	

Australia 2nd innings		R	M	B	SR
JL Langer	not out	**100**	199	146	68.49
ML Hayden	run out (Anderson/✝ Jones)	**37**	67	41	90.24
✸ RT Ponting	not out	**60**	131	85	70.58
Extras	(lb 4, nb 1)	**5**			
Total	**(1 wicket dec; 45.1 overs; 199 mins)**	**202 (4.47 runs per over)**			

Did not bat DR Martyn, MEK Hussey, MJ Clarke, ✝AC Gilchrist, SK Warne, B Lee, SR Clark, GD McGrath
Fall of wickets 1-68 (Hayden, 15.3 ov)

Bowling	O	M	R	W	Econ	
MJ Hoggard	11	2	43	0	3.90	
JM Anderson	9	1	54	0	6.00	
A Flintoff	5	2	11	0	2.20	(1nb)
SJ Harmison	12.1	1	54	0	4.43	
AF Giles	5	0	22	0	4.40	
KP Pietersen	3	0	14	0	4.66	

England 2nd innings (target: 648 runs)		R	M	B	SR
AJ Strauss	c sub (RA Broad) b Clark	**11**	51	31	35.48
AN Cook	c Hussey b Warne	**43**	128	94	45.74
IR Bell	lbw b Warne	**0**	11	4	0.00
PD Collingwood	st ✝Gilchrist b Warne	**96**	216	155	61.93
KP Pietersen	c Martyn b Lee	**92**	227	155	59.35
✸ A Flintoff	c Langer b Warne	**16**	37	26	61.53
✝GO Jones	b McGrath	**33**	68	48	68.75
AF Giles	c Warne b Clark	**23**	55	38	60.52
MJ Hoggard	c Warne b Clark	**8**	49	35	22.85
SJ Harmison	c McGrath b Clark	**13**	31	18	72.22
JM Anderson	not out	**4**	7	8	50.00
Extras	(b 8, lb 10, w 2, nb 11)	**31**			
Total	**(all out; 100.1 overs; 445 mins)**	**370 (3.69 runs per over)**			

Fall of wickets 1-29 (Strauss, 10.4 ov), 2-36 (Bell, 13.2 ov), 3-91 (Cook, 29.2 ov), 4-244 (Collingwood, 63.3 ov), 5-271 (Flintoff, 71.4 ov), 6-293 (Pietersen, 80.4 ov), 7-326 (Jones, 87.1 ov), 8-346 (Giles, 92.5 ov), 9-361 (Hoggard, 98.2 ov), 10-370 (Harmison, 100.1 ov)

Bowling	O	M	R	W	Econ	
B Lee	22	1	98	1	4.45	(7nb, 1w)
GD McGrath	19	3	53	1	2.78	(3nb)
SR Clark	24.1	6	72	4	2.97	
SK Warne	34	7	124	4	3.64	(1nb, 1w)
MEK Hussey	1	0	5	0	5.00	

Toss Australia, who chose to bat first

The middle of the bloody day and not a bone in the truck

ADELAIDE

AS I stood on the Southern Concourse at the Adelaide Oval, shaking with almost visible rage as Ricky Ponting and Mike Hussey picked off an England that had completely lost the plot on the final day of the second Test, an Australian turned to me and said: "How good is this?"

"Not very," I mumbled, hoping I could strangle this communication at birth.

"Pardon, mate," he replied, not so easily shaken off.

"Not very," I said again, this time a little louder, a rise in decibels that enabled him to clock me.

"Hey, you're not from Adelaide, then?" he probed.

"Er, no," I responded, my nationality becoming dangerously apparent.

"Oh, you're a fucking Pom," he came back, the glee undisclosed. (Well done, Sherlock, you win, I thought) "I didn't pick up the accent; it's not very thick."

"Unlike England's management team," I observed, trying to locate some grim humour in the situation as Ashley Giles failed again to find the rough outside Ponting's leg stump and Andrew Flintoff looked surprisingly surprised as the Australian skipper eased another single into an off-side field so lacking in attacking intent that even with nearly 100 runs still needed, it seemed England's three lions had rolled over, purred deeply and allowed Ponting and his team of ringmasters to rub their tummies.

"It's worse than '94," I added, referring to my previous visit to these shores to watch another inept England team be blown out of the water.

"No!" my inquisitor boomed, hardly able to believe that I could compare these 2005 Ashes heroes, OBEs still dangling from their necks, with the no-hopers that Mike Atherton had had under his watch 12 years earlier.

But, yes, this was worse. It was worse because we had expected something of this team, unlike Atherton's men, whose predilection for self-inflicted damage was some act to follow (Devon Malcolm caught chicken pox in Brisbane, Alec Stewart broke his right forefinger in Melbourne, England lost two one-day matches to the Australian academy on successive days, and watched as Australia A beat them to the final of the one-day quadrangular tournament. But they still won in Adelaide and went close in Sydney). We might not have expected to hang on to the urn – with Australia having rid themselves of the 2005 complacency complex that dogged them after their easy victory at Lord's, it was always going to be a tough ask. But I did expect more than this, 2-0 down after two Tests, tickets, hostels and travel fares to Perth, Melbourne and Sydney already destabilising my bank balance.

It was said that this team, like that of 2005, had not been bowed by the experience of failure. Maybe so, but on the final day they played as if they were. Or, if not the experience of failure, the fear of it. The worst thing, perhaps, about a worst-case scenario is that the more you consider its possibility, the more likely it becomes; it's the closest cousin of the self-fulfilling prophecy. So when England went back to their hotel on the fourth night, they knew they could probably not win this Test match, but they knew, with Shane Warne starting to turn it, they could lose it.

It only needed Steve Bucknor to open the door, with his appalling bat-pad decision against Andrew Strauss, for the rest of the England team to go filing obediently through it. And with Warne appealing with a hysteria totally at odds with the spirit of the game, you always knew that his second or third plea would be answered in the affirmative. That is not to disparage another great performance from the greatest of all spinners, but it did at least highlight some common ground between me and my newly-made acquaintance.

"He's great Warnie, isn't he?" the Australian said, before, to my surprise, he completely changed tack, adding. "But I can't stand the man, he's a total cockhead. If he walked into my local, I'd smack him straight in the face."

At that moment, I knew exactly what he meant.

—〽—

It hadn't in all honesty started promisingly for us in the so-called festival city. An oversight on my part meant that we were swapping, quite literally, Somewhere to Stay for nowhere to stay. While I had booked our flight from Brisbane for November 28, I had booked our next hostel, Annie's Place, a misleadingly cosy-sounding establishment that turned out to be squeezed between a fish factory, a shooting range and a Harley Davidson shop, only from November 30. A hurried perusal of wotif.com, a website promising discounted accommodation, was not encouraging, although we eventually secured the last room at a modest motel in Glenelg, Adelaide's beach area about 20 minutes from the city centre by tram. It was one of the few premises that hadn't raised its prices threefold for the duration of England's visit.

Two nights later, we checked into Annie's after a short

disagreement with the management about en suite facilities. It was an old Victorian building, adjacent to a pub that bewilderingly shut at around 8.20pm each night. In addition to the dorms in the main house, Annie's had a series of modern double rooms in an extension reached through a courtyard and up some stairs that looked like they were also the only route out in the event of an emergency. One of the rooms was destined to be ours for the next week, so we clanked our bags up metal steps in plus 30-degree heat before pausing for oxygen at the top and looking back down on the courtyard. There sat a small collection of listless bodies, so rendered by the combination of music loud enough to blister your ears booming from an invisible stereo system and the wearisome wait for a rumbling bank of washing machines to disgorge their clean laundry.

It was not a place to linger long in and we were soon out exploring, walking up to Rundle Mall, a gaudy shopping precinct with an interesting line in sculpture – a bunch of brass pigs seemingly running amok – to pick up tickets we had ordered but had never received. It took some time, principally because whenever I rang the office to find out exactly the building the agency was housed in, I could not hear their directions on my hopelessly inadequate mobile phone. Eventually, I settled for being old-fashioned and used a phone booth.

Relieved to have got that chore out of the way, we returned to the hostel, happy to find the air conditioning, faulty when we had arrived, was working, showered, and slipped next door to have dinner in the pub that bewilderingly shut at 8.20pm every night. It was about 6.45pm so we had about an hour and a half's grace. Sue first ordered a Victoria Bitter and was delighted to be told by the friendly barman to wait for a moment while he retrieved the free gift that went with it. It was a scratchcard which, after scratching, revealed that she had won a top prize. She was less delighted when the friendly barman reached beneath the pumps and produced it: something dark, substantial and, most disturbingly, hairy.

"What's that?" she shrieked, withdrawing her hand immediately.

"It's a Boony," said the barman.

"A what?" Sue seemed none the wiser.

"A Boony," the barman said again, laughing and passing the offending article to me. "It's a promotion; a free Boony moustache with every winning VB scratchcard."

"Boony," I said. "From David Boon, the Aussie cricketer. You know I've told you about him. Legendarily drank 58 cans of the stuff – or Fosters or Four X depending on who's telling the story – on the flight from Australia to England before an Ashes tour."

"Of course," said the friendly barman, "you could have won a stubbie holder or figurines of Boon and Ian Botham that talk to each other through the use of infra-red technology. Still, never mind.

"What about you mate?" he added, addressing me. "Another VB?" He raised a questioning eyebrow. "Another chance to win."

"Well, there's only so much cricketers' facial hair I can take," I said, casting my eyes round the bar looking for alternatives. "I'll just have a Coopers. What do you do food-wise?"

"Well sit down and I'll get you a menu," he replied, "but I can tell you, the chef's pretty proud of his chicken parmagiana."

After dinner, which we finished just as the landlord was clinking his keys and casting knowing looks in our direction, we decided to go and hunt for the Barmy Army. I had finally got my hands on a free *Barmy Harmonies* magazine outside the Gabba on the last day in Brisbane. Its cover shot was a manic-looking Matthew Hoggard inviting you into his world of insanity and occasional outswing in a portrait that made him look as if he might axe a hole in your bedroom door, Jack Nicholson-style in *The Shining*, and shout "here's Hoggie" if you turned him down.

But most important, it contained the information that the Army had arranged for a couple of pubs in each Test match city to be their drinking headquarters. Worries were beginning to crowd in on me that Adelaide could be just as bad as Brisbane and I needed someone to talk to who could put some optimism back in my breast. We had a choice of The Cathedral which, as its name would suggest, was situated by St Peter's, north of the cricket ground, or PJ O'Briens, which appeared to be to the east of the city centre: its address, on East Terrace, was a clue. The Cathedral was offering choir practice – presumably a test run of Army ditties for newcomers to the tour – but because we were not singing types we opted for PJ's, which promised a pre-Test party, a ladies' night and a DJ all in one package.

Yet it turned into another of those fruitless searches that seemed to occupy too much of our time in Australia because of our – or should I say my - tendency to take a quick glance at a map rather than give it total concentration. It should have been only a fifteen-minute walk. An hour later, we had still failed to locate it and Sue's feet, encased in the flattest of flip-flops, were beginning to trouble her. My guilt complex flared again and after almost totally circumnavigating the business district, we managed to find our bearings in Victoria Square and sloped disappointedly home for an early night.

On 29 January 1937, Neville Cardus, the doyen of cricket writers, was approaching the Adelaide Oval for the fourth Test of the Ashes series through parkland from the north when his attention, until then focused on the behaviour of the local bees, was distracted by something on an altogether grander scale. In the

nascent morning sunshine, a group of gentlemen appeared close by, clothed themselves in smart jackets, removed a variety of musical instruments from their cases and started to perform a Beethoven symphony. Cardus, a music critic as well as a sports journalist for the Manchester Guardian, was in heaven and sat down on the grass to listen for a while.

I had come across this snippet of information in the British Library while researching a separate book shortly before leaving for Australia and had envisaged that, once clear of the buildings and into the greenery surrounding the Torrens Lake that separated the city from the ground, I, too, would be able to detect the distant sound of music on the wind. Sure enough, I thought I could. But it was no Beethoven. It was formed of a series of high-pitched bleeps with no discernible rhythm, a cross between Stockhausen and Radiohead with a guest appearance from Kraftwerk. On arrival, however, it was clear that the only digital sampling taking place was that performed by the stewards, whose hand-held machines emitted the annoying atonal sound every time they ran them over the bar code on a match ticket.

Before Sue or I could undergo the screening – and the associated bag search – a slim, attractive Australian blonde promotions girl plonked a visor on my head. I didn't have the chance to protest – and she smiled so enthusiastically that I didn't want to – but on further inspection I realised it bore the legend 'Tonk a Pom'. The phrase had been all the rage in Brisbane – part of Cricket Australia's strategy to encourage home support – and every time Ricky Ponting or one of his merry men had had the audacity to flay our bowling to the boundary, it had appeared up on the giant replay screen alongside a picture of Matthew Hayden shading his eyes with one hand as he stared into the distance. I resolved to cross out the word 'Pom' as soon as I got to my seat and scribble 'Aus' in its place but as a one-man protest it would have carried little weight. Inside, I was also offered a giant inflatable hand with 'Go Aussies' on it, but declined, and an Ashes urn badge that was raising funds for the Royal Flying Doctors Service. Having had a bit of a crush on Lenore Smith, Kate Wellings in the 1980s TV action soap based on the service, I promised to part with my $5 later, although shamefully never did.

The first news as we take our place square on to the wicket in the Chappell Stands about 20 rows back is that England have won the toss and have chosen to bat; it is news received with relief and a rousing cheer by the visiting supporters, who are much more visible than at the Gabba. There is a Barmy Army stronghold to our right, in front of the famous old scoreboard, separated by about a metre from a bunch of The Fanatics, their Australian counterparts, and a huge group away to our left rolling back from the Southern Concourse on to the grass of the Southern Mound and into the South Mound Stand. The back of the stand is a mural of Union Jacks, marking attendance from far flung parts of the United Kingdom. Some smaller villages must have been left ghost towns.

The next news is not as well received as Flintoff tells Mark Nicholas, compèring for Channel 9, that England are going in with the same team; it means, once again, that there is no place for Monty Panesar, while Geraint Jones is still being relied upon to do his thing, whatever that may be, at No 7. Nicholas tries to york Freddie with a question on Panesar's absence. "So this bloke who's been in the papers for the last four days doesn't get a gig?" he queries, the surprise in his voice plain. Flintoff flinches momentarily, but jams his bat down on the awkward delivery just in time – a reasonable stroke in the circumstances. "As I say it's the same team," he mumbles a little too quickly, a sure sign that he knows it's a controversial decision. "I think the combination we've got is right, we've just got to perform a bit better."

There is no mistaking where the Aussies think they can get our opening batsmen. With perhaps the shortest square boundaries in world cricket, and possibly the longest straight ones, the Adelaide Oval is perilously close to being considered the Adelaide Rectangle, but it positively pleads for players to pull and hook and England have required no invitation to do that on this tour. Strauss is going to need to muster all his powers of concentration if he is not to be lured into lifting one to the two men stationed on the boundary by Brett Lee and Glenn McGrath for just that purpose. McGrath tries to tempt him early, releasing a bouncer, and even from 60 yards away you can see Strauss straining every sinew to prevent his muscles producing the involuntary reaction that usually follows such provocation.

With Strauss reining himself in, England make a timid start, five runs in four overs; it's not quite the all-guns blazing approach they had adopted after defeat in the first Ashes Test of 2005 and we could have done with now to tilt the balance of power. But I am not too unhappy with that. The parallels with Edgbaston 2005, so prominent in the media ahead of the game, have proved irrelevant. McGrath's heel injury has, er, healed and besides, while England had 10 days to regroup after Lord's, they have flown straight down to Adelaide for this Test.

There is a myth, perpetuated mainly by people sitting in commentary booths with microphones pressed to their lips, that players should always play their natural game, but this is nonsense: if a batsman plays constantly on instinct he will fail to spot the bowler's variations, the very things designed to disrupt that natural game. Giving a player carte blanche to play his natural game deprives him of responsibility. And there is a double standard at work here too, for it is a phrase that seems to be used only when that natural game is an attacking one. No one defends Geoff Boycott for having played his natural game. In fact, he was dropped by England after scoring a double century because it was considered too slow and created a media backlash. But if Kevin Pietersen plays his natural game, and lobs one of his trademark pull-slogs just out of reach of mid-on – as he will do with the penultimate ball of the first day here – he is pardoned on the basis that "it is the way he plays".

To my mind, Strauss is showing genuine regard for team rather than self when he declines the opportunities to cross-bat McGrath and Lee. It is his misfortune that his mistakes at Brisbane seem to have invoked the wrath of the cricket gods and as he attempts a cautious clip off Stuart Clark he gets the slightest of leading edges and is snapped up smartly by Damien Martyn at mid-wicket. The first-wicket partnership has at least got into the 30s here, but not by much, and when Alastair Cook pushes at one wide outside his off stump and gets a thin edge, Clark has figures of 4.5-0-5-2. The depression sets in again: we will be relying on Bell, Pietersen and Collingwood, all of whom scored runs in Brisbane, if not enough of them, to dig us out of a hole.

Unusually for the first session of a Test, the spinner is brought on early – the 18th over - a worrying development when that spinner is Shane Warne. There is immediate turn, and no small measure of it although it is the vocal reaction of those behind the bowler's arm and watching the replays on the televisions in the corporate boxes with their televisions that tell us so. The barometer of the Victorian's hold over Bell is apparent even from our seats, however, when Bell gets in position to sweep, quickly realises his error of judgement, and is forced into an ugly readjustment which ends with him manufacturing an approximation to a forward defensive.

Nobody's fooled, least of all Warne, who decides to toy with his prey once more with a slider, or top-spinner, depending on who you believe, which Bell reads as a conventional leggie, leaves and is no doubt mightily relieved to watch drift an inch wide of his off stump.

Lunch comes after 28 overs, with England 58 for two. It has been hard going, fours early on from Cook and just before the break from Collingwood rare highlights in another session Australia have largely controlled. Off the field, the main cause of concern in our section of the ground is the fate of a baby bird which has flopped out of its nest high up in the rafters of this marquee-styled stand and landed about eight rows in front of us. Nobody is quite sure what to do, especially with the mother in a noisy flap above us, but eventually an English couple take responsibility and gather the chick up in their England flag and carry it off to safety – maybe to the flying doctors service. The afternoon is better, with Collingwood and Bell defiant if unable to up the scoring rate markedly, although the Warwickshire player shows increased signs of confidence when he reads the length of Warne perfectly for once and lofts him straight down the ground. We go to tea with an unusual sense of symmetry, both batsmen on round 50s, and the considerable and unexpected boost of having gone through a session without losing a wicket.

Bell's growing sense of ease is reflected in consecutive boundaries off Lee shortly after the interval, one through the covers that is a technical and aesthetic treat. But how confidence so readily becomes over-confidence: bounced next ball, he hooks, but beaten by Lee's pace, only succeeds in sending it directly up. Lee has time to complete his follow-through, glance up, shout 'mine' about three times as Langer tries to get in on the act, before taking the ball above his head. The two men set deep on the leg-side for the shot are not required.

It is another hammer blow and so unnecessary. Lee has not been bowling particularly well; indeed, it is often a genuine pleasure to see him taking the ball because you know there'll be some serious action. There will be stuff sufficiently loose and fast to encourage strokeplay and bolster the scoring rate; the flipside is that, as now, he is always likely to pick up a wicket. However, Kevin Pietersen is determined that the slight change of momentum is not lost and, despite the placement of two fielders in unorthodox positions on the leg side – a man forward of square leg and a shortish mid-wicket – he pulls his second ball between the straighter of the pair and mid-on for four. McGrath, his pace well down on his average – perhaps his heel is not in as pristine condition as he had made out – gets clouted through extra cover and when Warne takes up the battle, Pietersen's response is to hurry down the wicket and lift him with the spin, inside out, over the fence at long-off. He even has to stretch to reach a couple of wide deliveries from a tiring Warne, cutting them to the boundary, while Collingwood, faced with the leg spinner coming round the wicket steps back and pulls them powerfully.

As it's heating up in the middle, though, it's getting decidedly cooler in our stand, where the breeze has strengthened and is sweeping through where the sun can't reach. It is officially the first day of the Australian summer today, but you could be forgiven for forgetting. The official temperature of 25C is offset by a wind chill factor that makes it feel more like Manchester in mid-winter. Not so much a case of balmy army then, as a shivering one. Sue has vacated her seat to shelter behind the stand, while a bloke in front of me is huddling under a blanket he has obviously pinched from Emirates Airlines. Thoughts of beer are turning to thoughts of Bovril.

I check on Sue and then scamper back up the steps to the Southern Concourse to watch the last couple of balls. Insanely, Pietersen, still playing his natural game, tries to pull Lee, gets it high up the bat and the ball drops towards McGrath. Painful heel and, like Warne, his partner in crimes against England over 13 years, wicketless for the day, the New South Welshman still looks like having the final say. But unbelievably and to the massive relief of the visiting contingent, the ball clears the scampering McGrath, whose outstretched arms can not haul it in and lands just short of a flock of seagulls, presumably immune to the drama until he sends them scattering.

It was with a bit of a spring in my step that I left the Adelaide Oval that night. I explained to Sue that she had just witnessed a day of Test cricket for the connoisseur: the early difficulties of a team low on confidence, followed by the staunch rearguard action of Collingwood and Bell that blossomed finally in the flowering brilliance of Pietersen, who for the second time in two innings, had got the better of Warne.

Strangely, not everyone saw it that way. Listening to ABC the next morning, I hear Jonathan Agnew, a rare and welcome Pommie voice on a station of gnarled and grizzly Australian whines, grumbling about an article in *The Australian*. Agnew is outraged by Malcolm Conn's story, which has characterised England's approach on the first day as boring. I make a mental note to track down a copy of the paper because the piece sounds completely out of step with how the rest of the media have seen it. "The battlers of Britain" is the headline on the front page of my chosen reading, the *Adelaide Advertiser*, and pictures an English couple, the female half of whom is wearing, I'm pleased to note, a revealing St George's Cross bikini top, celebrating in front of the scoreboard. Compare if you will, extracts from the two pieces:

"England has put the spine back into its Ashes defence, much to the delight of thousands of fans who descended on Adelaide for the second Test. Buoyed by Andrew Flintoff winning the most important toss of his brief captaincy, England turned the Test into a brutal streetfight. Collingwood reprised his fruitful Gabba partnership with Kevin Pietersen, who provided a turbo-charged, unbeaten knock of 60."
and
"Anticipation was replaced by anticlimax as England unveiled its secret

weapon to retain the Ashes – boredom. England had the world at its feet but could barely move for much of the day. Indeed, one of the greatest moments of animation and excitement from the touring party came before a single ball was bowled, when captain Andrew Flintoff won the toss and batted on one of the most benign pitches ever presented."

Methinks that Mr Conn must have been spoiled by watching Australia for 15 years since being appointed chief cricket correspondent.

Benign pitch or not, and to be fair to Conn, the *Advertiser* also savaged curator Les Burdett's stodgy creation, there is a genuine sense of optimism in the air among English supporters at the start of day two. Collingwood is on the verge of a hundred for the second time in the series – surely he will get there this time – and there's the prospect of more Pietersen. Our tickets today are out in the sun, four rows back from the front of the Southern Concourse, a better vantage point to see how much Warnie's turning it and just behind long-on or a very fine third man.

I'm willing Collingwood, on 98, not to repeat his rush of blood from the second innings of Brisbane and give us the carthasis of clapping an English century. But shortly before he pushes the ball through wide mid-on for three, a sudden wind shift lifts my sun hat off my head and sends it hurtling back into the seething mass of English supporters on the grass to my rear. Now these things are not cheap – it's a Greg Chappell one with the wide, stiff brim that cost me $25 from the Bradman Museum in Bowral and, according to the Australian Cancer Council, has earned a 50-plus rating for ultra-violet protection – so it is a significant piece of merchandise.

I'm forced to clamber over a series of legs to get to the end of my row, an annoying task at the best of times, but greeted now with a string of tuts from spectators irritated that I might block their view of Collingwood's big moment. As soon as I turn to face the pile of half-naked bodies strewn across the grass, Collingwood does it. If finding a hat amid a crush of prone humans in various states of undress surrounded by beers, flags, backpacks, and helpings of pea-floater – an Adelaide speciality – is difficult enough, it becomes nearly impossible as they all leap to their feet to acclaim the Durham man. Nobody is interested in my loss; they are all looking beyond me to where Collingwood is being hugged by Pietersen.

I start scouring the grass, aware that I'm missing out on one of the emotional high points of the tour, and finally, by the feet of two women at the edge of the turfed area, I notice a hat that bears a remarkable similarity to mine. Well, it's a Greg Chappell one, anyway. I try to study it inconspicuously for distinguishing marks that could identify it, afraid that people will think I'm taking advantage of the distraction to indulge in some thievery, but this isn't school and I haven't written my name inside it. In the end I just stoop down, smile and babble something incomprehensible above the din, and whisk it away in one movement before they can raise any objections. If it wasn't mine before, it is now. And it fits.

Pietersen, meanwhile, has got his eye in again and is picking up where he left off on Friday night. The famed flamingo shot, where he whips the ball wristily through mid-wicket off his front leg, is resuscitated, but just to be showy, he lets the top hand lead and leathers McGrath through extra cover from a balletic position on his front leg. For good measure, two balls later, he pleases the purists with a straighter, technically perfect, off drive for four. And a pull from McGrath's fifth ball of the morning takes him to within 15 of his century. The field is beginning to spread.

By lunch Warne has gone for more than 100 and has still to take a wicket. As the afternoon progresses, he as good as admits defeat, something which must come very hard to the Australian, by adopting the Ashley Giles attack, round the wicket, into the footholes, such as they are, outside Pietersen's leg stump, hoping to bore him into an indiscretion. Pietersen meets the challenge by padding away ball after ball, refusing to be tempted. And this battle within a battle of the egos appears destined to end in a goalless draw. I hope Mr Conn is taking a decent note of this up in the press box. Another full house of around 30,000 is not happy. There are boos from the crowd – but I'm not sure who's the intended target, Warne for his negative bowling or Pietersen for his refusal to play ball. Pietersen, 102 not out at lunch, is still 102 not out five overs later and it is Collingwood who takes up the attack, such as it is: he adds eight runs in the same time. Some Aussies are referring to "boring boring England". The words kettle and black come to mind. It is 14 overs before the Warne and McGrath wicketless partnership is broken up. The man known as the Pidgeon is removed and Brett Lee replaces him. Perhaps there'll be a bit more action now. There is: nine runs from the first over of his new spell. Warne bowls one more and Pietersen kicks it away. Drinks. I'm sure they need them.

Michael Clarke replaces the knackered Warne and it is from one of his flat orthodox left-armers that Collingwood, on 199, advances and smacks him back over his head for four. It is his first double-century for England, the first double century for any Englishman in Australia, unbelievably, for 70 years. I'm doubly excited because I think that might mean it was in the Test match that Cardus witnessed after his orchestral manoeuvres in the park in 1937. That would be some coincidence and lend a magical harmony to the event. But it transpires that that innings, Wally Hammond's unbeaten 231, was at the Sydney Cricket Ground. Checking it out at the end of the day's play, though, there is an encouraging omen. England declared at 426 for six, bowled Australia out for 80 in the first innings and needed only four days of a supposedly timeless Test to complete an innings victory.

But for the moment I am wrapped up in the emotion, explaining the significance to Sue: that despite the presence of some of the greatest talents in the English game appearing on this ground in the intervening seven decades, it is Paul Collingwood, poor, underrated Paul Collingwood – a man who might not even have got a game had Marcus Trescothick not flown home; and the only man, I had once read in an interview, convinced he would succeed at this level.

A drive minus any foot movement brings his downfall the last ball before tea – an anti-climax – but he has done his bit and England are dominant now. The only question is how long they will push on. With Pietersen and Flintoff at the crease we might be entitled to expect some fireworks after the break. I scrutinise opinion by spending the tea interval switching between the radio and television commentaries. I hear the suggestion that England should not declare but bat Australia out of the game and ensure they go to Perth still, at worst, 1-0 down. I can't agree with this view, although it is given an abundant airing amid the recriminations after the match, but feel that Flintoff will be thinking of a win. It is not every day that England make 500 or more against the Australians – in fact, it emerges, it's the first time in 20 years - and if that's not a potentially-winning position, I'm not sure what is.

However, in the overs of the final session, the strategy is not entirely clear. Pietersen completes his 150 but on 158, having equalled his highest Test score for the third time, he takes off on a single to short mid-on that is so suicidal he might as well run straight for the pavilion. Ponting swoops in and underarms from a couple of yards and Pietersen is yards short, walking off with an incredulous half-smile, mildly rebuking himself, no more, but mainly with his head held high. One of the things I like about Pietersen is his demeanour when he's out: there is no sloping of the shoulders, no slow walk back, no smacking his pad with his bat as if he's a slightly naughty schoolchild. If no one told you, you would think he was just wandering to the pavilion for a change of gloves; he refuses to adopt the countenance of failure even when he has failed.

And that, I think, must have some influence on the opposition: the analogy's not perfect but it's the batting equivalent of Shane Warne's riposte when he was asked, early in his career, what he thought when he was hit for six. "The ball's always got to come back to me and I've got another chance to take a wicket," was the gist of it. Pietersen's body-language, similarly, says; "Well, ah-ha, you've got me this time, but I'll be back in the second innings to give you another working over."

It crosses my mind, though, and not for the last time on the tour, that he has put a minor personal glory ahead of the team ethic. That might be an unfair judgement on a man who has restrained himself for overs against Warne but is a subject that is given legs later in the tour when John Buchanan, the Australia coach, suggests something similar.

Flintoff and Giles come together after Geraint Jones, Shane Warne's favourite wicketkeeper-batsman, gives the spinner a first wicket in his 47th over. Urgency does not seem their first priority, even after the 500. Englishmen and women throughout the ground are beginning to do mental calculations and again the commentators are split on whether to declare or not to declare. Suddenly, though, the plan becomes evident and we go into one-day mode; Giles gets a full one from Warne and thumps it over mid-on, two bounces, to the ropes. As Warne adjusts, dropping shorter, he leans back and leathers him through extra cover. McGrath is recalled, but looks as reluctant as never before to take the ball. Giles slashes his first ball to third man for four and when Flintoff gets down his end, he steps across his stumps and lifts the Australian into the crowd at square leg. Twenty-nine runs have come in three overs, the Australians look done and dusted and once the 550 is passed, Flintoff runs off, eschewing the personal landmark of a fifty that is there for the taking, and signifying that he knows where the momentum is.

It means a tough nine overs for the Aussies and, for the first time, the boot is on the other foot: they're under the pressure and we're going to make the most of it. Of course, that pressure could very quickly be eased if our opening bowlers don't do their stuff and there is a sense of apprehension that Steve Harmison will repeat his waywardness of Brisbane. I discuss the prospect with an Australian next to me, one of the few of his nationality who isn't revelling in the Durham bowler's tribulations. I tell him that I'd heard a rumour before the Test that Harmison was going to miss Adelaide, instead being sent for remedial work at the academy in Perth, where he would be stripped down by experts in biomechanics, have his parts reassembled as close to those of the 2005 model as possible, revved up and sent out to mete out revenge on his tormenters in the third Test. Admittedly, my source was not necessarily a good one – a loud-mouthed, middle-aged England fan sounding off in the departure lounge at Brisbane airport, no doubt trying to impress his friends with the breadth of his inside knowledge. The Australian beside me thought it, as I did, an unlikely plan.

"He's inconsistent, but you never know when he might come good again. I just hope it's not tonight," he joked.

It was possible, though, that the know-all at the airport had been reading cricinfo, where Tim de Lisle had put forward a cogent thesis for resting Harmison and provided the statistics to back it up: in his previous 11 Tests overseas he had got only 27 wickets at an average of 52, capturing no more than three wickets in any one innings. He dismissed the main argument against dropping him, that the absence of England's so-called strike bowler would give Australia a psychological lift, by contending that his erratic showing at the Gabba had done just that. Fair enough. But he seemed to be taking the argument too far in his insistence that in a perfect world we would have available Jon Lewis, a nailed-on swing bowler, who he christened the 'English Stuart Clark'. To me Lewis was 'the other English Matthew Hoggard', just not as accurate.

Certainly, though, Harmison's position in the scheme of things is exercising the minds of the England hierarchy – to the extent that when the team takes the field, the opening bowler finds himself not opening the bowling, while Jimmy Anderson, handed the new ball for the second innings in Brisbane, is also sent to graze in the outfield. Hoggard is first up from the Cathedral End and the England voices give way to their Australian cousins as Langer leans into a straight drive. But the roar that greets that four is as nothing compared to the energy released by the Barmy Army when Flintoff, awarding himself the Harmison role, gets Langer playing at one that climbs, but merely to guide it into the hands of the finer of two gullies, where Kevin Pietersen continues to show that he can catch.

Now, if we can just get Ponting tonight.

There's apparently a fair bit of chat going on out in the middle and Tony Greig, a man who's always keen to share a bit of the mid-pitch discussion, turns up the stump microphone on Channel 9. Flintoff, bowling with his tail up further than a dingo on the hunt for a baby breakfast, turns the Australian captain square on as he tries to drive. "I wouldn't fancy being you if you get out tonight, lad" we clearly hear Flintoff say. On the Shane Warne sledging scale, where a ten is Warne's observation to New Zealand batsman Matthew Sinclair to "f*** off, you buck-toothed f*** (as alleged in Paul Barry's biography of the great bowler) it probably barely registers, but the very fact that he thinks he's in a position to have a go at his opposite number is a shot in the arm.

The *Sunday Mail* made pleasant reading the next morning, where I learned in a feature by Robert Craddock that Paul

Collingwood is the son of a caravan factory worker, asserting his working-class hero status. More worryingly, John Buchanan, the Australia coach, has refused to concede that the best his side can hope for now is a draw. "I'm a bit of an optimist and I still think there's a win on offer," he is quoted as saying in the previous night's press conference. "Our job is to go out there and negotiate the new ball, get through that and build our partnerships – make 700 and bowl them out for less than 150 on the last day." What does he know that the rest of us don't? Has he got a special deal with the same cricket gods that are giving Andrew Strauss such a hard time?

Sue has decided on a lie-in – well at least until being awakened by the hostel's resident hip-hop band in the courtyard – so I have wandered up to the ground on my own. I'm slightly nervous, not just with apprehension about the day ahead – can we grind home our advantage? – but also because I have in my wallet a ticket that I'm not sure is going to gain me entrance. It was bought off Ebay and the Australian authorities have been making much of the fact that tickets acquired that way will not be honoured. It may just be tough talking because I can't work out a method whereby they could trace them, but I'm taking more interest in the sounds emitted by the steward's hand-held devices this morning. For all I know, the atonal bleep will erupt instantaneously into a prolonged screech of alarm, shutters will crash down and trap me the wrong side of the Victor Richardson gates and armed police with sniffer dogs will move in, cuff me and drag me away, screaming, to be deported.

I also arrive extra early because my ticket today guarantees only ground admission. That means slumming it on the grass at the Cathedral End but at least that will give me a close-up of the rivalry between the Barmy Army and the Fanatics. When I arrive I find that the area immediately in front of the scoreboard, where most of them are massed, is the alcoholic zone: an area further round is a booze-free neighbourhood, in front of which are a few banks of seats. Fearing that it could turn ugly as the liquid flows, I decide to cross the line to the region where liquor is not permissable. I try to mark out my personal kingdom for the day, spreading myself pretty much full length and placing my backpack to allow for room for Sue should she come up later, but my territory slips away quicker than the British Empire as the crowd builds up. A teenage Australian couple, greased up in the green and gold, plant themselves straight down on my backpack, so I tug it out from underneath them and give them a glowering look that goes straight over their sombreroed heads.

Ponting may have got through to the close last night but we've got another chance this morning. Fresh bowlers, batsmen yet to get set – and a very unorthodox field for the Australia captain when he faces up to Hoggard, again coming from the Cathedral End.

Flintoff's field placings are – like Winston Churchill's observations on Russia – an enigma wrapped in a riddle and shrouded in mystery. At first, they have appeared innovative, inventive, symbols of a captain in touch with a plan and his intuition. But as the series has progressed it is beginning to look as if he has simply borrowed some ideas from chaos theory, instructing the players to go out and pick a spot to stand at random.

As Hoggard comes in for his first ball, there are two slips and a gully – so far, so traditional – but there is also a man at short mid-wicket and two guys close together in front of the wicket on the off side. All the attempts I've made to teach Sue the fielding positions could be rendered obsolete by this so I'm lucky she's not here and in need of an explanation. I would be forced to make up names, introducing to the cricket lexicon such terms as the short forward cover point or deep silly point, forward short extra cover and deep silly mid-off. Giving Flintoff the benefit of the doubt, it could be a ploy to make Ponting think twice about driving on the up on this sluggish surface.

Whatever, his first act of the morning is to waft outside off stump, missing a swinging delivery and encouraging me to leap to my feet in excitement. Get an edge you bastard, I find myself saying under my breath, realising that this is not the behaviour of a man in love with his sport. Here is one of the best batsmen in the world, one of the great entertainers and I want to be entertained by his downfall. What kind of lunacy is this? I suppose it's the lunacy that comes from the desperation to win, but I'm slightly ashamed all the same. But then, having watched him bat for five minutes short of ten hours in Brisbane, there is barely a stroke in his repertoire that I don't know by heart.

It's not Ponting, but there is an early breakthrough, just what the doctor ordered, when Hoggard strikes at the end of the fourth over of the morning, tempting Hayden into a poor shot outside the off stump to a ball that doesn't follow its natural curve into the left-hander. I'm up again, along with many others around me but the Barmy Army don't need to follow our lead. They're already there. They spend their day on their feet. All of it. Whatever the temperature and whatever the quantity of beer they've consumed. Then, at the end of the day, they go to a bar and do the same all night. Perhaps it's one of those military initiation ceremonies you hear about. If the team can show the same stamina, the Ashes are in the bag.

Damien Martyn doesn't really seem to have his mind on the job – he could get in to the England team on this showing – and having scored a timid 11 from 33 balls he stretches for one that shapes away from him, again from Hoggard, and almost loses grip with his bottom hand as he sends it low to Bell in the gully. It's 65 for three!

Cautious runs are added as Michael Hussey comes to the crease but not without some discomfort, especially when the faulty

Harmison radar clocks on to Ponting's head at around 93mph and although failing to make contact, puts the momentarily shaken batsman on the floor. No-ball, says Mr Bucknor.

Maybe he's still traumatised minutes later when he rocks on to the back foot to Hoggard and rather lazily swivels to help the ball down to deep backward square leg. Waiting there, in front of the George Giffen stand, the historic George Giffen stand, erected as the members' pavilion in 1882 and subsequently named after a man thought by many to be the world's first great all-rounder – nine times he scored a hundred and took ten wickets in the same match – is Ashley Giles, who has yet to have a stand named in his honour, was once likened to a wheelie-bin and is considered a great all-rounder only by Duncan Fletcher.

"That's out," Tony Greig screams in my ear, but it's a premature ejaculation. "Correction," he says in his clipped South African tone. Giles, a few yards in from the fence, misjudges it, ends up having to jump higher than he would like and spills it. It all happens so quickly, we hardly have the chance to process what it all means. But the effect is strangely subliminal. At some deep level, before it has reached full consciousness, we realise the awful significance: Ashley Giles, poor, unlucky, injury-prone and often undervalued Ashley Giles, a man with one of the safest pairs of hands in the business, may have cost us the Ashes.

Of course, apply rational thought to the equation and that is nonsense; catches may win matches, but one dropped catch cannot decide a series, there are far too many variables. But that is what it feels like. I'm torn between wanting to brain the incompetent Warwickshire blockhead and going over to give him a big hug and tell him everything's going to be all right. Those of a less sympathetic disposition – so that probably means most of the Australians in the crowd – launch into a chant for Monty Panesar. It would have been 78 for four. The nagging sense of missed opportunity harasses the mind. Never mind, lads, positive thinking, there'll be another chance along in a minute. Yeh, right. But there is – are – two. And they come at eight run intervals. On 86, Ponting drives loosely at Anderson and the ball takes a thick outside edge and lands inches short of Bell in the gully; agony; on 94, he plops a ball from Flintoff into the on-side, and sets off for a quick single. But Collingwood, at square leg, is out of the traps like a shorter, squatter, very much more ginger Carl Lewis and hurls at the non-striker's end. Ponting is out by yards, but it misses and there are overthrows into the bargain.

We're going to suffer for this and we do. Ponting on 35, 42 and 48 at the time of his respective let-offs, finds his range and pummels 12 fours on his way to another bloody hundred, 142 to be exact, before Hoggard, the tireless workhorse, gets him to edge the new ball to Jones. By this time Hussey has moved on to 77 and Australia need only 90 or so more to save the follow-on. Hussey plays on before the end, again short of a deserved century, to boost English spirits but there has to be a feeling of what-might-have-been.

Starting day four on 312 for five, our best hope is to keep the Aussies on the back foot, tie them kangaroos down, sport, and get ourselves a handsome lead of about 170 or so, but Adam Gilchrist, unable to buy a run in England in 2005, and shot out by Hoggard third ball in Brisbane, has other ideas. With that high grip of his that allows him the longest and freest swing of the bat, he starts to pillage until he sweeps to Bell just in front of us in the Chappell stands. He's scored 64 in a partnership of 98 with Michael Clarke, who without doing anything fancy, purrs his way to a third Test century – this boy drives so cleanly you'd think he had a couple of brand new General Electric motors attached to him – while Warnie offers valuable support with the bat, even finding time to exchange belligerent words with his favourite Englishman, Paul Collingwood, between overs.

By the time McGrath edges behind to give Anderson a barely

merited wicket, the Aussies have cut our lead to a meagre 38.

On a wicket as unresponsive as this, though, that should be a springboard for another decent England innings. We lose Alastair Cook before the close, again aiming an unconvincing shot to Stuart Clark, but at 59 for one, Andrew Strauss on 31 and Ian Bell on 18, we're 97 runs to the good with just a day to play. Barring a miracle we can't win, but neither should we, barring a disaster, lose.

Tramping to the ground on the final day – we took a different route round the back of town to enjoy the walk alongside the Torrens river, pausing to reel off some snaps of the Canadian geese and a distant shot of the Adelaide Oval – there was a sense of anti-climax. We thought we English would probably outnumber our Australian counterparts at the ground – in fact, the attendance would prove to be 10,000 down on the first three days and nearly 5,000 down on the fourth, but even the 20,355 that was finally recorded could only have been boosted by locals emptying out of the city as news filtered through of what was unfolding on the hallowed turf.

But the sense of anti-climax was present because of the likelihood that we would dutifully preside over a draw. That in itself could be seen as a positive after the events of Brisbane – and something we would all have probably accepted, as football managers say, had we been offered it before the start of the match and even at lunch on the first day. However, after the morning session on day three, when there was tangible hope of victory, it was still a disappointment.

I'm nothing if not a masochist, though, because I realised that if England lost a couple of early wickets it would make the day more interesting from a purely cricket point of view. But, in typically English fashion, we couldn't just lose a couple of wickets and raise the level of excitement a couple of notches. We had to go the whole hog and collapse in quite spectacular style. It was nothing less than an implosion, a swallowing up of hope into an enormous black hole.

The history of Australia as written by the Aborigines would be quite different from that written by the white settlers and succeeding generations. So, too, the history of the Adelaide Test as seen through the eyes of Australians or the English, if not as bloody. I'm not quite sure when I understood that we were watching history, good and bad, in the making, but I think it might have been when Ian Bell was run out. But to put the history in context, you must understand what came just before and happened just afterwards.

Twelve balls before Ian Bell is run out, Strauss is given out erroneously by Steve Bucknor when he advances down the pitch, fails to make contact by several inches and the ball balloons to Hussey at short leg. Six balls *after* Bell is run out, Kevin Pietersen is bowled by Warne. So, in the space of three overs we have lost three of our best batsmen for the addition of three runs. But it is the circumstances surrounding Bell's dismissal that make me realise that something dreadful and debilitating and disastrous is in the air.

Two rows back in the Southern Concourse, on the line of backward point, we see it unfold horrifically before us. Bell plays a comfortable defensive shot off Warne in our direction, Collingwood, at the non-striker's end, thinks there is a chance of a single. Or does he? Bell has started, but he's not so sure. He sees Michael Clarke moving to pick it up. No, he doesn't want the run, but now Collingwood, even if he's no longer convinced it's on, starts to sprint down the pitch. They have looked at each other and away from each other and prevaricated for too long. Bell eventually decides he has no option but to go, but Clarke has picked it up in his natural left-hand and although his throw to Warne is well off target, the leg spinner catches it and has time to underarm it on to the stumps with Bell still well short. We deflate like pricked balloons.

Pietersen, in his effort to get off the mark, almost runs himself out third ball, but when he does go, I cannot understand how he has done it. He goes to sweep and suddenly there is the clink that you hear when a slow bowler has hit the wicket. Just a clink, not the fully formed death rattle you get when stumps are uprooted. For a moment I think it's an attempted stumping but Adam Gilchrist is already jumping and running down to embrace Warne. Pietersen didn't look out of his crease and we're close enough, with these short boundaries, to see it clearly. But in my ear I hear Bill Lawry or Mark Taylor or Peter Roebuck (no, discount that last one, I'm sure it is an Australian voice), exclaiming that he's bowled him round his legs. Not possible. From our angle, what has happened seems unthinkable according to the known laws of physics. But then I see the replay and all becomes clear. The ball has pitched just outside leg stump, Pietersen, who for hours on the second day refused Warne's temptations to sweep, has succumbed to the first offering and played all round it. Humiliatingly, it has not just gone round his legs and clipped the outside of leg stump, it has turned so far that it has taken out his off stump.

None of this, though, has happened until the final ball of the eleventh over of the morning. But a strangely subdued England have not come out fighting; if anything, they have come out frightened. Ricky Ponting has signalled where this match may be won by bringing Warne straight into the attack from the Cathedral End. He's laid open England's fears of the leg-spinner on a five-day old pitch from the very start. In ten and a half overs

– the dependable Stuart Clark has been given the River End – England have added just ten runs. The scent is in the Australian nostrils and as the heat rises, both figuratively and literally, England's batsmen are giving off an awful lot of sweat.

We are 74 for four and have two batsmen on nought. And soon Brett Lee is coming into view, replacing Clark. It's Lee versus Flintoff, another pair who are supposedly best mates after Flintoff's sympathetic reaction to Lee's despondency at Edgbaston. It takes the Australian only 12 balls. The first over is runless, apart from a no-ball and the second in similar provocative vein: balls of good pace just outside the off stump, inviting a stroke, testing patience, testing nerve, teasing - and finally seducing. The captain drives, lured into the trap, the outside edge is taken and Gilchrist is leaping in the air again. "Great bowling," says one commentator. "Bad batting," corrects another. Flintoff looks aghast but, from another angle, glad to be out of it. Is that dereliction of duty?

It's 77 for five and, as is becoming tediously apparent, when England are five down, it's as good as game over. There is fear and disgust and rage all mixing with one another in my stomach. I have probably sworn. I have probably sworn more than once. Sue is getting worried about me. Rational thought is impossible as the Australians in the crowd find their voice. "Warn-ie, Warn-ie," they intone, the chant picking up impetus as it travels round the ground, rather like a vocal Mexican Wave. For God's sake, it's 77 for five *from 40 overs*. Lunch seems a long way off, although it can't be. Collingwood works a four off his hips from Warne in the penultimate over before the break, but the man who became the first Englishman for 70 years to score a double-century in Australia in the first innings, had scored just one run from 42 balls before that. He seems mesmerised, perhaps still blaming himself for the Bell run-out, perhaps unsure whether he should throw caution to the wind – but look where that got him against Warne in Brisbane – or just stick in there. He has either decided on the latter course of action or he is in a state of shock.

After lunch, Jones picks up two boundaries from Lee's bowling, but when he stretches for a ball that starts wide and swings away, he does just enough to get wood on it but has no chance of controlling where the ball goes from there. It's gully, and it's out. Giles is given almost the full gamut of Warne deliveries but it is a shorter, turning one that gets him, forcing him on to the back foot and square on and the ball takes the shoulder of the bat and is gratefully clasped by Hayden. Then the Victorian makes Hoggard look like a chump, throwing up a series of sharp-turning leg breaks, inviting the big shot for the next ball, which is a googly, and the haggard Yorkshireman drags it on to his stumps from a foot outside.

Harmison and Anderson go to McGrath lbws, 129 all out. Australia need 168 from 36 overs. They come out all guns blazing. The rest is history.

That evening, I didn't have much interest in eating but Sue insisted. However, we'd missed the window of opportunity provided by the pub that bewilderingly shut at 8.20pm each night. It meant we had to journey further afield, towards the city centre, and after we had found somewhere suitable, we sat down to peruse the menu. It quickly became obvious that we had stumbled upon the restaurant that bewilderingly shuts at 8.50pm each night.

"Sorry, mate, we're closed," said a sympathetic waitress.

As we sought ever more desperately for some food we wandered past a bar, from whose door was emerging the The Man Who Isn't Called Darren, glass of beer in hand. We commiserated with one another over the result – it was nice to share the pain – and he told me that he had been standing with the Barmy Army for the whole match. He didn't think he would be going as far as Perth – he didn't have a ticket and wasn't confident of getting one. So, our conversation exhausted, we asked him if he knew a good place to get dinner at this time of night.

He wasn't sure, but eventually pointed us in the direction of a small Italian café where, unpromisingly, a middle-aged woman was wiping down a table. I poked my head in the door. "Are you still open?" I asked hopefully.

"Well, not really," she said, "but what are you looking for?"

"Oh, nothing special," I replied, guiding Sue into a seat before the woman could regret engaging us in dialogue. "What have you got?"

"Well, I suppose I could rustle you up a couple of chicken parmigianas," she said, disappearing into a darkened kitchen.

The following day we tried to forget about England's catastrophe with an early start on a day tour to Kangaroo Island. It wasn't easy. As we waited to board the coach that would take us to Cape Jervis, where we would be met by a ferry for the 30-minute crossing to Australia's third-largest island, I couldn't help but notice the headline on a paper in a nearby newsagent's. "THE INCREDIBLES" it trumpeted, focusing more on Australia's brilliance than England's failures. As far as I was concerned, it could just as easily have read "THE CRUSHINGLY INEPT" – we'd have known to whom they were referring. Back home, I was sure, such phrases – and less subtle ones - would be landing on doormats up and down the country.

We weren't the only English cricket supporters on the trip. In fact, the party of a couple of hundred, which would be divided up and put on separate buses on arrival in Penneshaw, the island's ferry terminal but a pleasant town nonetheless, was comprised almost entirely of people wearing blue and red Vodafone replica tops, sad flattened county cricket sunhats that had spent too long at the bottom of a suitcase, or polo shirts bearing the emblem of the cricket tour group they were with. Doug, our driver and guide, who had lived on a farm on the island before moving away to pursue a career in engineering, only returning home on his retirement, was proud. "I've got half the Barmy Army with me," I heard him confide to a receptionist at the visitor centre of the Flinders Chase National Park on our final stop.

Doug was about 105 years old and had a dodgy hip. In fact, as he welcomed us aboard his bus I worried about his clutch control. As a depressing coda to the cricket disaster we had witnessed, I had visions of us careering off an unsealed highway, ending up, head gasket steaming, halfway up a gum tree – from which there seemed an infinite variety to choose, although personally I couldn't tell the difference between a South Australian blue, a rough-barked manna or a red forest one – with a startled koala looking down from on high wondering who'd disrupted his lunch.

Despite his disability, Doug was a mine of information about his native island and as good an exponent of multi-tasking as you could wish to see. As he swung his 52-seat vehicle round some narrow and testing bends, he would point outside at an echidna – a hedgehog-like creature that would roll up in a ball and do its best to burst your tyres before waddling off into the bush to hoover up some small insects (it is commonly known as a spiny ant eater) – or launch into a despatch about the koala management system. This programme involved sterilising a proportion of the furry marsupials or relocating them to other parts of south-eastern Australia because their voracious appetites were threatening the eucalyptus habitats of other endangered species such as the white-naped honeyeater – a bird to you and me, admittedly a very colourful one. Koalas were not native to Kangaroo Island, he explained, and the original population of 18 introduced for conservation reasons from Victoria in the 1920s, had grown to

27,000 by 2001. There had been some serious koala incest going on.

Doug's solution to the problem was quite simple: "I think if all the tourists took one home each that'd sort it out," he said.

Doug also had an interesting line in extraordinarily long-winded jokes, so long-winded in fact that by the time he got to the punchline everyone had forgotten the beginning, so nobody laughed. He didn't seem bothered. Why should he have been? He was the archetype of the best sort of Australian: enthusiastic, genuinely friendly, interested in life and people – and rarely mentioned the cricket. When he was completely lost for words he turned to his impressive collection of Pam Ayres tapes, which not only had the effect of transporting us back instantaneously to the mid 1970s, when talent shows were decided on the outcome of a clapometer rather than a premium-rate phone line, but also allowed us to try out our individual impersonations of West Country accents – and it's always good to have an excuse to do that.

Our whistlestop tour – the island really deserves more leisurely investigation – took in, among other sights, Seal Bay, a glorious beach whose length, despite its name, is colonised by wild sea lions holidaying after protracted fishing trips, and Remarkable Rocks, a naturally occurring phenomenon overlooking the Southern Ocean on the west coast that looks like something Salvador Dali might have produced had he shown more interest in geology.

At each stop, Doug would be first off the bus, clambering down from his seat and leading the way across awkward terrain to the place of interest, hobbling at every step. The only place that defeated him was Admirals Arch, a walkway descending hundreds of steps down a rugged cliff face that takes you to a spectacular rock arch where fur seals play.

But it was only a temporary defeat for Doug. "I'll look forward to seeing you next time," he said as he waved us off at the end of the day, "and then nothing'll stop me. I'll have a new hip."

I had been sending some of my observations on the tour to *The Times'* cricket blog Line and Length, manned heroically by my colleague Patrick Kidd, in London, who would burn the midnight oil from his sofa in Blackheath, writing pithy comments on the state of play throughout the wee hours, fending off the often disagreeable opinions of gloating Aussies, and occasionally posting my contributions. While we had been away in Kangaroo Island, Matthew Hoggard had been writing the latest instalment of his Times online diary – and it made inflammatory reading. We had planned to wile away our final hours in Adelaide before boarding the train for the 38-hour journey to Perth late in the afternoon with a spot of café hopping and second-hand book shopping but I felt compelled to respond to Hoggard's words. So instead of a spot of idle browsing we took up position in an internet centre, Sue e-mailing some friends, while I tapped out my angry response. What emerged was reactionary, sexist, some might say mysoginistic – but I hoped people would see that my tongue was at least partly tucked in my cheek.

'The final paragraph in Matthew Hoggard's piece said it all about this England side and why they were doomed to failure,' I wrote. *'They were just too well-adjusted. He said: "The one consolation for me – other than the drowning of sorrows last night – was that we will be back on an aeroplane tonight to fly to Perth where Sarah, my wife, will be waiting for me. We haven't seen each other for more than a month and she will know exactly how I'm feeling after our performance in Adelaide. I think I need a good hug after a game like that."*

'Precisely, I thought. This team was just too touchy-feely. In the aftermatch of the 2005 Ashes series, the players became not just national heroes but lifestyle icons. They were lauded for their sensitivity, the

image that cemented that impression being Andrew Flintoff's show of sympathy for Brett Lee after England had won the perilously close second Test at Edgbaston.

'Suddenly, these were not just international sportsmen concerned with winning an important contest at all costs, but real people with real feelings who could identify with an opponent's suffering even in their own moment of success. And we have had countless examples in recent years of senior players knocking off in the middle of a game, home or abroad, to be present for the births of the first, second or even third children.

'These 'new men' may prove popular with the modern woman, even perhaps the occasional modern man, but they cannot be relied upon to bring back the Ashes against an Australian side that has rediscovered the ruthless streak it left at Lord's last year. These Australians, far from wanting to be present when their wives go into labour, would get on the blower, order them to stop making such a fuss and tell them to have their dinner on the table when they got home.

'On the eve of the second Test; well, at about three o'clock in the afternoon to be precise, we had wandered up to the café at the Adelaide Festival Centre, the arts complex a river crossing from the Adelaide Oval. There, sitting at a table, with pushchair, wife and infant in tow, was Andrew Strauss. I sat down at a table nearby, while Sue ordered some drinks, reasoning that all the practice to rid him of the instinctive need to hook had been done that morning and hoping that I could eavesdrop on England's plans to level the series in the upcoming match. Unfortunately, all I caught was some minor domestic tittle-tattle and the England vice-captain engaging in baby talk with his offspring.

'My problem with this is that the night after he had spooned a catch to mid-wicket to put England in early trouble, he would have been able to fall into the comforting arms of his wife, who would no doubt have assured him that even if the cricket media was questioning his shot selection, even if the whole sporting world was against him, she was still on his side.

'Touching, and what Hoggard is seemingly seeking on arrival in Perth. The Australians, though, didn't prepare for this series with a night out with their other halves: they went to a bush camp, suffering the severe deprivations of the Outback, even if Shane Warne did complain about John Buchanan confiscating his mobile phone. It seems like it was time well spent, with the team bonding and more important, clarifying in their minds what this series meant to the people of their nation.

'England need to eat, sleep and breathe cricket, with few distractions if they are to compete here. They need to decide whether they want to be professional cricketers at the top of their game with all the benefits – and some disadvantages – that implies, or househusbands. It's time for England to get macho!'

I later heard a rumour that Hoggard, a seven-wicket hero in defeat, had been severely censored by his ghost writer. If what the Yorkshireman had really said about his team-mates had been reported, it wouldn't have got past the lawyers in a family newspaper. Well, not without liberal use of the asterisk.

It was the middle of the night on 1 February 1995, and Denis Compton was crying out for help. It is not every day that your presence is demanded by a cricketing legend, so I stepped gingerly from my single-berth first-class cabin on the Indian Pacific, the iconic train that bridges the Australian continent from Sydney in the east to Perth in the west, wondering whether the former Middlesex and England batsman and Arsenal and England winger, by chance allocated the sleeping quarters next to mine, was having a nightmare. Perhaps his presence in Australia had awakened a repressed memory about the first Test against Don

Bradman's Invincibles at Trent Bridge in 1948, when in a desperate rearguard action, Compton had narrowly failed to guide England to safety, over-balancing in response to a short ball from Keith Miller and falling on his stumps on 184. The Australians went on to win the series 4-0 and remained unbeaten in the 32 matches they played on the tour.

My other thought was that he was suffering a health emergency. He was 76 now, walking with a stick and wearing a ruddy complexion that spoke of his love for socialising. I was no first-aid expert so I hesitated outside his door but before I could decide on my next move, he had thrust it open, pointed at the toilet bowl that flipped down from the cabin wall when it was in use and returned to its upright position, hidden beneath the basin, when not, rather like a foldaway bed in a studio flat, and asked loudly: "What am I supposed to do about this?" I had hoped that my first discussion with one of England's most maverick and best-loved of sportsmen would have been less prosaic: he might have let me in on the secrets of his 300 for MCC against Transvaal, the fastest triple-century to this day, which must have been some three hours of mayhem. But no, it was to be to do with the curious workings of the lavatories on a long-distance train.

Or it would have been had not a member of the train staff, also alerted by Compton's exclamations, arrived in the nick of time. She smiled to indicate that I could stand down and she would handle things from here on in. Mildly disturbed, but back in my cabin, I could hear her unsqueamish explanation about the unsophisticated nature of the flush mechanism through the partition. "You just lift it back up into the wall," she said, "and gravity does the rest." It was one way for a sporting luminary to leave his mark on the Outback.

I didn't see much more of Compton who, like me, had joined the train at Adelaide, but I often heard him acceding to requests to sign autographs and pose with other England fans who had learned of his presence on board and had left their cramped accommodation in coach class to seek him out. It was probably just as well: I doubt whether, following the night's events, we could have looked each other in the eye in the cold light of day.

Compton was not the only celebrity making the journey with us. Thousands of fans reinvigorated by England's victory in Adelaide that, after the nail-biting draw at Sydney, had revived the series, had decided to travel to Perth to see if we could square it, even though the Ashes, held by Australia, could not be wrenched from their grasp.

One of them was Sir Tim Rice, the lyricist and mad keen cricket follower, who I had crossed paths with a few days earlier. Sir Tim, later to become president of MCC, his Australian friend and I had found ourselves in a short queue of three at the Keswick Rail Terminal, Adelaide's interstate station. I was confirming my booking on a $500 rail pass that permitted me to travel first-class on any train in the country for a total of 30 days in any 90. For a backpacker, it was an absolute bargain, one so good that the rail authorities have since dispensed with it. He offered me a ride back into town in the taxi that was waiting for him and asked me if I was a member of the Barmy Army, which, although at its formative stages in this series, was shortly to gain temporary corporate recognition in the form of sponsorship from Mitsubishi. "We're Atherton's Barmy Army" memorably became "We're the Mitsubishi-sponsored Barmy Army" when it was sung at Perth. I replied that I wasn't. I should have asked him what he thought of their lyrics.

The next time I saw him, some days later, was in Kalgoorlie, a Western Australian mining town, where the Indian Pacific stops for a couple of hours shortly after darkness falls to re-stock, and passengers are encouraged to go on a coach tour of the goldfields to get them out from under the feet of the train staff. I eschewed the tour, instead walking into town, where I stopped and watched a floodlit bowls match for a while. Then I returned to the platform where I decided to investigate just how long this beast of transportation was. I counted 26 carriages and it took so long to get to its far end that by the time I had, I felt as if I had passed an Aboriginal rite of passage.

It was one carriage in particular that interested me, however: flooded with light and life while all the rest were empty and dark, dinner was being dished up. I couldn't see what was on the menu, but it was silver service, with a waiter in a starched white shirt and black bow tie performing the honours. Moving closer, but staying in the shadows to avoid detection, I tried to identify the guest list. It wasn't hard. There, at the head of the table, was Sir Tim and taking advantage of his hospitality was DCS Compton and Mark Nicholas. Sir Tim had obviously not been booking a first-class cabin at Keswick Rail Terminal but a first-class *carriage*. Still, I think I might have paid to listen in to that dinner conversation.

It was experiences like these that had persuaded me that I wanted to share similar ones with Sue. She would have been happy to fly to Perth – "I get on a train and commute to work every day," she complained. "I don't really want to do it when I'm on holiday" – but as we sat at home in August planning the expedition, I managed to convince her of the romance of rail travel.

"What about those documentaries on TV," I said. "You know, the ones with people like Clive Anderson, or Clive James – Clive someone or other, anyway. They're *Great Railway Journeys of the World*, not Great Plane Journeys of the World. I mean, on the Indian Pacific you can travel across the Nullabor Desert on the *longest stretch of straight track in the world*."

I hoped the emphasis on this phrase would clinch it. I wasn't sure why it should though, really. It's one of the strange things about tourism, that even the most minor of idiosyncracies is played up for all its worth. I worked in Bermuda for nearly three years and it always bemused me that despite its gorgeous beaches, its quaint, brightly-coloured houses and a proliferation of golf courses squeezed on to a tiny island, the tourist literature and guide books often pointed to one unique selling point: it had the world's smallest drawbridge. Exactly who this would have swayed to visit Bermuda, rather than, say, cheaper destinations in the Caribbean, I was never sure, apart perhaps from the odd bridge engineer.

"*The longest stretch of straight track in the world, eh?*" Sue repeated to me, hiding her obvious admiration well beneath her sarcasm. "What, no bends at all?"

"None," I said, "not for 478 kilometres at least," and got on to Great Southern Railway's UK agents.

The news was not good. All the first-class cabins, now rebranded Gold Kangaroo Service, had been sold for our chosen travel dates – not that we could have afforded one – and we could only get on to the waiting list for a Red Kangaroo sleeper. This left us facing the prospect of sitting upright for nearly two days. I wasn't too bothered: I envisaged plenty of good conversation with like-minded cricket fans, the chance to imbed myself in at least one of the 14 or so books I was bound to take to last me round Australia and, failing that, the opportunity to get roaringly drunk or catch up on some sleep (perhaps one would even lead to the other).

About a month before our departure for Australia we got an update: we couldn't have a Red Kangaroo sleeper because they would not be available on our train, which had been designated the Christmas special. We were keen to know what this meant. Would we get presents delivered to our seats by the Great Southern Railway chief executive in a Santa outfit? That would be a nice gesture. Or a festive non-stop cabaret involving dancing girls and comedians with a scathing Australian wit? Christmas pud at mealtimes?

The truth was even more surreal than we could have imagined: we were to witness an ageing boy band step down from the train in the middle of the Nullabor desert, attired in evening dress at 9 o'clock in the morning, to sing a collection of their greatest hits to an audience of Aboriginal children, who had travelled in minibuses and 4x4s since the early hours to get there. If this was the Australians' idea of a Christmas treat for the indigenous population, they surely had a few kangaroos loose in the top paddock. The children, having travelled for three hours across one of the widest and flattest landscapes in the world, appeared totally nonplussed to be confronted by Human Nature's observation that there *Ain't No Mountain High Enough*. And although the dance steps were enough to make Mark Ramprakash proud, they were equally confused when the group finished by singing that they were leaving, now, on a *Midnight Train to Georgia*.

It was a cloying clash of separate cultures and difficult to work out who looked more embarrassed, the Aborigines or Human Nature. Just when you thought it couldn't get any worse, the children were encouraged to respond with a song of their own that they'd been practising at school. Most of them, though, were either too shy or overawed by the occasion and by the time they got to the chorus it was their white teachers, desperately trying to chivvy them along, whose voices were the most prominent.

The white teachers, to their credit, were doing their best, smiling through gritted teeth at the cameras. Yes, the cameras: there was a woman from Channel 9, a news crew from the BBC, writers from various Australian newspapers and correspondents from a bunch of travel glossies.

Now it all made sense: we couldn't get into a Red Kangaroo sleeper because they were occupied by pop singers and glamorous TV journalists, being given the full PR treatment to ensure they wrote or broadcast nice things about what the nice white people were doing for the poor downtrodden natives. Maybe I'm being harsh – the tourist literature describes the Christmas train, an annual event since 2000, as bringing cheer to remote Australian communities and as a gift to the locals for their support of the train.

That was probably more true of Cook, perhaps the hottest and sleepiest town in the Outback, a little further down the line. Cook once had a community of 120 people, many servicing the railway, but changes to maintenance methods meant that there were now just two couples living there, occasionally supplemented by train drivers, for whom it was a changeover point.

One of the residents, a large and jolly woman, was interviewed by the Channel 9 reporter while she dished out postcards and stamps in the souvenir shop. She seemed happy with her lot, thousands of miles in almost any direction from civilisation, although an article I found later on the internet described her disappointment when the hospital had shut. "I can't bear to go there now," she was reported as saying. "It's just so depressing when I think of how alive it used to be."

I'd have been more concerned about whether I could pick up the cricket. Apparently not. The ghost town was served by three TV channels received by satellite. ABC, the national broadcaster, was among them, but there was no Channel 9.

Ms Channel 9, meanwhile, had not travelled lightly: while we stepped out into the blistering 48 degree heat – heat that feels as if someone has turned a giant hairdryer on you at full power – wearing T-shirt and shorts, she emerged tall, blonde and brassy in a stunning outfit that could not have been easy to slip into in a relatively small train cabin; still, easier than trying to change in a shower cubicle in which you could barely stretch both arms out, as we were obliged to do. But I really had to hand it to the Channel 9 costume department because when we rolled up in Kalgoorlie and Human Nature did their thing to a population probably more familiar with their work, she was dolled up to the nines in yet another fashionable ensemble.

As we departed Kalgoorlie for our final night of discomfort, a

New Zealander, bronzed and blonded by too much sea and sun, was on a desperate hunt for a new challenger in his 38-hour arm wrestling competition. As he passed our seats, I lowered my head into one of my books, *It's Just Not Cricket*, the autobiography of Peter Walker, the former Glamorgan and England cricketer. I had interviewed Walker a few weeks earlier for an article about the number of ex-cricketers on jollies with supporter tours to the Ashes, of which he was one. I remembered him as an occasional presenter of John Player League matches when they were always played on Sundays and broadcast on BBC2 – a kind of poor man's Peter West, although that is not a reflection on his professional skills, which were as good as anybody's in my young eyes, but more a recognition that he never got the really big gigs. Thinking about it, he came across as a calmer Charles Colville and would have wiped the floor with most of Sky's analysts these days, apart perhaps from Bumble and Mike Atherton.

Walker had proved an engaging interviewee during our brief chat, if not an incredibly high-profile one, so when I spotted his book in a local shop I felt I should return the favour and buy a copy. I was a bit disappointed with the title, judging it to be a bit clichéd but further investigation proved that his life, literally, wasn't just cricket.

He'd run away from his native South Africa, gone to sea – where he honed considerable catching skills by juggling with potatoes on board – survived a murder attempt, fights with crocodiles and learned to play the clarinet, all seemingly before he'd got padded up. He sounded, in fact, exactly like the sort of person who could take on a Kiwi at arm-wrestling; indeed, the kind of person who might end a Kiwi's arm-wrestling career for good.

He would have been especially useful now, as the frustrated surfer-dude even tried to persuade a fellow passenger, who was clearly disabled, to take him on. I couldn't in all honesty tell whether he was serious and too stupid to realise he was severely disabled, or just taking the piss. Whatever, he was persuaded to leave the poor man alone by some friends, one who had obviously grown tired of his behaviour and an international incident was narrowly averted.

The peacemaker looked up at another member of their group, as she dished out a hand in a game of cards they were playing. "Remind me to take the plane next time," she said in a long-suffering voice. By then, I felt the same way.

The Ashes - 2nd Test

Australia v England

Played at Adelaide Oval on 1,2,3,4,5 December 2006 (5-day match)
Result Australia won by 6 wickets

England 1st innings		R	M	B	SR
AJ Strauss	c Martyn b Clark	14	63	44	31.81
AN Cook	c ✝Gilchrist b Clark	27	90	57	47.36
IR Bell	c & b Lee	60	189	148	40.54
PD Collingwood	c ✝Gilchrist b Clark	206	515	392	52.55
KP Pietersen	run out (Ponting)	158	377	257	61.47
✱ A Flintoff	not out	38	101	67	56.71
✝GO Jones	c Martyn b Warne	1	10	7	14.28
AF Giles	not out	27	63	44	61.36
Extras	(lb 10, w 2, nb 8)	20			
Total	**(6 wickets dec; 168 overs; 707 mins)**	**551 (3.27 runs per over)**			

Did not bat MJ Hoggard, SJ Harmison, JM Anderson
Fall of wickets1-32 (Strauss, 14.3 ov), 2-45 (Cook, 20.5 ov), 3-158 (Bell, 61.4 ov), 4-468 (Collingwood, 145.5 ov), 5-489 (Pietersen, 151.6 ov), 6-491 (Jones, 154.2 ov)

Bowling	O	M	R	W	Econ	
B Lee	34	1	139	1	4.08	(8nb, 1w)
GD McGrath	30	5	107	0	3.56	
SR Clark	34	6	75	3	2.20	
SK Warne	53	9	167	1	3.15	(1w)
MJ Clarke	17	2	53	0	3.11	

Australia 1st innings		R	M	B	SR
JL Langer	c Pietersen b Flintoff	4	9	8	50.00
ML Hayden	c ✝Jones b Hoggard	12	57	30	40.00
✱ RT Ponting	c ✝Jones b Hoggard	142	353	245	57.95
DR Martyn	c Bell b Hoggard	11	42	33	33.33
MEK Hussey	b Hoggard	91	298	212	42.92
MJ Clarke	c Giles b Hoggard	124	318	224	55.35
✝AC Gilchrist	c Bell b Giles	64	111	79	81.01
SK Warne	lbw b Hoggard	43	157	108	39.81
B Lee	not out	7	47	33	21.21
SR Clark	b Hoggard	0	9	7	0.00
GD McGrath	c ✝Jones b Anderson	1	25	21	4.76
Extras	(b 4, lb 2, w 1, nb 7)	14			
Total	**(all out; 165.3 overs; 718 mins)**	**513 (3.09 runs per over)**			

Fall of wickets1-8 (Langer, 1.6 ov), 2-35 (Hayden, 12.6 ov), 3-65 (Martyn, 22.2 ov), 4-257 (Ponting, 82.6 ov), 5-286 (Hussey, 90.4 ov), 6-384 (Gilchrist, 114.4 ov), 7-502 (Warne, 153.5 ov), 8-505 (Clarke, 157.1 ov), 9-507 (Clark, 159.2 ov), 10-513 (McGrath, 165.3 ov)

Bowling	O	M	R	W	Econ	
MJ Hoggard	42	6	109	7	2.59	
A Flintoff	26	5	82	1	3.15	(5nb)
SJ Harmison	25	5	96	0	3.84	(2nb, 1w)
JM Anderson	21.3	3	85	1	3.95	
AF Giles	42	7	103	1	2.45	
KP Pietersen	9	0	32	0	3.55	

England 2nd innings		R	M	B	SR
AJ Strauss	c Hussey b Warne	34	125	79	43.03
AN Cook	c ✚ Gilchrist b Clark	9	48	35	25.71
IR Bell	run out (Clarke/Warne)	26	85	73	35.61
PD Collingwood	not out	22	198	119	18.48
KP Pietersen	b Warne	2	8	5	40.00
✱ A Flintoff	c ✚Gilchrist b Lee	2	25	24	8.33
✚GO Jones	c Hayden b Lee	10	41	24	41.66
AF Giles	c Hayden b Warne	0	14	8	0.00
MJ Hoggard	b Warne	4	27	24	16.66
SJ Harmison	lbw b McGrath	8	25	21	38.09
JM Anderson	lbw b McGrath	1	41	28	3.57
Extras	(b 3, lb 5, w 1, nb 2)	11			
Total	**(all out; 73 overs; 324 mins)**	**129 (1.76 runs per over)**			

Fall of wickets 1-31 (Cook, 10.6 ov), 2-69 (Strauss, 29.6 ov), 3-70 (Bell, 31.6 ov), 4-73 (Pietersen, 33.1 ov), 5-77 (Flintoff, 38.6 ov), 6-94 (Jones, 48.4 ov), 7-97 (Giles, 51.6 ov), 8-105 (Hoggard, 57.5 ov), 9-119 (Harmison, 62.6 ov), 10-129 (Anderson, 72.6 ov)

Bowling	O	M	R	W	Econ	
B Lee	18	3	35	2	1.94	(2nb)
GD McGrath	10	6	15	2	1.50	(1w)
SK Warne	32	12	49	4	1.53	
SR Clark	13	4	22	1	1.69	

Australia 2nd innings (target: 168 runs)		R	M	B	SR
JL Langer	c Bell b Hoggard	7	12	8	87.50
ML Hayden	c Collingwood b Flintoff	18	31	17	105.88
✱ RT Ponting	c Strauss b Giles	49	95	65	75.38
MEK Hussey	not out	61	129	66	92.42
DR Martyn	c Strauss b Flintoff	5	4	4	125.00
MJ Clarke	not out	21	47	39	53.84
Extras	(b 2, lb 2, w 1, nb 2)	7			
Total	**(4 wickets; 32.5 overs; 161 mins)**	**168 (5.11 runs per over)**			

Did not bat AC Gilchrist, SK Warne, B Lee, SR Clark, GD McGrath
Fall of wickets 1-14 (Langer, 2.2 ov), 2-33 (Hayden, 5.4 ov), 3-116 (Ponting, 21.4 ov), 4-121 (Martyn, 22.2 ov)

Bowling	O	M	R	W	Econ	
MJ Hoggard	4	0	29	1	7.25	
A Flintoff	9	0	44	2	4.88	(2nb)
AF Giles	10	0	46	1	4.60	
SJ Harmison	4	0	15	0	3.75	(1w)
JM Anderson	3.5	0	23	0	6.00	
KP Pietersen	2	0	7	0	3.50	

Toss England, who chose to bat first

Up and down like a bride's nightie

PERTH

THE rumours started circulating at the Waca some time on Saturday afternoon and by lunchtime on the Sunday they were confirmed during a strange, stilted exchange with a security guard at the entry to Gate 6.

"Tickets for the Ashes?" he inquired. "Another 1,000 have been released. Two hundred for Poms. On sale tomorrow. Twelve o'clock. Ticketmaster. Wellington Street."

This was of interest to me for two reasons: I had no ticket for the first day of the third Test – the only one in the entire series that I lacked – which was now just four days away, and my hostel, at last a well-equipped, delightfully clean and friendly YHA one, was on Wellington Street. I could camp out overnight if necessary and nip back for a shower and some breakfast while Sue held my place in the queue, I reasoned.

Further investigation proved frustrating, however: hostel staff not only knew of no Ticketmaster outlet on Wellington Street, but also doubted whether there was one in the city at all. When I pulled up the agency's website, at least proving it was legitimate, it made no mention of these extra tickets, nor of a Perth address.

I turned, instead, to the Barmy Army, scrolling down their website forum until I hit a few posts that renewed my hope by attesting to the tickets' existence, but infuriatingly gave no details of where they could be obtained.

The hunt for the elusive bounty began to take on the essence of a John Le Carré spy novel as I was mysteriously advised to contact the Perth Tourist Information Office, hidden behind the city's main post office and which I quickly suspected of being a front for the Western Australian intelligence services.

One woman manning the desk seemed to be in the know. Taking me aside and tapping the side of her nose to suggest that it was seriously classified information, she directed me to follow a maze of side roads, join Hay Street – "the longest street in Perth," she announced proudly – until I reached His Majesty's Theatre.

"Her Majesty's Theatre?" I checked.

"*His* Majesty's Theatre, she corrected. "We're *that* old."

Once there, she confided, I was to seek out the nearby Cloisters newsagents where, if I passed a package of used notes over at the counter, I would be shown to the back of the shop where the clandestine transaction could be safely completed.

As a rule I'm a person who prefers to move at a steady pace – sedate some people might call it, others somnambulant – but now the race was on. I thanked the woman and breathlessly followed her instructions, hastening down Hay Street – it really was long - dodging office workers weighed down by a fresh week's responsibilities and cardboard trays of take-away cappuccinos, and nearly taking out a couple of elderly ladies as they window-shopped outside a menswear store, perhaps for new suits for a couple of elderly husbands.

But when I screeched to a halt at my destination, it appeared as though the tourist information office woman had not confided her information to me alone. It was only 10.30am and already there were at least 50 people, largely desperate Poms by the look of them, ahead of me in the queue, which wound its way out of Cloisters and through a small and neat shopping mall.

"How long've you been here?" I asked a group at the front of the line.

"Since nine," one replied.

Bastards, I thought, as I set off to the back, simultaneously doing a body count and dividing the number into 200. It wasn't promising. I became the 64th person on the waiting list.

We were an anxious audience but a captive one, too, with all the unexpected economic benefits that that can bring to small businesses at a generally quiet time on a Monday morning. So it was little surprise when the more wily entrepreneurial among the staff in the surrounding shops took the opportunity to promote their wares. One woman from a printing outlet passed along the line with a business card on which she had swiftly embossed a picture of Matthew Hayden in full flow. It was a good effort, but I couldn't help thinking she had misjudged her market. While it was no doubt emblematic of the state of play in the series so far, it was hardly likely to endear her to a bunch of England supporters growing more impatient by the minute.

When she offered her card to a shaven-headed, tattooed man beside me, he said: "No thanks, luv, but I don't suppose there's any chance of a coffee, is there?"

His mates laughed, freeing up the reluctant conversationalists among the queue-dwellers – and tales of cricketing disenchantment began to emerge. I listened in interest as one man in a red England football top told of how he had brought his 17-year-old son out to Perth for the trip of a young lifetime. "I paid for his flights, and I paid for all his accommodation," he said, "but he turned round after just one day and complained of being homesick. He took the next plane back to London."

I shared his incredulity, and would have sympathised with him had my peripheral vision not picked out a small group beginning to form a circle around a woman who obviously had something they could use, but who was also giving off a strange, dazzling aura.

"I've got four tickets," shouted the middle-aged Australian, whose hair, I realised as I approached, was in the process of being dyed an almost preternatural blonde. It transpired that she had been having it done in the mall's salon when the queue – now at least 100 strong – had started to stretch past its window. When the stylist explained the reason for the commotion, she had leapt from her chair, run into the mall, engendering a mix of excitement, anticipation and temporary blindness among those nearest by when she explained her business. Having negotiated deals with four members of the queue, she disappeared to get the tickets, all frustratingly for me for the third day, from her husband at home. I never saw her come back, though, and to my dying day, it will haunt me that I don't know whether she ever did get her blow dry or is still running around Perth with a multicoloured barnet.

Word began to sweep through the queue that only two tickets would be available for each customer. Anyone requiring more would have to rejoin the end of the queue. I began to feel guilty – some of these people were flying around Australia ticketless, hoping to acquire spares from touts in each city. I had the keys to the locks on the front door of practically every session of the Ashes, while they were hoping to pick their way through the tradesman's entrance.

Surely the right thing to do would have been to vacate my place in the queue; better, to offer up my tickets for the remaining three days, not necessarily to the highest bidder, but to the most needy. Such altruism would please Sue: she had begun complaining that we were not experiencing the "real" Australia and although I countered that being part of the crowd at a cricket match Down Under was as authentic an experience of the "real" Australia that you could get, she wasn't convinced. But I could probably subdue her grievances with a quick flight to Alice Springs to view Uluru at sunset or a drive north of Perth for a couple of days to the ancient desert rocks of the Pinnacles, best experienced at first light, which exposed them at their most silent and eerie. But cricket was my drug, and I was desperate for my next fix, forgetting, like addicts of every sort, that brief highs were followed by the most desperate and extended of lows – as Adelaide had shown us all too well. My tickets remained in my wallet.

My selfishness, however, was to earn me a dose of instant karma: when the desk finally opened, barely ten transactions had been sealed before the news came through that all tickets for day one were gone. I panickily decided on a new strategy. I'd bag a couple for day two or three and then try to use them as bargaining tools in a swap deal. Trouble was, nobody at the front of the queue who had bought the tickets I wanted had hung around long enough for me to put my plan into action, and when I finally got to the front of the line, only day four was left.

It all seemed like another kick in the stomach for England fans, who had endured the Australian cricket authorities' clumsy attempts to prevent them getting their hands on tickets in the first place by offering ten at a time to members of the Cricket Australia family. To qualify for the family, you simply had to reside in Australia and register. Those who did were given 18 days' priority booking. Some 161,000 seats went in the first six hours – and the CA website went into meltdown for a while. For touts, it was a second Australian gold rush.

By the time tickets went on sale to fans based in England, there were relatively few left. Before midnight on June 18 I had three computers – and three computer operators, my brother, my sister and me – in position. Switching from Venuetix in Adelaide, to Ticketmaster in Melbourne and Ticketek in Sydney, the story was the same over and over again: Allocation Exhausted, an infuriating PR synonym for Bugger off, we're Sold Out. In the event, we grabbed what we could – a couple of one-day internationals in Hobart here, a ground admission ticket there. The Barmy Army website forum became a veritable *Saturday Multicoloured Swapshop* of bartering.

My batch had eventually arrived courtesy of a work friend with contacts in Australia, some eBay bargaining and minimal effort of my own, although the Adelaide tickets remained worryingly in the vaults of Venuetix until the day before the Test started.

And now, in Perth, my salvation lay just around the corner: literally, as it turned out, at the Sheraton Hotel.

I had shared my frustration with *The Times'* blog and while it didn't arouse much sympathy among Australia readers – the Poms were universally blamed for grabbing tickets that were not rightfully theirs – it did touch the good nature of another colleague, Walter Gammie. His brother-in-law ran one of the companies conducting one of the more upmarket Ashes tours, and he contacted him to see if he had any spare tickets. He did, and, as luck would have it, in the top row of the Prindiville Stand, right behind the bowler's arm.

The Test in Perth, it turned out, was only the culmination of what the city bigwigs had designated a ten-day cricket festival. A one-day match between a Cricket Australia Chairman's XI and an England Invitational XI, which had not been on any of my fixture lists, was arranged for Lilac Hill, a regular starting point for international tours since 1990, and was played out as we chugged across the Nullabor on the Friday.

Our train having rendered us sleep-deprived and severely luggage-laden (we'd had to extract numerous items from our hold-alls and pack them in what looked like glorified shopping bags to meet health and safety limitations for baggage handlers) on the platform of East Perth Station early the following morning, we decided to skip the first day of England's next fixture. This was another anomaly on a tour full of them – a two-day game against

Western Australia that, barring some pretty sensational bowling and gruesome batting – the latter was always possible with England – would become effectively a one-innings contest. Indeed, when, on the second afternoon, England passed their opponents' score, they simply carried on batting until the close.

Yet there was interest in this encounter – just a 12-a-side one this time – and that was provided by the presence in the England team of Michael Vaughan, who was desperately trying to get match practice where he could in his rehabilitation from a serious knee injury. It was pleasing to see that it was not only his own supporters who longed to see him back at the England helm. When Geraint Jones was dismissed for a golden duck at No 3 in the latest, but fruitless, attempt to find somewhere in the order that he would score runs, the scoreboard operators swung rapidly into action, putting the Yorkshire batsman's name up alongside that of the undefeated Alastair Cook, even though the man striding to the middle, a stocky, short fellow, bore little resemblance to the elegant, upright opener.

The Australian spectators, though, in honour of his fine form in the 2002 series, when he scored three centuries against them, and his excellent leadership in 2005, gave him a genuinely affectionate welcome, even when he took guard left-handed and revealed himself to be Ed Joyce. Much as Joyce pressed his claims to strengthen the batting line up for the third Test, I, and many others I suspect, were desperate to see a Vaughan cameo. In fact, having got his half-century, Joyce seemed so determined to get himself out that the only conclusion that could be drawn was that he too wanted to witness the former captain leaning into a trademark cover drive. Yet wickets, and retirements – Alistair Cook completed his hundred before voluntarily calling a halt – came and went and still no Vaughan emerged. When Ashley Giles and Sajid Mahmood got the nod over him, it was the cue for most of us to leave.

But we were back on Tuesday – a gloriously sunny evening that you could quite as easily have spent in the adjoining Queen's Gardens with its fabulous water lily-filled lakes, formed from the pits left after the site's use in the late 19th century as a clay mine and brickworks – as were more than 17,000 others. The draw was a Twenty20 game between England Legends and their Australian counterparts. The brainstormers who had racked their grey matter for a way to promote the match had come up with a beautiful line: "Not just any old teams, but two very old teams," was the catchy synopsis in an advert in *The West Australian* newspaper.

I am not a big fan of these sorts of matches: the spectacle of ageing sportsmen running around trying to recapture the glories of their youth – and displaying a false kind of bonhomie when the passing of the years reveals their bodily limitations – is one I generally happily avoid. You won't catch me at Masters football or the Gentlemen's Over-45s doubles in the second week of Wimbledon. But there was an additional sadness watching this game, as a team representing England broke the habit of this tour and won by six wickets with seven balls to spare. The leading batting lights for the tourists were Graham Thorpe and Robin Smith, two middle-order masters who'd had, at least in my opinion, their international careers curtailed prematurely. Thorpe, banished after his hundredth Test, against Bangladesh, in favour of Kevin Pietersen for the subsequent Ashes series, was still young enough to fit snugly in at number four in the current line-up with Collingwood dropping to number six and Flintoff, still underachieving with the bat, one lower.

Thursday morning. It's a glorious morning weather-wise and I grab my ticket, my one ticket, leaving Sue to take in a couple of museums or do the washing – she decides on the latter, her choice – and walk to the Waca.

I'm trying to think now: is there any hope left? There wasn't after Adelaide but I've seen some strange sights since then – not least Angus Fraser chasing a ball to a boundary like a man with very painful veruccas on both feet; maybe time to stick to the writing now, eh, Gus? – and wherever there is life, even if it's hanging above a precipice by the fingers of one hand and an Australian's standing above it with some nail scissors, there has to be hope.

Theoretically, of course, we can still retain the Ashes; two wins out of the remaining three will do it. But surely it is not going to happen. The last day at Adelaide had sucked the life out of the England team, as surely as if they had happened upon a vampire on Halloween, and had changed everything. England now know, and what's more know that Australia know, that however well things are going for them, however far ahead they get, however many wickets they take in a session, it can all be turned round in the blinking of an eye. Or a flick of Shane Warne's wrist.

I take my seat in the Prindiville Stand after climbing five exhausting flights of steps and am pretty pleased with my position. I look around for signs of members of the tour group from whom I've acquired my ticket and spot Mike Gatting, their star guide, mingling, no doubt discussing the previous day's wine excursion which I know to be another part of this particular group's tour experience. I feel quite privileged to be in such company, and settle down to enjoy the day – that is, until Flintoff loses the toss. We really needed him to win it, but the "specially-minted" coin that is being used in this series teeters around on its edge when it lands, rolls across the pitch and comes down tails when he's called heads – or the other way around. Freddie comments on this to Mark Nicholas when he realises that his side are going to face another hard day in the field. Still, there is a cheer when he reveals that

Monty Panesar will finally get his chance: after the press coverage of the intervening days I have a feeling that he and Duncan Fletcher would have been sought out by a lynch mob had that not been the case. Sajid Mahmood is also brought in, to replace his Lancashire team-mate James Anderson, for his extra pace on the Waca wicket. This seems like another misjudgement because for days we've been hearing that the pitch, formerly probably the fastest and bounciest in the world – this, remember, is where Curtley Ambrose took seven wickets for one run on the first day of a Test Australia ended up losing by an innings in three days in 1993 – has lost some of its fire in recent years. Certainly, there are greater tinges of green on it than you'd expect, although I'm only assured of this by the television commentary because the shimmering of the sun runs all the colours together on the distant replay screen and makes it impossible to tell.

"We are the England, the mighty, mighty England," sing the Barmy Army, one ball into the match, perhaps buoyed by a nice swinging delivery from Matthew Hoggard that Justin Langer has to work hard to get a bat on. But soon it seems like business as usual, as the ball starts to disappear to all parts. Langer seems especially de-mob happy; perhaps he's thinking of joining Damien Martyn – whose premature retirement we learnt about when a fellow England fan got a text message just west of Cook on the Indian Pacific – on a Hawaiian beach. Langer slices some ugly shots over the slips and gully – don't these sort of things usually find Australian hands when we try them? – and with Flintoff still grimly refusing to post a third man, we find the fours are flowing.

But then, in the eleventh over, and out of nowhere with the fifty partnership in sight, we are suddenly given something to cheer about. Hoggard's in-ducker holds its line and Hayden, playing towards mid-wicket, nicks it. A roar of approval rises from the huge contingent of English fans, but nothing like the one that goes up on the third ball of the thirteenth over. Harmison, introduced first-change, bowls a straight full-length ball which Ricky Ponting, as he is liable to do early in his innings, looks to work to leg. He misses and the ball thuds into the pad. He looks a fair way down but I appeal along with the rest of my compatriots despite my more objective side instinctively saying it's not out. But it is. Aleem Dar lifts his left index finger high above his head. Sajid Mahmood is the first to leap on to Harmison's back and the Durham bowler is acting like a wild man. Ever since the wide in Brisbane he has worn an expression ranging from mild terror to hangdog whenever he's been handed the ball, but now he's up and letting rip, fielders arriving from all points to share in a rare moment of delight.

Perhaps this is where the series will turn; we'll look back on the moment after the celebrations have died down in Sydney, the Australians humbled by the greatest comeback in Ashes history, and we'll say *that's* when it started. When Ponting, a little over-confident in the circumstances maybe, thinking he could wander across his stumps against an inaccurate Harmison, got his angles wrong. Harmison was unstoppable after that, we'll agree, and the strongest batting line-up in world cricket couldn't stay with him.

Will we buggery!

But it certainly looks that way in the aftermath of Ponting's departure. Harmison is hitting the bat hard, Michael Hussey taking one hand off it as he drops a rising ball, all 90mph of rapidly revolving red blur, down at his feet. Then the paceman slants one across Langer and induces the edge. We're off our seats as Flintoff dives low to his right at second slip and the ball comes loose, rebounding off Andrew Strauss. It looks like it's just fallen short but the replay will tell us. It does, and painfully, distressingly, Flintoff has got there - whack into his palm, but it doesn't stick. It would have been a great catch, we console ourselves. Harmison is clapping his captain's effort, but will that dent the confidence he has suddenly regained? I worry about the fragility of his mental state.

England are enjoying a period of ascendancy, and have allowed just 12 runs in seven tight overs when Monty Panesar is brought into the attack for the first time, a double change as Mahmood also slips on at the far end. The left-arm spinner's first over is tidy, Hussey playing him watchfully, and at the end of it, there is prolonged applause and cheering, even from the Australian spectators, pleased to have got a first proper look at the mythical turbaned one. Then, at the start of the second over, they see why he has become a national icon. He propels a regulation ball, over the wicket to Langer. The Australian props forward and plays a regulation defensive shot. Everything looks as exactly as it should do in the last over before lunch. Except... except for the incongruous fact that there's a clink, a bit like two champagne glasses brought together at a social gathering, and, well, hey, let's get the bubbly out because the sound is not from the corporate boxes but from the breaking of Langer's off stump. The Western Australian can't believe it but he's played inside a perfectly straight ball, perhaps anticipating some spin, perhaps playing with his bat a little behind his pad for fear of popping up a catch to the two men stationed in front of him at silly mid-off and silly mid-on.

Whatever, Monty's off on his celebratory gallop, applauding himself in his excitement and trying to find team-mates' hands to high-five with. We must be the worst team at high-fives; he fails to connect properly with anyone, clashing wrists with Paul Collingwood , accidentally head-butting two fielders to the ground and leaping into embraces first with Andrew Flintoff and Kevin Pietersen. High fives? Leave them to the Americans, I say.

But what a comeback: at 47 for no wicket after ten overs, we had been settling back to endure another morning of Australian domination, yet somehow, as at Adelaide, we've lifted ourselves back into contention.

The balance of power shifts again in the overs after lunch, however, if slowly. Michael Clarke, fresh from a hundred in

Adelaide, is finding the middle of the bat, not always for runs, but he appears supremely comfortable at the crease. With Hussey, he rotates the singles well and eventually a boundary or two comes. They have added just over 50 when England get a stroke of luck. And it's Harmison who takes advantage of it. Maybe he's just a little bit too quick on this occasion and Clarke's decision to pull is the wrong one. He is hardly halfway through the shot when the ball, on a decent length, meets the bat and is fired back at some pace at about waist height. It all seems very fast, but it could be that Clarke's connection has come a bit off the shoulder of the bat and Harmison, following through, plucks the ball out of the air to the left of his hip.

Another counter-attack follows, Hussey dismissing Flintoff through the covers, the face of his bat so full you could swear he's had it surgically enhanced. Andrew Symonds, Martyn's replacement, has much to prove at this level – his ten matches have brought him only 286 runs at an average of 19 – but he doesn't want to go too much into his shell, partly because it's not in the nature of a man who hunts feral pigs in his downtime, and partly because the Australian way is not to let a threat, in this case the new one of Monty Panesar, settle.

Consequently, after scratching around for a bit, Symonds takes the attack to Panesar. And what an attack it is. Six, dot, six, four are the bare statistics but they tell only half the story. The two sixes are two of the straightest, flattest sixes you will ever see. In fact, in my years of watching cricket, I think I've only ever seen two sixes hit as hard or as flat, and strangely both were against Surrey at Guildford – one by Richard Hadlee and one by Rob Bailey, the former Northamptonshire batsman and now an umpire. And that makes me think of one of the other great things about this sport: neither of those shots were played in matches with a significance beyond that particular contest – mid-table Sunday League matches both if I remember rightly and I couldn't tell you the scores – yet they remain in the memory for their sheer singularity years after the event. Both times then, I was side-on to the action, but each time now the ball is careering down towards me in the Prindiville Stand and although landing in the bottom tier, the straight boundaries at the Waca are the shortest and I feel almost under physical threat. The crack as bat connects with ball is so bone-shuddering that it feels as if, somewhere in the reaction, gunpowder is involved.

The man is a brute, but a brute in clown's clothing, which makes him even more dangerous. The expansive dreadlocks erupt up and out from the top of his head like some sort of hirsute lava and the application of excessive white sun block around his lips and chin give him the look of someone who does not expect to be taken too seriously, but don't be fooled. He's no big-top jester, more a high-wire act who's prepared to do without a safety net. Despite the precariously-balanced state of the game, and some concerns on what it might do to Monty's confidence, I find I'm positively enjoying watching an Australian wreak havoc with the bat for the first time in the series.

And a word of praise for Flintoff's captaincy here. It would have been easy for the skipper to protect his raw spinner, take him out of the firing line for a spell, but he knows that the head on Panesar's 24-year-old shoulders is much more advanced than most of his age. Flintoff's confidence in his man reaps its reward almost immediately. Panesar, whether by accident or design – possibly he's hoping to forestall Symonds' progress down the pitch and the bludgeoning that has accompanied it – drops one wide and short, it draws the Queenslander into the cut stroke, but he gets a thin top edge through to the wicketkeeper. It's a cheap wicket and leaves me a little disappointed but not so disappointed that I can't enjoy Adam Gilchrist's dismissal, a fine diving catch by Bell at short leg which follows in Monty's next over. Warne goes after tea, cutting at one too close to him and Michael Slater is among the commentators, on radio and TV, coming up with the predictable: "Where was this guy in the first two Test matches?" he rants – or words to that effect. "It's ridiculous to think he's had to wait this long." There's the welcome sight of Warnie shaking his head in despair as he walks off – he hasn't hung about for his 25 – although he's obviously annoyed with himself rather than the decision because he seemed to set off without waiting for the finger.

Brett Lee it is who provides Panesar with his fifth victim, it's a pad-first-bat-afterwards decision, but the fast bowler has got a decent stride in as well and it is a surprise to me to see Aleem Dar's finger go up. It's no less a surprise to the Channel 9 commentary team but, on reflection, it's not so different to Warne's dismissal of Ian Bell in the second innings at the Gabba. It's 234 for eight, beyond our wildest dreams 50 minutes into the morning session and it emerges that Panesar's haul is the first five-wicket one by an English spinner in a Test at the Waca, although the fact that the ground didn't stage its first Test until 1970 – 80 years after it was built – puts the achievement into a more reliable context.

Harmison cleans up, demolishing Stuart Clark's leg stump and then having McGrath caught at silly mid-off from a bouncer that the No 11 actually plays very well, but can't stop Rudi Koertzen giving despite the ball rebounding off his shoulder rather than his bat. It's a crowd catch, in all honesty, and not even the most patriotic Aussie is going to argue over his demise. But as his tall figure stands there, perceptibly shaking his head, although perhaps not so perceptibly that the match referee will notice, it strikes me that I'd swap his dismissal for the equally rotten one Andrew Strauss got at Adelaide.

So just how well has Monty bowled? My opinion is not that well; a couple of the Aussies have got themselves out and he'll bowl better for little reward. But maybe it's his sheer aura and charisma that have done the trick. The following morning's papers were keen to play up his impact, headlines ranging from the slightly unimaginative "MONTY SPINS LIFE INTO ENGLAND" to the alliterative "PANESAR THE PANACEA" and Steve Waugh's judgment that "even his appeals appeal", but Michael Hussey, who remained undefeated on 74, pointed to his patience and control as the critical factors. "There wasn't a lot of spin out there, " Hussey said, "so he bowled with good discipline, which is a pretty tough art, and got the rewards. He's got a good knowledge of his game and understands discipline is a big part for a spinner."

There's even praise for Harmison, who at least temporarily loses his tag of "farce" bowler, but although Andrew Strauss and Alastair Cook have got us off to our customary bullish start, boundaries flowing in our rapid advance to 30, the game is back in the balance after the late losses of Cook and Ian Bell. The first session of the second day is going to be crucial, but I've got a feeling we've said that too many times already.

Offensive at times they may be, if moderately amusing in their observation that all Australians "live in a convict colony" but the Barmy Army are also, at worst, gender neutral. I've yet to come across an Army song that disparages the women folk of the Sunburned Country; in fact, I think we can safely say that the female Australian has rather been taken to the collective bosom of the English male. We make no secret of our love for Kylie, we fully appreciate the acting and musical skills of the former *Neighbours* star Natalie Imbruglia, and some of the sadder among us have even been known to tape whole editions of *Aerobics Oz Style*, Sky Sports' mid-morning alternative to *Homes Under The Hammer*.

Imagine my shock, then, when I discovered the following ditty in the tour handbook of The Fanatics, the Australian answer to the

Barmies. Entitled *Ode to a British Girlfriend*, and designed to be sung to the tune of *Living Doll* by Cliff Richard, it went like this:

"Got myself a mingin', borin', pasty, naggin', whingein' Pom/
Got to do your best to leave her just cos she's a whingein' Pom/
She's got a lazy eye and big fat thighs from all those chips and pies/
She's not the only borin', pasty, naggin' whingein' Pom."

I guess it was a mistake to show this to Sue, now back in tandem, over a honey nut cornflakes and toast breakfast at our hostel on the second morning, especially when I followed up by informing her that our tickets were for a temporary stand housing The Fanatics. Maybe our mainly Asian fellow guests, feasting on giant, intricate, noodle concoctions that looked as if they could sustain the workforce of a small Far Eastern economy for many months, would provide sterner opposition for them. Brits Alone, we would be hopelessly outnumbered.

I thought we should go undercover.

"A hint of mascara should sort out the lazy eye," I advised her, "but I'm not sure about the thighs. The Shroud of Turin, perhaps? A hot air balloon?" And received a faceful of marmalade-laden invective for my trouble.

In truth I feared close proximity to The Fanatics. It was one thing to be stuck among a throng of Barmies, singing, drinking and flag-waving as if there was no tomorrow – although, unfortunately, in this series, there always was – but at least they were your own. Caught up with The Fanatics, we could expect rampant piss-taking at best and outright hostility at worst.

Thankfully, because of The Fanatics' inability to sell all their tickets (call themselves Fanatics? More like the Moderately Interested), we found ourselves high in the stand with plenty of British company and within reach of only those Fanatics that could climb what seemed like the hundreds of stairs to the top of a rickety construction that felt as if it was held together by the last scaffolding in Australia and a bloke underneath with some masking tape.

Positioned behind the East Grassed Area, it was so far from the action that, by early evening, we could turn round and pick a winner in the trotting race meeting on the adjacent Gloucester Park course between balls. Its placement was such that we were also above and behind the ground's only scoreboard and the replay screen on the far side was so distant that it had the appearance of an ever-changing postage stamp. Only if one of us turned on his pocket radio – and the batteries on mine had worn mercifully low – would we know what was unfolding before us. Instead, as English batsmen came and went with alarming rapidity, we could go deep into denial.

It was even better for one spectator sitting behind me who had mislaid a contact lens. "I can't see a f***ing thing," he moaned as Geraint Jones plastered a wide half-volley into the grateful hands of gully ten minutes before lunch, "I'm watching through one eye." It was better than two, which, had they been in working order would have seen Paul Collingwood go for the addition of three runs – just the start we didn't need – Strauss flay an over-confident drive at Clark – Rudi Koertzen's decision to give him out is roundly jeered when the Barmy Army see the replay – and Flintoff, most unforgivably, give a slip chance to Warne off Symonds. Innocuous medium pace it may have looked, but innocuous medium pace it did not prove. Oh no, not to our batsmen. And when Jones went to the same bowler, 51 for two overnight had become 122 for six by the interval. Thoughts of a lead of 100 or more were being hurriedly recalculated. Now, we would just be happy with parity.

Pietersen might get us that. For at least he is still there. But, with a tail starting with Sajid Mahmood at No 8, he is going to have to employ some inventive manipulation of the strike. When he does this, and Ponting responds by sticking all his fielders on the fence, it upsets the one Australian in our midst, one who has survived the assault on Everest and slipped in to the top left-hand corner of the stand and planted his flag, obviously while our sentries were off duty.

Pietersen is content to stick his big left foot down the pitch and smash the ball into the outfield without the slightest intention of taking a single. This incenses the Australian who, predictably enough, starts up with his solo chant of "Boring, boring England". This of course, incenses me, and after his third intervention I can no longer stay silent. "Are you completely thick?" I turn and say to him. "Do you know nothing about cricket?" This is far from the red rag to a bull that I expect it to be and he ignores me, cups his hands round his mouth and hollers: "Booooo…"

"What do you expect him to do?" I continue, "give you catching practice on the boundary. You're the ones being negative. Why doesn't Ponting try to get him out?"

Sue is giving me that "why do you have to get involved?" look.

"Just leave it," she says. "He's an idiot."

But I'm in no mood to stand down. "If he's an idiot he needs to know about it," I reply in a strong whisper. "You can't just let idiots be idiots or they just go on being idiots."

"But it's not your job to show them."

I suspect it is, but for the moment do as I'm commanded.

I hate these tactics and think it is the senior batsman's duty to bluff until the defending captain gets tired of it. Pietersen, however, seems to get caught in two minds and in between turning down singles, launches some spectacular and rather ungainly slogs, one a pull off the front foot with the bat perpendicular after taking two steps down the wicket to McGrath. The Australian bowler is rendered speechless. In normal circumstances he would exchange a few words with the batsman, but on this occasion he can't form a retort suitable for the situation, so he ignores Pietersen, and rather irritably instructs, by pointing, the umpire to give him his cap and sunglasses. A few minutes later, he drags a Brett Lee ball horribly from a foot and a half outside off stump and it swirls into the air on the leg side. The negativity of Ponting's approach is highlighted as three fielders run from off the fence at square leg, mid-wicket and long-on and end only able to stare helplessly at each other as the ball lands short of them all.

People have criticised Pietersen for being a predominantly bottom-handed player and he as good as corroborates this analysis when he clears mid-wicket with a stroke off Warne. The follow-through is huge but curiously his left hand has come completely off the bat handle. The last time I saw a shot like that was in a match between Effingham under 14s and their Epsom counterparts, of which I was one. But the bloke had a good excuse: he didn't have a left arm.

An inside-out lofted drive, another Pietersen trademark, is spilled by McGrath running around at long-off just in front of the sight screen, which gives me an opportunity to mock the lone Australian behind me, and when Warne tosses one up wider of off stump, the batsman finds the middle for once and carts it murderously over extra cover for six. The English in the The Fanatics' Stand are all on their feet, making it shake disquietingly and when I turn round the Australian is up and cheering too. I can't work them out, these Aussies.

Eventually, though, the fun has to end and having twice smashed Brett Lee unsuccessfully into the covers, he puts his whole body and soul into the next one. The height is all right, but the length is lacking and Andrew Symonds comes running off the boundary at long-off to pouch the catch. He ends up falling forward on to his knees but it's safely in his enormous hands, a relatively simple move for a trapeze artist.

At 175 for nine, we are still 69 adrift of the Australians, but there is life in the last-wicket pair of Steve Harmison and Monty Panesar, in his first Ashes innings. Harmison we know has a few good swings in him, but Monty's batting has been most unfairly maligned. I've been arguing for his merits in this skill of the game against an almost unanimous nationwide opinion that he is completely useless with a piece of wood in his hand. This reputation had gone before him. Even in Brisbane, where he didn't get a game, there were Australians wearing T-shirts proclaiming: "Monty Panesar: can't bat, can't field, bowls left-arm spin – are you Phil Tufnell in disguise?"

Anyone who saw Phil Tufnell's attempts to keep out Shane Warne at the Gabba in 1994 – I still have pictures of him, sat on his backside, legs splayed, bat on the ground, after being defeated by another big-turning leg break – and then compares it with Panesar's compact forward defensive, solid wafts to leg and a classy, there's no other word for it, drive down the wicket off Clark in a snappy innings of 16 here, will know that the two cannot be bracketed together.

He plays an important part in ensuring that England trail by only 29 on the first innings and when Harmison is the last man out, top edging Clark to Lee at mid-on, English hopes have been lifted again.

It's probably right that we should pause at this juncture, at the nominal halfway stage of the Test series, to consider the impact of Clark. It is not enough to call him a McGrath clone, although he would probably not mind the comparison. But he has little of the sullen, chuntering side of McGrath, which shows itself, sometimes quite unpleasantly, when things aren't going to plan (which, in itself, is rare). Clark, rather, is amiability itself in his manner and mien. He ambles up to the wicket as if about to deliver a loosener in an undaunting club net session and his delivery stride can barely be called that – he skims through the crease like a hover mower, just grazing the top of the grass, and lets go of the ball from a relaxed grip. The subtle movements from his loose fingers effect a destruction far beyond their apparent threat: he is a stealth bomber, a baby-faced assassin and, in Bill Lawry's words "the best seamer we've had since Terry Alderman".

He has 14 wickets in the series so far and it is he who comes to mind when I cast my thoughts back to an incident at the beginning of the series. Two nights before the start of the Brisbane Test we were wandering down Boundary Street on the lookout for a place to eat when we passed a small, independent bookshop, which was advertising a reading and question and answer session with the Australian cricket writer Gideon Haigh. It seemed too good an opportunity to miss: I might get some material for the blog and Sue could quench her thirst on the complimentary wine. It was a pleasant and interesting hour, spent in the courtyard at the back of the shop among an audience of about 50, and Haigh, who was promoting *Silent Revolutions: Writings on Cricket History*, was perhaps only a bit more modest and self-deprecating than an author who's written about twenty books in nine years should be.

But the highlight for me came with the last question of the session, when a local audience member put to Haigh a query that had always puzzled me. "You know the writer CLR James and that quote 'what do they know of cricket who only cricket know'," he said in what I presumed to be a grizzled Queensland accent. "Does anyone know what the fuck that means?"

Apart from being amused by the pithy presentation of the enquiry – a no-bullshit typically Australian one – I was keen to discover if it really was just one of those phrases that cricket people tended to use, and nod knowingly at each other, without completely understanding. I had never read CLR James's *Beyond a Boundary*, the tome from which the quote was drawn, despite it being an acknowledged cricket classic, so had never thought about it deeply and worked it out for myself.

If Haigh was shocked by the question, he didn't show it, and launched into a literate and plausible reply that cricketers today were too one-dimensional, appreciating little of the outside world.

If so, Clark was the exception to this rule. He was studying for a Masters degree in commerce and planned to study law with a long-term aim to work in finance in the future. Perhaps this was a strategy forged from injuries that had afflicted him after he had won his first Cricket Australia contract in 2001-2, forcing him to look outside the confined world of the game, or evidence of his ability to put the sport into a truer, and healthier, context.

Sue, having exhausted all the possibilities of protection from the fierce rays of the sun – lotion, sun hat, long trousers and a towel draped round her shoulders have failed to provide adequate screening – has opted for the air-conditioned deliverance of our hostel, but, as the Australian second-innings gets underway, I am queueing for an ice-cream, impatiently actually, because these could be crucial overs. If we can get some early wickets, we will have the momentum. So when a roar goes up almost immediately, I instantly forget about my desire for a large '99 and run back, accompanied by a mass of people who have been milling around seeking refreshment, or bladder relief in a repository that isn't as stifling as the one I've just left – an experience similar to that had by a bunch of Chinese asylum seekers crammed into the back of a container lorry.

Hoggard has, it becomes clear as we reach the top of the steps leading on to the grassed viewing area, removed Justin Langer with his first ball, a perfect inswinger that finds the gap between bat and pad and bowls him. However, by the time I've happily taken up residence back at the peak of the Fanatics' Stand, Ponting and Hayden have swung the game back in the Australians' favour. Ponting, after a rare first-innings failure, announces himself in time-honoured fashion, cutting Hoggard's third ball backward of square for a boundary and by the 15th over, the hosts are dealing only in four-balls: Hayden has struck eight in his 32 and Ponting six in his 30. Hayden works the last ball of the day from Harmison to fine leg for a four, taking him to 57, a score on which he joins his captain.

It is 119 for one and England are going to need some of Panesar's first-innings inspiration to work their way back into the game, although I sense it has slipped away from us already.

Oh bugger! I should have been there, but I wasn't. A bloke hits the fastest century in Ashes cricket, nearly breaks the record for the quickest in Test history and I'm not there to see it, even though I have a ticket – one that other Englishmen, and Aussies, might quite happily have sold their granny into slavery for. A cruel chain of events has combined to create this sad state of affairs.

We pasty-faced Brits are often described as turning beetroot with too much exposure to sunlight; this is not entirely accurate. After an ill-advised half hour of baring my rarely-revealed torso to the elements on a windy Scarborough Beach on the eve of this Test, I resemble more closely a richly-textured strawberry blancmange. Apart from rendering me almost sleepless at night, destined to restlessly relive Ian Bell's run-out at Adelaide as I toss and turn in an ever-more desperate hunt for a patch of flesh to balance myself upon that will not send me whimpering for some of Sue's cool moisturising milk, the agony meant that I would not be in good enough condition to take much more heat for a while.

With my third-day tickets giving us access only to seats at the top of the roofless Fanatics' stand, the Perth thermometer predicted to hit 42C and the Australian second innings promising to rise to similar extremes, we opted instead to check out the atmosphere at the giant screen that had been erected in the city's entertainment district in Northbridge.

And some giant screen it was, too, about 20 feet wide and 15 feet high: it could be seen from some way off on the approach. Unfortunately, as we got closer, screwing up our eyes to scrutinise the action, we realised there wasn't any: it had, it emerged, blown a fuse.

I nearly joined it.

Adjourning to a nearby café for a late breakfast, I was little more than a mouthful into my scrambled egg, when the screen burst back into life. Tony Greig's vocals boomed out from the amplifiers either side of it and a movie-sized Matthew Hoggard trundled in to bowl to Michael Hussey. This was good news: it meant a wicket had already gone down, and as the camera scanned back to reveal Matthew Hayden at the other end, joy filled my heart. Ponting had gone. When Hayden then cut Panesar into the grasping hands of Paul Collingwood at slip, so grasping that it took him two touches to bring it under control, it seemed as though England might yet pull something out of the fire.

We hurried over to the grass, where a few England fans had mustered, trying to find a comfortable position that wasn't blocking the view of anyone else and willed England to take another wicket: they might have done, had Geraint Jones not fumbled a stumping chance against Michael Clarke in the last over before lunch and had Michael Hussey, who continued to drive through the off side with that deft placement of his and pull with violent aplomb, been given out when he seemed to poke Panesar to Alastair Cook at silly mid-off.

It was enough to send more and more Poms crawling back from their sunbathing positions into the shade and shelter of the marquee that had been helpfully provided nearby, put their backpacks on the ground, rest their heads on top and fall asleep.

It was only the arrival of Adam Gilchrist after tea that provoked them back to life, and also awakened an interest among those out for a pre-dinner stroll in an area surrounded by bars and restaurants.

If England aren't out of it with Australia on 365 for five when he replaces Symonds, out for just two, they soon will be. He sets about the bowling with such gusto that Clarke's hundred seems lost in the cyclone of strokes. And in the time that Clarke goes from 100 to 106, the Australian wicketkeeper goes from 11 to 73, although it is the category-five carnage of over number 107 that really makes the difference. Monty Panesar does not realise, when his first ball is met by perfect defence, that he's about to be at the centre of a serious storm. It's as if Hurricane Gilly is sitting just offshore, uncertain which direction to take. Second ball, it makes landfall, taking two through extra cover to record a fastest Test fifty, and third ball, it gives an illustration of its strength with a blast down the ground, six rows back. Monty hasn't heeded the warnings and tosses the next one up, but bat meets ball with the sound of a thunderclap and now the spinner knows the eye of Gilly is upon him. The fifth ball is just a four, over mid-wicket, two bounces, an apparent lull, but the full fury returns for the last, deposited just to the leg of straight, the ball gaining a height almost equal to its length.

He has 73 off 44 balls and Mark Taylor, by now almost blasting out of the speakers, reminds us that the fastest hundred in Test cricket, by Viv Richards, is within his grasp. He needs 27 in 11 balls and I can't help wanting him to do it, even amid my total despondency with England.

This time Flintoff doesn't show the same confidence in Panesar that he displayed when Andrew Symonds put him to the sword in the first innings, and replaces him with Hoggard, but bowlers, slow and faster, are all coming alike to Gilchrist now. It is as if the

England attack have, in their own individual ways, personally affronted his family. Hoggard, from round the wicket, finds his way on to the meat of the bat and disappears for a six wide of long-on that might even be the biggest yet.

The countdown is on: he needs 11 off seven, seven off six, four off two, and now, with that four needed off two, and Harmison running in to deliver, the picture, which has been breaking up at regular intervals throughout the afternoon, freezes. There's a collective sigh and only one thing for it – a handful of us dash across the road to a pub which is also showing the cricket. By the time we get there, alas, the record has come and gone; Gilchrist has just missed out, but he's reached his hundred anyway from 57 balls. Surely the declaration will follow and it does.

I thought I should head back to the hostel to see how Sue, who had left me halfway through the afternoon, was getting on. With the ten minutes between innings I figured I could get to another pub en route in time to see the start of England's reply, even though a target of 556 runs is out of reach. How wrong I was. As I slipped in through the door of this more up-market bar, I was greeted by the sight of Andrew Strauss walking disconsolately back to the pavilion. He had lasted just four balls.

They had come to bury England, but left having to praise them – well, a little anyway. At 19 for one overnight the Australian supporters were sensing the blood of their old foe, the return of the Ashes to their possession within only 15 months of losing them – and after only 14 days of this series. (I knew it had been a mistake to free the urn from under lock and key in the Lord's museum and send it on a tour of Australian cities: give them a sniff of the prize, display it in venues in their own backyard, and they'll move in for the kill.)

However, thanks to Alastair Cook, Ian Bell, and, later, Kevin Pietersen, many a Perth employee was left wondering how to excuse themselves from their daily duties on a Monday morning and hotfoot it down to the Waca for the last rites.

Cook's effort – he made 116 from 290 balls in five and a half hours – was a monumental one; not pretty particularly – he only smote nine fours – but one to rank with that of Mike Atherton in Johannesburg in 1995, even if it was unlikely to bring about such a desirable outcome for English supporters. To play with such watchfulness and concentration for close to three sessions after a day in the field in searing temperatures, was not an achievement to be underestimated. And he showed, in his duel with Shane Warne, that he had learnt from earlier battles in this series – a trait that any emerging player needs to display if he is to become regarded as one of the best. Picked up by the leg spinner in Brisbane when he played around the front of his pad, he tried to operate mainly on the back foot, giving himself a moment extra to deal with the Victorian's variations, and using the punch through the vacant covers from that position to keep his score ticking over.

Of course, he was helped in the execution of his defiance by the determined spirit and occasionally sumptuous strokeplay of Ian Bell. Bell is a force to be reckoned with when he allies his natural fluency with single-minded resistance, and he spent long enough at the crease to gain sufficient confidence to twice lift Warne over the ropes. What a shame that after sharing a second-wicket partnership of 170 in 56 overs with Cook, he should fall, driving uppishly enough for Langer to cling on to a sharp chance at short extra-cover. Even when Collingwood went cheaply, a victim of the irrepressible Clark, there was a feeling that it had been England's day.

Tickets had not been sold for the final day, but as the shadows lengthened, announcements were being made that they could be obtained from the windows outside Gate 6, a walk almost halfway around the ground for me. I had already decided that if five wickets or more were down by the close, I would not return for the final day to watch Australia hoover up the tail and parade the Ashes to great fanfare. It would be just too much, too disappointing, too much of an association with unbridled failure. But Cook and Bell had done what they shouldn't have been allowed to – they had planted fresh seeds of hope. I phoned Sue, who was again struggling with the heat, and told her that we were only three wickets down and tickets were going on sale at $30 a time. Should I get her one? Yes, she finally decided after much prevarication. So I left my position high above The Fanatics and began the walk round the Concourse to the box office.

I had reckoned without Glenn McGrath. How much misery had that man caused me over the years? Could each wicket be measured, like the furtive puffing on a single cigarette, in a reduction of five minutes in lifespan? I suspected so, but he had proved surprisingly ineffective in this innings, sending 16 overs down at the expense of 38 runs and no reward in the wickets column. He had last seen action at the end of the 44th over but was brought back to bowl the 90th. I had made it as far as third man when he struck with the second ball of the 94th. Cook, a weary Cook, hung out a fatigued bat at a ball angled across him, feathered it, and Gilchrist did the rest. The standing ovation hardly touched the young batsman's dismay. There was only one response: Matthew Hoggard, nightwatchman. I watched one ball on tenterhooks before moving into line right behind the wicket. I saw it all as if it was slow motion: the perfect yorker, swinging just a little away from the batsman, a death rattle that went straight to my adrenal glands. I was in a quandary then. Did I want the tickets or not. At the start of the over it had been a simple equation but by the end, after I had moved not much more than

50 yards, my thinking was muddled. I watched transfixed from the same position, while Pietersen and Flintoff, the latter painfully unsure in McGrath's corridor of uncertainty, survived until the close.

What do I do now? I thought. Sod it, I'd buy the bloody tickets!

We walked to the Waca the next morning like people going to their own funeral. Pietersen and Flintoff are together and, realistically, our last hopes. But I'm fed up with thinking about that word: hopes. Too often they have been raised, only to be dashed again and if I had a dollar for each time I've started a sentence with the word 'if' – "if KP and Freddie can just stay together for the first hour" etc etc – I'd have been able to book us in for a few nights at the Sheraton.

We take our rather resigned places in Block 7 of the perimeter seating in front of the Prindiville Stand, a perfect view from behind long-on. We need only another 292 for victory, Australia need five wickets to take back the Ashes. Clark is on for the first over and it's a maiden. No worries. But the second over is a different matter. Flintoff is so out of form it's almost implausible, his feet anchored to their places either side of the batting crease, and although McGrath beats him twice with venomous deviation, you don't get the sense that he needs to do much more than put it on a line outside off stump and the England captain will feed the wicketkeeper or slips. He is looking so out of his depth it's incomprehensible. Hard to believe that not more than a year ago, Flintoff and Pietersen would have been most people's idea of a fantasy partnership. Yet they have never really hit it off when batting together, almost as if neither is quite sure who should play the leading role. Maybe it would help if one of them was smaller. At 6ft 4in each and built like a pair of concrete dunnies, these are not men interested in quick singles and dabs behind square. They are constructed for big shots.

Pietersen has already realised this and punched Clark for four behind point and before it is too late Flintoff seems to register that this is more the way he should be playing. His technique is so shot, after all, that to hang around embarrassing himself further strikes him as not the best option. Suddenly, with the removal of McGrath and his replacement by Brett Lee, the Lancastrian bursts into life. First, he smacks him straight back over his head for four, then he aims over extra cover with enough strength, if not timing, to get back for two. Two balls later comes the shot of the morning; Lee pitches it fullish, but six inches outside the off stump and Freddie just picks it up and pummels it over mid-wicket, right out of the middle of the bat. "Four more to the Engerland," chorus the Barmy Army before a shot off the back foot brings him three more. By the time he's banged Clark through the covers for three successive boundaries in the next over, he has collected 25 runs from his previous nine balls. Thoughts of what Adam Gilchrist can do, Freddie can do better enter my mind. The 300 is up, the Barmy Army is up even more than usual, and I'm up too, enjoying it while I can do.

It's a race to see who'll get to his fifty first. Pietersen had a 35-run lead at the start of play, but he's been caught up in the forties. However, he makes it by moving his feet deliciously and driving Warne through mid-wicket, while Flintoff is temporarily subdued by the return of McGrat h. But a risky late cut and an inside edge bring Freddie his own half-century. "He wants to double that score if not treble it," says Mark Taylor, teetering on the brink of the bleeding obvious in the Channel 9 box.

But he can't even add to it. Warne is employing the in-out field that has served him so well as a tactic in this series. There are close fielders and deep fielders, but few infielders – just a backward point and mid-wicket – so that timidity is as likely to be punished as any over-adventurousness. The leg spinner tosses one up with a bit of drift into the right-hander, it pitches and Flintoff is bowled. It has turned a little admittedly but the batsman hasn't helped himself by aiming a bit of a bottom-handed boosh at it and playing all over it.

That's it. I know it. And the luckless Geraint Jones confirms it. On the third day, after missing the chance to stump Michael Clarke, he was so desperate to justify his position in the side, do something to contribute, that he chased manically down towards long leg when Hussey skied an attempted hook off Harmison, even though Hoggard, coming towards it from the fence and Kevin Pietersen, running sideways from square leg, were favourites to take it. In the end, the outfielders demurred to the desperation of the man with the gloves and watched in horror as he dived headlong, his hands outstretched, and failed even to make contact with the plummeting ball. Now, coming out on a pair, and facing a fourth duck in succession in all cricket, it is hard to believe that his anguish can intensify. But Murphy's Law is in operation and when he gets down low to sweep Warne, he is so distracted by the spinner's exaggerated lbw appeal that he fails to notice that he has dragged his back foot out of his crease. Ponting, at silly mid-off, has though and collects the loose ball, dives forward and throws down the stumps. Warnie's confused but after a referral to the third umpire and a replay on the big screen everyone can see what's happened and Jones is off, on his way to the pavilion, and out of Test cricket, probably for good.

The lbw appeals are coming thick and fast now: Sajid Mahmood is hit full on the foot by Stuart Clark's inswinging yorker and it's Goodnight Charlie, as Tony Greig would say, while Steve Harmison lasts one ball, done by Warne, despite the ball apparently pitching outside leg stump. The Barmy Army are mocking Warne's outlandish appealing but he waves them away dismissively as he takes up position at first slip for the next over. They probably don't even notice but I do and patriotism takes possession of me. "Oh, that's all right Warnie," I shout. "Dismiss England now, but you'll be happy to take Hampshire's cash when the summer comes. You like England then."

Three Australians turn round to stare at me and I feel momentarily exposed. "It's not England he likes, mate," one of them says. "It's your nurses."

I'm lost for words and have nowhere to direct my fury. I suggest to Sue we leave – and, distressed to see me making an exhibition of myself again, she's all for that. But Monty Panesar survives the last three balls to lunch and some strange unknowable force, the last drop of hope in my blood, compels me to stay. What for? To yell obscenities at England's failures? To watch Australian triumphalism when the last wicket falls, as it must? Or to just be sure? So we sit through the lunch break, hardly talking, and wait for the players' return.

Warne takes up the attack and Pietersen laps his first ball down to fine leg for a single, bringing Panesar down to face him. Monty has had some success with a kind of lap sweep in the first innings and he decides this is the way to go. Warne bowls, Panesar sweeps expansively and the ball turns and clunks into his stumps. It's over.

The Ashes have gone.

England tour of Australia

Western Australia v England XI

Played at W.A.C.A. Ground, Perth, on 9,10 December 2006 (2-day match)
Result Match drawn

Western Australia 1st innings		R	M	B	SR
CJL Rogers	c ♱Read b Anderson	66	154	117	56.41
DC Bandy	c ♱Read b Anderson	5	33	25	20.00
SE Marsh	c ♱Read b Mahmood	59	141	120	49.16
✱ MJ North	c Joyce b Mahmood	18	40	29	62.06
AC Voges	lbw b Harmison	31	76	72	43.05
L Pomersbach	not out	101	179	139	72.66
♱L Ronchi	c Strauss b Panesar	3	8	8	37.50
AK Heal	run out (Panesar)	28	46	42	66.66
BR Dorey	c & b Anderson	2	22	11	18.18
TP Macdonald	not out	4	38	26	15.38
Extras	(lb 1, nb 4)	5			
Total	**(8 wickets dec; 97.3 overs)**	322 (3.30 runs per over)			

Did not bat SJ Magoffin, BM Edmondson
Fall of wickets 1-17 (Bandy, 8.4 ov), 2-119 (Rogers, 40.4 ov), 3-140 (Marsh, 46.1 ov), 4-155 (North, 50.1 ov), 5-207 (Voges, 66.5 ov), 6-212 (Ronchi, 69.2 ov), 7-267 (Heal, 81.6 ov), 8-289 (Dorey, 87.4 ov)

Bowling	O	M	R	W	Econ	
JM Anderson	24.3	6	53	3	2.16	
SJ Harmison	21	1	99	1	4.71	
SI Mahmood	19	2	67	2	3.52	(4nb)
MS Panesar	25	6	69	1	2.76	
AF Giles	8	0	33	0	4.12	

England XI 1st innings		R	M	B	SR
✱ AJ Strauss	b Heal	88	171	110	80.00
AN Cook	retired out	106	215	171	61.98
GO Jones	c North b Heal	0	1	1	0.00
EC Joyce	c Marsh b Macdonald	73	109	97	75.25
♱CMW Read	not out	59	129	107	55.14
AF Giles	c Rogers b Edmondson	4	22	15	26.66
SI Mahmood	not out	20	33	30	66.66
Extras	(b 2, lb 1, nb 3)	6			
Total	**(5 wickets; 88 overs)**	356 (4.04 runs per over)			

Did not bat MP Vaughan, MS Panesar, LE Plunkett, JM Anderson, SJ Harmison
Fall of wickets 1-183 (Strauss, 41.2 ov), 2-183 (Jones, 41.3 ov), 3-219 (Cook, 52.6 ov), 4-299 (Joyce, 74.3 ov), 5-320 (Giles, 80.3 ov)

Bowling	O	M	R	W	Econ	
BR Dorey	13	1	57	0	4.38	
SJ Magoffin	14	3	40	0	2.85	
BM Edmondson	15	1	72	1	4.80	(1nb)
TP Macdonald	10	2	57	1	5.70	(2nb)
AK Heal	20	0	61	2	3.05	
MJ North	6	0	20	0	3.33	
DC Bandy	4	0	23	0	5.75	
AC Voges	6	0	23	0	3.83	

Players per side 12 (11 batting, 11 fielding)

The Ashes - 3rd Test
Australia v England
Played at W.A.C.A. Ground, Perth, on 14,15,16,17,18 December 2006 (5-day match)
Result Australia won by 206 runs

Australia 1st innings		R	M	B	SR
JL Langer	b Panesar	37	116	68	54.41
ML Hayden	c ✝Jones b Hoggard	24	48	33	72.72
✱RT Ponting	lbw b Harmison	2	19	11	18.18
MEK Hussey	not out	74	244	162	45.67
MJ Clarke	c & b Harmison	37	62	67	55.22
A Symonds	c ✝Jones b Panesar	26	39	30	86.66
✝AC Gilchrist	c Bell b Panesar	0	7	4	0.00
SK Warne	c ✝Jones b Panesar	25	32	22	113.63
B Lee	lbw b Panesar	10	32	25	40.00
SR Clark	b Harmison	3	13	5	60.00
GD McGrath	c Cook b Harmison	1	4	2	50.00
Extras	(w 1, nb 4)	5			
Total	**(all out; 71 overs; 313 mins)**	**244 (3.43 runs per over)**			

Fall of wickets 1-47 (Hayden, 10.3 ov), 2-54 (Ponting, 13.3 ov), 3-69 (Langer, 24.1 ov), 4-121 (Clarke, 40.4 ov), 5-172 (Symonds, 49.6 ov), 6-172 (Gilchrist, 51.4 ov), 7-214 (Warne, 59.1 ov), 8-234 (Lee, 67.6 ov), 9-242 (Clark, 70.3 ov), 10-244 (McGrath, 70.6 ov)

Bowling	O	M	R	W	Econ	
MJ Hoggard	12	2	40	1	3.33	
A Flintoff	9	2	36	0	4.00	(3nb)
SJ Harmison	19	4	48	4	2.52	(1w)
MS Panesar	24	4	92	5	3.83	
SI Mahmood	7	2	28	0	4.00	

England 1st innings		R	M	B	SR
AJ Strauss	c ✝Gilchrist b Clark	42	101	71	59.15
AN Cook	c Langer b McGrath	15	26	15	100.00
IR Bell	c ✝Gilchrist b Lee	0	5	2	0.00
PD Collingwood	c Hayden b McGrath	11	45	33	33.33
KP Pietersen	c Symonds b Lee	70	180	123	56.91
✱A Flintoff	c Warne b Symonds	13	46	31	41.93
✝GO Jones	c Langer b Symonds	0	11	4	0.00
SI Mahmood	c ✝Gilchrist b Clark	10	24	18	55.55
MJ Hoggard	c Hayden b Warne	4	47	39	10.25
SJ Harmison	c Lee b Clark	23	56	33	69.69
MS Panesar	not out	16	41	26	61.53
Extras	(w 1, nb 10)	11			
Total	**(all out; 64.1 overs; 301 mins)**	**215 (3.35 runs per over)**			

Fall of wickets 1-36 (Cook, 5.6 ov), 2-37 (Bell, 6.6 ov), 3-55 (Collingwood, 17.2 ov), 4-82 (Strauss, 24.2 ov), 5-107 (Flintoff, 33.4 ov), 6-114 (Jones, 35.6 ov), 7-128 (Mahmood, 40.6 ov), 8-155 (Hoggard, 51.6 ov), 9-175 (Pietersen, 54.5 ov), 10-215 (Harmison, 64.1 ov)

Bowling	O	M	R	W	Econ	
B Lee	18	1	69	2	3.83	(6nb)
GD McGrath	18	5	48	2	2.66	(4nb)
SR Clark	15.1	3	49	3	3.23	(1w)
SK Warne	9	0	41	1	4.55	
A Symonds	4	1	8	2	2.00	

Australia 2nd innings		R	M	B	SR
JL Langer	b Hoggard	0	1	1	0.00
ML Hayden	c Collingwood b Panesar	92	252	159	57.86
✳RT Ponting	c ✟ Jones b Harmison	75	194	128	58.59
MEK Hussey	c ✟ Jones b Panesar	103	224	156	66.02
MJ Clarke	not out	135	251	164	82.31
A Symonds	c Collingwood b Panesar	2	9	6	33.33
✟AC Gilchrist	not out	102	103	59	172.88
Extras	(lb 15, w 2, nb 1)	18			
Total	(5 wickets dec; 112 overs; 514 mins)	527 (4.70 runs per over)			

Did not bat SK Warne, B Lee, SR Clark, GD McGrath

Fall of wickets 1-0 (Langer, 0.1 ov), 2-144 (Ponting, 39.4 ov), 3-206 (Hayden, 58.4 ov), 4-357 (Hussey, 89.3 ov), 5-365 (Symonds, 91.6 ov)

Bowling	O	M	R	W	Econ	
MJ Hoggard	20	4	85	1	4.25	
A Flintoff	19	2	76	0	4.00	
SJ Harmison	24	3	116	1	4.83	
MS Panesar	34	3	145	3	4.26	
SI Mahmood	10	0	59	0	5.90	(1nb, 2w)
KP Pietersen	5	1	31	0	6.20	

England 2nd innings (target: 557 runs)		R	M	B	SR
AJ Strauss	lbw b Lee	0	2	4	0.00
AN Cook	c ✟ Gilchrist b McGrath	116	389	290	40.00
IR Bell	c Langer b Warne	87	234	163	53.37
PD Collingwood	c ✟Gilchrist b Clark	5	45	36	13.88
KP Pietersen	not out	60	243	150	40.00
MJ Hoggard	b McGrath	0	2	2	0.00
✳A Flintoff	b Warne	51	96	67	76.11
✟GO Jones	run out (Ponting)	0	11	7	0.00
SI Mahmood	lbw b Clark	4	14	10	40.00
SJ Harmison	lbw b Warne	0	3	1	0.00
MS Panesar	b Warne	1	8	9	11.11
Extras	(b 7, lb 8, w 6, nb 5)	26			
Total	(all out; 122.2 overs; 529 mins)	350 (2.86 runs per over)			

Fall of wickets 1-0 (Strauss, 0.4 ov), 2-170 (Bell, 56.6 ov), 3-185 (Collingwood, 69.3 ov), 4-261 (Cook, 93.2 ov), 5-261 (Hoggard, 93.4 ov), 6-336 (Flintoff, 114.5 ov), 7-336 (Jones, 116.6 ov), 8-345 (Mahmood, 119.6 ov), 9-346 (Harmison, 120.2 ov), 10-350 (Panesar, 122.2 ov)

Bowling	O	M	R	W	Econ	
B Lee	22	3	75	1	3.40	(1nb)
GD McGrath	27	9	61	2	2.25	(4nb, 1w)
SR Clark	25	7	56	2	2.24	
SK Warne	39.2	6	115	4	2.92	
A Symonds	9	1	28	0	3.11	(1w)

Toss Australia, who chose to bat first

As miserable as a bandicoot

MELBOURNE

CULTURALLY instructive though it was, Melbourne's Immigration Museum was not where a smattering of my fellow travelling England supporters would have chosen to be on what should have been the fourth morning of an Ashes Test. It was perhaps why they were roaming its spaces and peering at its exhibits with an air of slight detachment.

The team's pathetic capitulation at the MCG the evening before had left them with an unexpected couple of days of sightseeing ahead of them and while their attempts to make the most of it had the city's tourism heads rubbing their hands in glee, most of them looked as if they knew they should be somewhere else.

I was there because it was the first place I thought to look for unsuspecting story victims on my way down to Flinders Street from our hostel – and where else would a mourning England supporter go apart from a place where they could ruminate on a time when the ten-pound Pom was a welcome addition to the industries of the Sunburned Country. Now, a Pom with ten pounds in his pocket would be lucky to get change for a middy of light beer and a pea floater. I had just received an email from the head honchos on the sports desk at *The Times*. They wanted a fan's view on the dead men walking that constituted our excuse for a Test team. To be honest, I wasn't sure whether they wanted a fan's view – ie mine – or the fans' view; the apostrophe could be all-important. I couldn't check because I had picked up the email about 12 hours after it had been sent and it was now some ridiculous hour back at Wapping headquarters. Besides, my mobile phone was in a typically disobedient mood. It could provide me with a video of some salacious girls wanting a hot date that I'm sure I had never deliberately downloaded, or tell me the time in Kabul, but when it came to dialling numbers outside Australia, it flashed erratically, made a high-decibel bleep and switched itself off.

I had probably missed the space the article was intended for, anyway, but what the hell, I thought, I had nothing better to do. I decided against composing a first-person piece in favour of a workout for my oft-neglected interviewing skills, and ventured out to grill some unsuspecting cricket tourists.

Museums, though, are not the optimum place for conducting an interrogation and having failed to catch the attention of even one eye that welcomed the intrusion of a man in scruffy shorts and a delicately poised notebook, took myself elsewhere. My next stop was PJ O'Briens, one of the two Melbourne pubs charged with replenishing the unquenchable thirsts of Barmy Army foot soldiers. It took some finding, hidden as it was inside an emporium of indoor food outlets on Southbank, a trendy dining and entertainment complex a footbridge away on the other side of the Yarra river. And when I did find it, I was distinctly underwhelmed. I had expected to come across the detritus of a drowning of Barmy Army sorrows, bodies slumped at strange angles against footstools or an ancient piano in the corner, a pile of pasty British carcasses piled one on top of the other, glasses pressed to their lips, through which they were sucking their last drops of Guinness.

I asked a barman if the Barmies had been in. "They were last night," he said in a strident and not altogether approving tone.

"Singing the same songs. It's all right but it gets a bit boring after a while."

So where were they, I wondered? Perhaps they had brought forward their journeys to Sydney. I sidled up to tables, listening out for English accents, action which proved more profitable. I managed to get people to talk but no one seemed prepared to give me the killer quote of blame and disappointment that I could massage as representative of the thousands of Poms Down Under.

Richard, from Nottingham, sitting at the bar with an English friend, was particularly sanguine. "There should have been better preparation," he agreed with my leading question. "But I think, to be honest, that whatever we'd done, we'd have lost."

Mm. Not helpful.

Ryan, his mate, who was now a Melbourne resident, suggested simply that England had not often got the rub of the green. "I think it's fair to say that we didn't have much luck with the umpiring decisions, he said, "but you can't really say that or you'll be accused of being a whingeing Pom again."

So?

David and his wife Libby, from Blackburn, were even less willing to be shunted down the avenue I was directing them towards. "I expected England to lose," David said. "Now we've got a couple of days of leisure."

Thanks a lot.

I dismissed him as untypical. He was lucky enough to have witnessed England's last overseas Ashes victory, under the captaincy of Mike Gatting, in the 1986-7 series and had been following the team around the globe since. He was either used to it or he saw so much Test cricket that a couple of defeats here and there didn't bother him too much.

At this rate I was going to have to quote myself. But then I struck gold in the form of Harry from Cheltenham. "I'm disappointed in the coach for not standing up and at least saying sorry to the fans who've spent a lot of money following the team," he said. "He's always in the background, not taking the blame. There was a lack of preparation and England were not a team unit. They all had their wives and girlfriends out. They were all individuals going off doing their own thing. They're not together as a bunch of lads."

This was more like it, I thought, although I couldn't help wishing Harry could have been a bit more emotional about it. He spoke calmly and without rancour throughout, when what I wanted, what I really, really wanted, was a good deal of rancour. Still, substitute the odd "thundered" for "said" and stick an adjective such as "angry" in front of his name and nobody would know the difference. It didn't matter. I was too late to make the main paper and the piece went out, unread and unloved, on the blog.

We had flown into Melbourne in the early hours of December 20 and were deposited in the north of the city at an official youth hostel I soon recognised as one I had frequented years earlier. We were booked in there for three nights before moving a few blocks away to a serviced studio apartment, where we would spend Christmas.

Martin, the manager, reacted to our arrival as if he'd been lost in a jungle at the end of a war and we were the first humans with whom he'd had contact for several months, giving us the kind of meticulous attention that might be visited on royalty. He gave us a detailed rundown of the apartment, pointing out the sumptuous bed – well, sumptuous by the standards to which we'd become used – the cushions on the sofa in the small lounge area – cushions? Blimey – and an exhaustive display of how to handle most of the kitchen utensils. As much as we appreciated his thoroughness we were both in desperate need of a long lie-down, but Martin hadn't finished with us yet. An innocent question about eating out brought an extended summary of the local possibilities and a lengthy resumé of their menus. His greatest enthusiasm was reserved for the nearby Redback Hotel and in particular, their chicken parmigiana, for which he had such vivid praise that we felt he must have his own restaurant column in *The Age*, the city's main paper – either that, or he was on commission.

This regular worship of chicken parmigiana was beginning to sound like some sort of national obsession. From down-to-earth pubs to top establishments with five-star service – yep, we did splash out from time to time – it seemed to be a staple of most forms of eatery. What was it about this simple dish of crumbed chicken or veal topped with ham, napoli sauce and cheese and most readily served with chips and salad that captured the imagination Down Under? I determined to find out. This was to take me into very disturbing territory, most worryingly when I came upon the existence of the superparma.com website, dedicated to the search for the perfect parmigiana in the state of Victoria. It had a section devoted to "rating criteria" with marks for size (out of five), quality of sauce (out of four), quality of meat (out of three), the amount of cheese and sauce, quality of side order (chips or wedges) and, for the absolute connoisseur, the percentage of meat to crumbing. A total of 222 establishments were ranked, with the Australian Hotel, in Shepparton, the fifth-largest city in Victoria, bringing up the rear with a miserable nine out of 20. PJ O'Brien's, the Barmy Army haunt, was a disappointing 199th, while the Redback, Martin's favourite, came in at a respectable 55th.

But there was something worse than finishing last in the league table: not serving chicken parmigiana at all. A Hall of Shame named the guilty parties, all five of them.

Shane Warne looked like the kind of chap who'd enjoyed the occasional parmigiana in his time, although no pubs in his native Upper Ferntree Gully made it on to the superparma.com pages. Residents in his birthplace would probably have been more concerned with his cricketing legacy. Four days before Christmas, he gave a press conference announcing his retirement at the end of the Ashes. We first heard word of it on the taxi radio from the airport but I thought we could wait until the following morning to learn the whole story, and I'm sure Sue did, although she at least appreciated the significance of the news, something she probably would not have done two years earlier, perhaps even two months earlier.

I'm sure the coverage at home was huge, but in Melbourne it was the only tale in town. There was immediately talk of the great man being immortalised in a bronze statue outside the MCG or having a stand named after him, and politicians on both sides of the divide lined up to laud him; there were the inevitable references to The Don – he was the bowling Bradman, some suggested - but nestling beside these were those who seemed almost traumatised by his going. Allan Border said he was in a state of shock, Mike Gatting said he was surprised because he thought he had more petrol in the tank. And Merv Hughes's moustache turned up at each end. He was even described as "irreplaceable as The Beatles". Thank god there weren't four of him.

I would be laughed off the page if I was too cynical about one of cricket's greatest-ever bowlers, but so close to Christmas, this Messianic glorification left a bit of a sour taste – and I'm an agnostic. That said, of course, until Warne had come along, there were people who weren't sure if they believed in leg spin. They had heard rumours, and were told that Richie Benaud had been a master of the art – but it was only Warne's ball to Mike Gatting at Old Trafford in 1993 that convinced them. I was a disciple, however, because I was brought up on Intikhab Alam at the Oval, had bowled them myself as a schoolboy, even knowing the joy of bowling a 12-year-old round his legs from round the wicket before unimaginative coaches convinced me that off spin was the only way forward. Perhaps, as much as anyone, I should have been lining up to pay my respects. Perhaps, if he'd been English, I would have been.

Rather, it brought out the Ebenezer Scrooge in me, and far from willing him to take his 700th wicket on his home ground – he was only one away from doing so – I thought it would be fun if

England's batsmen, in a desperate and belated attempt to extract some cruel comfort from the lopsided series, did everything in their power to ensure that he didn't – even if that meant gifting their wickets to some minor asteroid in the Australian bowling solar system, such as Michael Hussey, running themselves out more clownishly than Ian Bell at Adelaide or being timed out.

OK, so I wasn't being entirely serious, but with Warne, and, it was shortly to emerge, McGrath planning to quit at the end of the fifth Test, the remaining matches risked being an anti-climactic Australian love-in. I wasn't sure I could endure the endless re-runs of their achievements on the replay screens, accompanied no doubt by the kind of crass music that had dominated the series and tested the ears of even the tone deaf: I could already hear The Young Divas warming up in the wings.

I suppose my grouch with Warne was his bowling persona: that despite his prodigious abilities he was still prepared to put pressure on umpires with appealing that was quite frankly ludicrous, shouts and cries and facial expressions of contempt that he used to get into officials' minds and make them think they were idiots when they didn't decide in his favour. If the umpires had upheld even half of his appeals, he would probably be approaching 3,000 wickets, not 700.

The best way to understand his impact, though, is to realise that throughout the series, I had felt stone cold terror in the pit of my stomach as soon as he had come on to bowl. I knew that, one or two players excepted, he was always going to be too good for us.

Sue had always wanted to spend Christmas abroad, but I don't think this was quite what she had in mind. Christmas Day was the coldest and wettest in Melbourne for 70 years. Typical. I think London was warmer. The Barmy Army were putting on an outdoor party but it hardly seemed the weather in which to enjoy it; besides, tickets were needed. Instead we attired ourselves against the wind and the rain, and with as much festive spirit as we could muster, skipped up the road to the youth hostel for a three-course Christmas dinner with wine at a very reasonable $19 a throw. Then we headed back to the apartment, stopping at a garage to stock up on some nibbles and cheap champagne. I fell asleep and Sue dyed her hair. We knew how to party.

The following day, the start of the Boxing Day Test, the damp was still creeping into the bones. We took the No 59 tram to Flinders Street and walked for 25 minutes to get to the MCG – a ground on an altogether bigger scale than any we had experienced before. It was like they had taken the Gabba, blown it up to three times the size and plonked it down in the centre of Melbourne. The last time I had been here, there were wooden benches up high; now it had the same uniformity as Brisbane. We found our seats, four rows back at ground level, checked that Dave, my colleague from work and the Australian-based friend he was staying with were not already there, and slipped back under cover from the spitting rain.

The start is delayed, but despite the conditions, Andrew Flintoff elects to bat and Ricky Ponting suggests he would have done the same had he won the toss. The only good news to greet English ears – and there are more English ears here than at any other of the venues – is that about the replacement of Geraint Jones by Chris Read behind the stumps. Again, at least a Test late but at least he is getting his chance now.

The floodlights are on from the start, which, combined with the cold and damp, gives the whole occasion a surreal feeling. The first over, from Brett Lee, is a maiden, as in fact are three of the first four. "It might do a bit in the first hour, then it should be good for batting," Flintoff has assured Mark Nicholas. By the time the fifth over has come, the drizzle has grown heavier and the umpires are conferring about the weather. Dave and his mate slip into their seats next to us. "What time do you call this?" I mock. They have got their timings wrong. "Schoolboy error," Dave admits. The fifth over is a maiden too; they have not missed much. By the end of the sixth over, England are two for no wicket, batting as miserable as the conditions. We have to wait until the fifth ball of the ninth over for a boundary, a fine extra cover drive from Alastair Cook, but even then Andrew Symonds, who seems to employ the triple jump before diving full length, almost claws it back from the rope. A ball later, they all adjourn for drinks.

It does our openers no end of good: five balls later Cook is out, trying to leave Brett Lee outside the off stump but failing to get his bat out of the way quickly enough and giving a straightforward catch to Gilchrist. A few overs later, rains forces the players off. Dave and his mate rush off quicker than Olympic sprinters to be first in the queue for a beer and, unforgivably, neglect to include us in the round. In the race for shelter, we have proved to be also-rans, so, bedraggled and beerless, we stand shivering, trying to make conversation in a crowded passageway.

I can tell Sue is not enjoying this, so when lunch is taken early, she scoots off to find a taxi, the cold and rain defeating her as surely as the heat has elsewhere. She will miss the historic high point of the match: no, not Andrew Strauss's first fifty of the series, but Warnie's 700th victim.

Ponting, though, is being a bit of a tease; knowing that everyone – well, every Australian – wants Warnie on, he seems to be deliberately keeping him in reserve. It's like waiting for the headliners at a music gig; Ponting keeps raising the tension and expectation another notch. He even joked with the press the night before that he might play four seamers and leave Warnie to carry the drinks. As if. Even Andrew Symonds is getting a go, like the support act that's largely ignored while concertgoers enjoy another drink at the bar. At the end of the 38th over, Langer joins in the fun, playing the roadie putting the last guitar in position by creeping up on Warne, snatching off his cap and eliciting an enormous roar from the 97,000 crowd. But Warne retrieves his cap and takes up his position in the slips for the next over. In honesty even Symonds is finding enough nip off the pitch to justify sticking with the seamers but at the beginning of the 38th over, Warnie really does seem to be warming up. By the end of the over, the irritating chant of "War-nie, War-nie" is echoing round the stadium.

Finally, at the start of the 41st over, Ponting gives in to the demands of the Australian public and Warnie is pulling off his jumper, picking up the bowling marker and readying to turn his arm over. He rubs his left hand through his hair and his right hand on the earth in front of the batting crease, looking for grip. An unstoppable wave of Warnie worship is being whipped up and the crowd are on their feet. There are home-made placards with 699 and 700 written on them being waved; yellow-shirted Fanatics are bowing. If this is the ovation he gets when he comes on, what's it going to be like when (if?) he gets that wicket? And then, the first ball. What frenzy there will be if he gets it with his first ball. Every other element of the script has come together, why not this? Why not? Well, because, instead, he delivers a full toss. Collingwood might have slammed it to the boundary but with the England score creeping along at about two an over, he is unable to switch immediately into attack mode and Warne gets away with it. Fifth ball, though, and the Durham man reminds the bowler that he is not afraid to hit against the spin, hastening down the pitch to lift him high over wide mid-on for four.

Every ball brings the same expectation but those who have come to praise Warne are made to remain patient for another couple of overs and the first landmark, if a more modest one, is reached by Strauss, as he turns Warne off his legs to pick up a half-century; it's been a battle: he's hit only one four, been dropped by Matthew Hayden at gully and hardly makes up for some of the decisions he's received throughout the series, but it's something to cling on to, even if only a sideshow to the main event. In the same over, Collingwood hints at renewed confidence in the England camp, sweeping Warne for a four and three, bringing up, it should be mentioned, the tourists' 100. The leg spinner's three overs have cost 15.

But woe betide that England should get ahead of themselves: just when I'm beginning to think that we've seen off the best that Australia can throw at us, I'm tripped up with two wickets in three balls. With the last ball of the third over of his spell, Brett Lee strikes, a climbing ball outside off stump helped on its way to second slip by Collingwood.

Warne starts another over: Strauss comes forward to his first ball, hides his bat behind his pad, but gets away with it. Warne gives his second ball a little more air, it pitches on a full length, and turns just enough to defeat the half bat that Strauss offers to it as he tries to work across it to leg. The bails are off, there's a moment of suspended animation as the reality strikes home – and then Warne's off on a celebratory run, a little bit girlie if you ask me, and that's more or less the last thing I see for a few minutes, as the crowd rises as one in front of me and around me. Dave and his mate are up on their feet, applauding and grinning but the curmudgeon that I've become remains seated, more annoyed that Strauss hasn't gone on to make more of his innings. If I stand up then I will see Warne surrounded by his team-mates somewhere around deep mid-off where his run of delight has run out of steam. But I don't so it is only later, on the news, that I see it. And, quite frankly, it's a bit of an anti-climax. You'd think the Aussies would have thought up something special, a routine of some sort – after all, they've had long enough to think about it – but they haven't and the reliance on spontaneity is a bit of a let-down. When Warne emerges from the huddle, Brett Lee doffs his cap to the living legend, the replay screen says simply and starkly –

SHANE WARNE
700
TEST WICKETS

and Ricky Ponting reminds him to lift the ball above his head and acknowledge all parts of the MCG. By tea, England have slumped to 117 for four. Within 22 more overs, we are all out for 159 and Shane Warne has five for 39 and 704 Test wickets.

Australia start their reply with a devil-may-care attitude, but Matthew Hoggard cares a lot, especially when two plumb lbw appeals against Hayden are turned down. Only the spirit of Andrew Flintoff rescues another dismal day for England as he takes two wickets in two balls, even if one is of nightwatchman Brett Lee.

Come morning, a sweeter, sunnier morning, Flintoff has a close appeal of his own and although it looks as if the ball would have taken out Ponting's leg stump, Aleem Dar is not remotely interested. Fortunately, Ponting doesn't last that long, his usually reliable pull shot letting him down and giving a straightforward chance to Alastair Cook at mid-wicket.

Hoggard then gets some reward, making a horrible mess of Michael Hussey's stumps, while the Harmison of old is briefly resurrected as he gets his second ball of the innings to lift and leave Michael Clarke and Read takes the catch. Dave's timekeeping is as poor as on the first day, and, with Sue taking up the option of a wine tour to the Yarra Valley, I'm left to enjoy it on my own.

Eventually, Dave finds his way to the second deck, where we have seats side-on to the action, and atones for his tardiness by getting the meat pies in. The Australians are very fond of their pies, many considering them their national dish, with an average annual consumption of 12 per person, although that must fail to take into account the huge numbers thrown down, with the mandatory plop of ketchup on top, at the cricket or other great sporting occasions. I'm very fond of their pies, too, but in the interests of health – a 2002 study found that some versions contained as much as 35 grams of fat – have largely restrained myself on the tour so far. I also remembered 1994-5.

Then, starting out a sprightly 11 stone before the cricket got under way, I had met a sweet Indonesian girl in a Perth hostel. She was studying English in the city but was pretty much a beginner and communicated with me mainly through an electronic translating device. When, back in the city for the final Test, I bumped into her again as she sold copies of *The West Australian* newspaper, she had obviously noticed that my staple diet while on the road had been wanting.

"Are you fat?" she said after taking a moment to recognise me. I thought it was nice that she should solicit me for my own opinion rather than coming straight out with it, but then realised that, despite the improvement in her language skills, she had got her verbs and nouns the wrong way round. She wasn't asking me, she was making a statement of fact.

Pies consumed, we start to wallow in Australia's present difficulties: Clarke's dismissal has left them 84 for five and 159 is beginning to look a better total than anyone could have imagined. And next into the fray is Andrew Symonds, still trying to prove himself with the bat in Test cricket. In the overs up to the lunch break, Symonds looks a shadow of the big shot-maker we know him to be in other forms of the game, playing and missing, prodding and poking, even edging one ball from Harmison just short of Collingwood at second slip. It takes him 21 balls to get off the mark and he's advanced to four by the time the interval comes with Australia on 107.

Hayden completes a fortuitous fifty and then almost runs himself out, but the biggest surprise of the afternoon session comes when Flintoff turns to Monty Panesar almost immediately. The ground has clouded over and after bowling without luck earlier, Hoggard is surely the automatic choice, and I mention this to Dave at once. Later, it transpires that Hoggard had slipped off before lunch with a bit of a side strain and has only just sauntered back on, but short of this knowledge, I'm incredulous.

By the time Hoggard does return, Symonds has reverted to type and although a couple of horticultural drives fail to get him full value, he soon finds his range with successive smashes through and over extra cover that dispirit the Yorkshireman further. Eleven overs into the session, they have passed England's total. Symonds' example rubs off on Hayden, who begins to raise his own scoring rate. Symonds brings up his fifty from his 79th ball which means that after getting off the mark he has scored at nearly a run a ball.

He's even playing proper shots now, a drive off Flintoff through extra cover, skirting, as the textbook says it should, across the top of the turf.

That's been the difference in this series: under pressure the Australian has come through, the Englishman has not. Or it could be something to do with the umpires. Monty comes back into the attack and with his second ball, hits Symonds on the trailing pad as he misses a sweep in the most ungainly fashion. Even Bill Lawry admits: "That's out." But it isn't: Rudi Koertzen has obviously had his slow motion finger of death bitten off by a Tasmanian Devil at Melbourne Zoo.

To add insult to injury, Symonds and Hayden take 11 runs from his next four balls, the last one clattering into the sightscreen without bouncing, while the replay of the Panesar appeal elicits a chorus of boos from the England faithful. Flintoff can do little but shake and shake and shake his head.

The six has taken Hayden within touching distance of a 27th

Test century and the first ball of Panesar's next over takes him there, a testosterone-charged drive over mid-on doing the business.

Tea is taken with Australia on 226 for five. Stumps are drawn with Australia 372 for seven. Despite our attempts to allow the final session to disappear in a haze of alcohol, pies – yes, another couple – and ice cream, we are cognisant of Symonds pummelling his way through the 90s to reach his first Test century – who else would it come against apart from England – and Hayden completing his 150. When Hayden goes, for 153, Symonds has almost caught up with him. Gilchrist doesn't last long, as Sajid Mahmood gets a second wicket when he edges, full bloodedly, to second slip, but the partnership between Hayden and Symonds, of 279, means that we have gone almost six hours without a wicket.

On the third day of Christmas, and, by coincidence, the third day of the fourth Test, my true love said to me: "Do you mind if I don't come to the match today." Sue was suffering the after-effects of Yarra Valley wine-tasting and an exhaustive run-down from Martin, on her return to the apartment, of the items he and each member of his family had consumed at their Christmas lunch. (Chicken parmigiana, for once, did not figure significantly). There was little to be gained from forcing her to the MCG and so it was that Dave and I – well I, because Dave was delayed again by a complicated tram route (a weak excuse) – took our seats for the next instalment.

It's fairly dispiriting despite the early loss of Symonds as Warne, maestro with the ball, starts to show his abilities with the bat. He races through the 30s, dealing dismissively with Sajid Mahmood, whose bowling is unequivocally judged "absolute garbage" by Tony

Greig, and raising speculation among the radio commentary team that he could make his first Test hundred. You wouldn't put it past him.

Mahmood cleans up the tail, saving us from that fate, and with it, records the vastly flattering figures of four for 100 (Greig has fallen into silent disbelief, a rare occurrence) and England's opening pair confidently reduce the deficit by 28 by lunch. In fact they have advanced to 41 before the collapse gets underway, their highest opening partnership of the series. In fact, with the exception of the second innings in Perth, their stands have been remarkably similar: 28 and 29 in Brisbane, 32 and 31 in Adelaide and 36 in the first innings at the Waca. Remarkably suggestive of an inability to concentrate.

Cook plays on to Stuart Clark, Bell is caught in front by one that breaks back from Glenn McGrath, probably out but certainly not as clear cut as a few in the Australia innings that Rudi Koertzen failed to respond to, and Pietersen, promoted to No 4 on the back of public demand, drives ambitiously at Clark, who squeezes it through the gap between bat and pad. That's it, we think. Game over. From 41 for no wicket to 49 for three in minutes.

We go to tea at 90 for four, Collingwood having driven Brett Lee to short extra cover, and straight after the break, Lee gets Andrew Strauss to flay at one outside the off stump and it's 90 for five. Strauss, who has resisted for almost three hours, is gone again. As Ian Chappell notes, he's looked in good form for most of the series but has got precious little to show for it. Little more than 20 overs later, England are staring down the barrel. The three lions are waiting for the vet's final poison dart, which is delivered by Lee, who yorks Hoggard. Only Chris Read, the man who can't bat according to Duncan Fletcher, has stood defiant in the final hour, finishing with 26 not out.

Dave and I can't get out of there fast enough; while Warne plays out a rather longer farewell in the outfield, we say swift goodbyes, hoping that Sydney will have something, anything, to console us.

That night, I persuaded Sue to go to the cinema to see the latest James Bond, *Casino Royale*. I convinced her with assurances that Daniel Craig, in his first Bond role, featured regularly in a pair of very brief swimming trunks. I had a slightly different motive: I was desperate to see at least one Englishman doing things with ruthless efficiency.

The Ashes - 4th Test
Australia v England
Played at Melbourne Cricket Ground on 26,27,28 December 2006 (5-day match)
Result Australia won by an innings and 99 runs

England 1st innings		R	M	B	SR
AJ Strauss	b Warne	50	206	132	37.87
AN Cook	c ✝Gilchrist b Lee	11	49	37	29.72
IR Bell	lbw b Clark	7	46	30	23.33
PD Collingwood	c Ponting b Lee	28	115	82	34.14
KP Pietersen	c Symonds b Warne	21	104	70	30.00
✱ A Flintoff	c Warne b Clark	13	36	31	41.93
✝CMW Read	c Ponting b Warne	3	28	17	17.64
SI Mahmood	c ✝Gilchrist b McGrath	0	11	9	0.00
SJ Harmison	c Clarke b Warne	7	11	12	58.33
MS Panesar	c Symonds b Warne	4	27	19	21.05
MJ Hoggard	not out	9	15	10	90.00
Extras	(b 2, lb 1, nb 3)	6			
Total	**(all out; 74.2 overs; 324 mins)**	**159 (2.13 runs per over)**			

Fall of wickets 1-23 (Cook, 10.5 ov), 2-44 (Bell, 20.5 ov), 3-101 (Collingwood, 45.6 ov), 4-101 (Strauss, 46.2 ov), 5-122 (Flintoff, 55.5 ov), 6-135 (Read, 62.6 ov), 7-136 (Mahmood, 65.4 ov), 8-145 (Harmison, 68.2 ov), 9-146 (Pietersen, 70.2 ov), 10-159 (Panesar, 74.2 ov)

Bowling	O	M	R	W	Econ	
B Lee	13	4	36	2	2.76	(2nb)
GD McGrath	20	8	37	1	1.85	(1nb)
SR Clark	17	6	27	2	1.58	
A Symonds	7	2	17	0	2.42	
SK Warne	17.2	4	39	5	2.25	

Australia 1st innings		R	M	B	SR
JL Langer	c ✝Read b Flintoff	27	45	29	93.10
ML Hayden	c ✝Read b Mahmood	153	418	265	57.73
B Lee	c ✝ Read b Flintoff	0	2	1	0.00
✱RT Ponting	c Cook b Flintoff	7	37	28	25.00
MEK Hussey	b Hoggard	6	37	20	30.00
MJ Clarke	c ✝Read b Harmison	5	6	5	100.00
A Symonds	c ✝Read b Harmison	156	327	220	70.90
✝AC Gilchrist	c Collingwood b Mahmood	1	10	8	12.50
SK Warne	not out	40	75	54	74.07
SR Clark	c ✝Read b Mahmood	8	34	24	33.33
GD McGrath	c Bell b Mahmood	0	9	6	0.00
Extras	(lb 6, w 1, nb 9)	16			
Total	**(all out; 108.3 overs; 505 mins)**	**419 (3.86 runs per over)**			

Fall of wickets 1-44 (Langer, 9.2 ov), 2-44 (Lee, 9.3 ov), 3-62 (Ponting, 17.3 ov), 4-79 (Hussey, 24.1 ov), 5-84 (Clarke, 25.2 ov), 6-363 (Hayden, 90.4 ov), 7-365 (Gilchrist, 92.3 ov), 8-383 (Symonds, 99.2 ov), 9-417 (Clark, 106.5 ov), 10-419 (McGrath, 108.3 ov)

Bowling	O	M	R	W	Econ	
MJ Hoggard	21	6	82	1	3.90	(1nb)
A Flintoff	22	1	77	3	3.50	(8nb)
SJ Harmison	28	6	69	2	2.46	
SI Mahmood	21.3	1	100	4	4.65	(1w)
MS Panesar	12	1	52	0	4.33	
PD Collingwood	3	0	20	0	6.66	
KP Pietersen	1	0	13	0	13.00	

England 2nd innings

		R	M	B	SR
AJ Strauss	c ✝Gilchrist b Lee	31	173	107	28.97
AN Cook	b Clark	20	64	46	43.47
IR Bell	lbw b McGrath	2	21	11	18.18
KP Pietersen	b Clark	1	7	8	12.50
PD Collingwood	c Langer b Lee	16	52	38	42.10
✱ A Flintoff	lbw b Clark	25	60	45	55.55
✝CMW Read	not out	26	127	77	33.76
SI Mahmood	lbw b Warne	0	3	2	0.00
SJ Harmison	bw b Warne	4	44	26	15.38
MS Panesar	c Clarke b Lee	14	20	19	73.68
MJ Hoggard	b Lee	5	21	20	25.00
Extras	(lb 12, w 1, nb 4)	17			
Total	**(all out; 65.5 overs; 301 mins)**	**161 (2.44 runs per over)**			

Fall of wickets 1-41 (Cook, 14.5 ov), 2-48 (Bell, 19.2 ov), 3-49 (Pietersen, 20.5 ov), 4-75 (Collingwood, 31.4 ov), 5-90 (Strauss, 37.5 ov), 6-108 (Flintoff, 45.5 ov), 7-109 (Mahmood, 46.3 ov), 8-127 (Harmison, 56.5 ov), 9-146 (Panesar, 61.2 ov), 10-161 (Hoggard, 65.5 ov)

Bowling	O	M	R	W	Econ	
B Lee	18.5	6	47	4	2.49	(3nb)
GD McGrath	12	2	26	1	2.16	(1w)
SR Clark	16	6	30	3	1.87	(1nb)
SK Warne	19	3	46	2	2.42	

Toss England, who chose to bat first

Walking the Wallaby Trail

SYDNEY

I'D never read my own obituary before, but there it was, in black and white in *The Times'* Line and Length blog: Henderson: Missing In Action. In a piece penned by friend and colleague Dave Townsend, whose company I had enjoyed throughout the Melbourne and Sydney Tests, I was being laid to rest, a result, I should add, of my failure to show for the crushing, closing moments of the series.

"In the end," he wrote, *"poor old Nigel couldn't face it. He had sat through the opening humiliation in Brisbane, endured the agony of Adelaide, only missed one day in Perth and stayed to the very end (of Day Three) in Melbourne... but the final act was too much for him.*

Having become increasingly agitated over the six days we sat together since Christmas, and prone to increasing outbursts such as 'That's pathetic, England', 'Show some fight' and my favourite, 'For fuck's sake Strauss', he was a beaten man. When I left him at Sydney's best pizza restaurant on Thursday evening, he promised me he would be there at the ridiculous starting time of 10.10am.

Perhaps he did reach the ground, only to turn away in disgust when last hope Kevin Pietersen surrendered third ball of the morning. Perhaps he couldn't face the journey from his hostel in Newtown.

Whatever, Nigel Henderson was missing in action for the final session of the series.

Although I missed his company, I couldn't blame him. After 20 days of abuse, he deserved a break. I'm not sure how many England fans, like Nigel, followed the whole tour, but those who did are owed an apology by the players and the ECB. Those of us part-timers who turned up for the last two Tests should get our money back too. What has passed for an Ashes defence has been pathetic. Those in the crowd around me today who weren't beaming under green and gold hats were using words like 'disgrace', 'hopeless', 'gutless' and 'embarrassing'. We all knew it would be a tough series, Australia were always likely to win... but 5-0? The Queen should demand those MBEs back. England, you've let us all down."

I was touched, although less so when Patrick mentioned on the blog that he had received "literally several" enquiries about my whereabouts. It was all quite simple, really: for the first time on the tour I had got properly pissed. This had followed a night out in Paddington with Dave, Walter and John McNamara, yet another friend from *The Times* sportsdesk who had made it out to Australia. John was perhaps the luckiest of all, having clung on to the coat-tails of a mate who had won a competition to the Sydney Test, although the downside was that he had to live on a cruise liner for several days with Allan Lamb before the vessel turned him into a veritable victim of projectile vomiting as it rolled and tossed its way across the Bass Straits for a stop-off in Tasmania. Lamby had sensibly opted for dry land by then.

At 4-0 down, and despite my assurances to Dave in the pizza restaurant, I had promised myself I would not bother going to the fourth day if England were five or more wickets down overnight. There was sound reasoning behind this: five down and England were as good as all out. Australia had known it all along, despite Duncan Fletcher's baleful attempts to hide the fact behind Geraint Jones, Ashley Giles and later, Sajid Mahmood. By a strange sense of symbiosis I think Andrew Flintoff knew of my predicament, otherwise what would have led him to get out moments before the close on the third evening to a stumping of scandalous stupidity?

The day has started so hopefully with James Anderson, back in for the injured Hoggard, bowling at his best in the series, tempting Michael Hussey into a Cook-like fish outside off stump with his second ball; Dave, arriving late for a change, needs an update and I supply it as we cover our faces, especially the protruding parts, with lashings of sun cream. Hussey's dismissal has left Australia 190 for five, still 101 adrift of England's first-innings score, and when Panesar lures Symonds into an ugly swing across the line, they are 260 for six. Warne comes in to rampant applause – the phrase "the Bradman of the ball" gets another airing in a commentary box rapidly running out of superlatives - and then, within six balls, England have two chances to send him back to the pavilion for the penultimate rather than final time. Warne is determined to go out with a bang, so he sweeps Monty's first ball fine for four and belts the next for six over mid-wicket. Two dot balls follow but with the final ball of the over, Monty tosses it up on a perfect line and turns it enough to brush the underside of Warnie's glove. There is a huge appeal; Chris Read, who has taken the catch, Monty and his close fielders all convinced it is out. Even Warnie, perhaps guiltily, stumbles forward, as if setting out on the walk back to the pavilion, but he soon stops and looks suitably dismayed, hurt even, that England should be claiming that he got a touch. And Aleem Dar buys it.

The next ball, delivered by Sajid Mahmood to Adam Gilchrist, who's on 42 and in the kind of state of focused hostility that greeted Monty Panesar in Perth, is carved out to deep cover and becomes a symbol, a microcosm, of everything that's been wrong with England on this tour. Alastair Cook runs in, and seeing Gilchrist wanting to turn it into two, throws to the non-striker's end, which Warne is struggling to reach. Now. Call me old-fashioned, but in clubs and schools up and down the land, are not youngsters being instructed that in such circumstances they should take up position behind the stumps to which the ball is being thrown, adopt a position of crouched readiness and cup the return in soft hands before whipping off the bails? Perhaps the library budget didn't stretch to the MCC coaching manual at North College, Bolton, where Mahmood received his education because the loose-limbed fast bowler fails to do any of these things and as the ball flashes in, he half-heartedly sticks out a hand as it passes the stumps. Warne, who is barely in the picture, goes on to make 71 and Australia's last four wickets add 133 to give them a lead of 102.

Billy Cooper's faint strains of Jerusalem are heard above the general din, but it seems a parody of itself in the circumstances. There really is nothing for us to trumpet. In fact, I'm almost beginning to see the Barmy Army as part of the problem.

"We are the Army, the Barmy Army
We are mental, we are mad,"

they sing, quite regularly, and no one would disagree with those sentiments. But it is the accompanying rhyming couplet to this tune that has worried me increasingly as the series has progressed. It goes:

"We are the loyalist (sic) cricket supporters
The world has ever had."

The point is: where does loyalty end and blind faith begin? I have watched in admiration as the Army has responded to each England setback with the call to arms of Vic Flowers, their vocal leader, and the demand for a rousing fanfare from Billy while I've been burying my head in my hands, groaning deeply and exchanging banter of a not always friendly kind with my Australian neighbours.

But sometimes I wish they would be less sporting, less keen, maybe, to be liked. They've no-balled Brett Lee a few times (no doubt upsetting Justin Langer again) and they've continually reminded Australia that a Republic may still be some way off, but when Andrew Strauss plays a second suicidal hook shot in a match, offers half a bat to Shane Warne when he's a wicket away from 700 or slashes at a wide one moments after tea, should they be applauding him back to the pavilion or giving him a verbal reminder of the standards expected from an international batsman?

England's players seem to play lip service to the Army's unwavering support, too. They will, when interviewed, praise their singing and how they spur them on. Yet, on the pitch, there is little or no sign of this. I have observed the Army stir every hour or so throughout this series and belt one out from their back catalogue – the theme from *Only Fools and Horses* even got an airing on the third and final day at Melbourne – but the players have seemed shamefully unmoved.

Maybe it's time the Army stood down some of its active members and left England to their own battles on foreign fields. Perhaps then the players and management will realise what they are missing and get the message that such support is never to be taken for granted.

It's heresy, I suppose, and I shouldn't even be having these thoughts, not when we're 166 for two on the first day and Pietersen and Bell are sailing along as happily as they've done all series. But all it takes is a wind shift called Glenn McGrath and some poor helmsmanship from the man the Aussies have come to know as FIGJAM (fuck I'm good, just ask me) and suddenly the spinnaker has broken loose and we're in danger of capsizing. Pietersen has already survived one of his trademark walks down the wicket where he then tries to pull a fast bowler off the front foot, looping the ball over Hussey at mid-wicket for two runs, but he does not learn. Two balls later he tries the same trick and this time McGrath bangs it in so short that he really can't get any leverage and the flamingo shot leaves him with a pink face as it's clutched by a leaping Hussey.

It's McGrath's first wicket in his final Test – his 900th international wicket in all – and he's got the bit between his teeth now and soon he has his second when Bell, the most elegant of our batsmen in this series and who has barely put a foot wrong in his 71, is bowled. We really didn't see that coming – and obviously neither did he – and from our angle it is hard to understand how he's missed it. The replay provides the answer: it has seamed back in with intent, caught a bit of an inside edge and gone on to clip the top of off stump. It's 167 for four, Flintoff's on his way to the middle and either he or Collingwood, who's only just arrived at the other end himself, preferably both, are going to have to produce something special to prevent another fall away towards the end of the innings. A statistical analysis reveals that England's bottom five batsmen have averaged 9.7 runs each in the four Tests to date – and that includes Flintoff's 51 in Perth, when he batted at No 7 to allow Matthew Hoggard to play nightwatchman.

The pair do well, guiding us to 234 for four by stumps, but the next morning is a different matter altogether. Once Collingwood has edged McGrath to Gilchrist, we add only another 46, mostly from Flintoff, who plays his best innings of the winter, as Chris Read, Sajid Mahmood, Steve Harmison, Monty and James Anderson muster the grand total of four between them.

So, by the fourth morning, waking up with a hangover, I'm caught between the promise I made to myself and the strange desire in my stomach, that little kernel of hope that usually wins in the battle with logic, to shuffle down the road, get on the No 53 bus and head down to the SCG to see KP launch a rescue act. Somehow, I hold out against this desire and for once, my intuitive sense that it will be futile proves correct, as I instead switch on the television and see McGrath catch Pietersen's edge with the day's third ball. I bury my head in the bedsheets. McGrath has drifted in and out of this series, but when he has drifted in to it, he has done so with impeccable timing that has had a devastating effect. His sense of occasion remains to the end, as he skids one low through Mahmood's defences – the 1,000th Test scalp claimed by he and Warne in combination – and, coming round the wicket, he forces the left-handed Anderson into an unconvincing drive-cum-chip into the on-side. "Now then," says Mark Nicholas on the commentary, "Michael Hussey's underneath it." The outcome is inevitable and I feel a lump growing in my throat. "And he takes the catch. Glenn McGrath takes the final wicket with his final ball in Test cricket." I wouldn't like you to think that I'm soft but there's a sadness creeping over me. It's the end – not only for two great cricketers, maybe three if you include Justin Langer, although personally I'd rank him with the very good, but also it's the end for England – and for me. If I had really thought it would end up like this, would I have gone to Australia? I don't think I had any choice. I had to be there. But did it also have to be, as McGrath began every series saying it would, 5-0?

Still, there were always the one-dayers.

The Ashes - 5th Test

Australia v England

Played at Sydney Cricket Ground on 2,3,4,5 January 2007 (5-day match)
Result Australia won by 10 wickets

England 1st innings		R	M	B	SR
AJ Strauss	c ♱Gilchrist b Lee	29	64	52	55.76
AN Cook	c ♱Gilchrist b Clark	20	88	47	42.55
IR Bell	b McGrath	71	194	153	46.40
KP Pietersen	c Hussey b McGrath	41	162	104	39.42
PD Collingwood	c ♱Gilchrist b McGrath	27	119	73	36.98
✱A Flintoff	c ♱Gilchrist b Clark	89	195	142	62.67
♱CMW Read	c ♱Gilchrist b Lee	2	13	9	22.22
SI Mahmood	c Hayden b Lee	0	2	1	0.00
SJ Harmison	lbw b Clark	2	51	24	8.33
MS Panesar	lbw b Warne	0	20	14	0.00
JM Anderson	not out	0	6	5	0.00
Extras	(lb 5, w 3, nb 2)	10			
Total	**(all out; 103.4 overs; 462 mins)**	**291 (2.80 runs per over)**			

Fall of wickets 1-45 (Strauss, 14.2 ov), 2-58 (Cook, 19.1 ov), 3-166 (Pietersen, 58.3 ov), 4-167 (Bell, 60.1 ov), 5-245 (Collingwood, 85.6 ov), 6-258 (Read, 88.5 ov), 7-258 (Mahmood, 88.6 ov), 8-282 (Harmison, 98.6 ov), 9-291 (Flintoff, 102.1 ov), 10-291 (Panesar, 103.4 ov)

Bowling	O	M	R	W	Econ	
GD McGrath	29	8	67	3	2.31	(2nb)
B Lee	22	5	75	3	3.40	(1w)
SR Clark	24	Ω	62	3	2.58	(2w)
SK Warne	22.4	1	69	1	3.04	
A Symonds	6	2	13	0	2.16	

Australia 1st innings		R	M	B	SR
JL Langer	c Read b Anderson	26	41	27	96.29
ML Hayden	c Collingwood b Harmison	33	113	77	42.85
✱RT Ponting	run out (Anderson)	45	96	72	62.50
MEK Hussey	c ♱Read b Anderson	37	120	100	37.00
MJ Clarke	c ♱Read b Harmison	11	39	24	45.83
A Symonds	b Panesar	48	138	95	50.52
♱AC Gilchrist	c ♱Read b Anderson	62	118	72	86.11
SK Warne	st ♱Read b Panesar	71	114	65	109.23
B Lee	c ♱Read b Flintoff	5	14	10	50.00
SR Clark	c Pietersen b Mahmood	35	55	41	85.36
GD McGrath	not out	0	6	3	0.00
Extras	(lb 10, w 4, nb 6)	20			
Total	**(all out; 96.3 overs; 432 mins)**	**393 (4.07 runs per over)**			

Fall of wickets 1-34 (Langer, 9.3 ov), 2-100 (Hayden, 25.3 ov), 3-118 (Ponting, 32.3 ov), 4-155 (Clarke, 43.1 ov), 5-190 (Hussey, 56.2 ov), 6-260 (Symonds, 73.1 ov), 7-318 (Gilchrist, 80.3 ov), 8-325 (Lee, 83.3 ov), 9-393 (Clark, 95.3 ov), 10-393 (Warne, 96.3 ov)

Bowling	O	M	R	W	Econ	
A Flintoff	17	2	56	1	3.29	(3nb, 1w)
JM Anderson	26	8	98	3	3.76	(1w)
SJ Harmison	23	5	80	2	3.47	(1nb, 2w)
SI Mahmood	11	1	59	1	5.36	(2nb)
MS Panesar	19.3	0	90	2	4.61	

England 2nd innings		R	M	B	SR
AJ Strauss	bw b Clark	24	68	45	53.33
AN Cook	c ✛Gilchrist b Lee	4	11	8	50.00
IR Bell	c ✛ Gilchrist b Lee	28	85	51	54.90
KP Pietersen	c ✛Gilchrist b McGrath	29	139	95	30.52
PD Collingwood	c Hayden b Clark	17	67	36	47.22
✶A Flintoff	st ✛ Gilchrist b Warne	7	31	21	33.33
MS Panesar	run out (Symonds)	0	27	19	0.00
CMW Read	c Ponting b Lee	4	26	17	23.52
SI Mahmood	b McGrath	4	13	11	36.36
SJ Harmison	not out	16	42	26	61.53
JM Anderson	c Hussey b McGrath	5	37	22	22.72
Extras	(b 2, lb 3, w 1, nb 3)	9			
Total	**(all out; 58 overs; 278 mins)**	**147 (2.53 runs per over)**			

Fall of wickets 1-5 (Cook, 2.3 ov), 2-55 (Strauss, 14.3 ov), 3-64 (Bell, 20.5 ov), 4-98 (Collingwood, 34.6 ov), 5-113 (Flintoff, 41.3 ov), 6-114 (Pietersen, 43.3 ov), 7-114 (Panesar, 47.2 ov), 8-122 (Read, 48.6 ov), 9-123 (Mahmood, 49.6 ov), 10-147 (Anderson, 57.6 ov)

Bowling	O	M	R	W	Econ	
B Lee	14	5	39	3	2.78	(1nb, 1w)
GD McGrath	21	11	38	3	1.80	(1nb)
SR Clark	12	4	29	2	2.41	(1nb)
SK Warne	6	1	23	1	3.83	
A Symonds	5	2	13	0	2.60	

Australia 2nd innings (target: 46 runs)		R	M	B	SR
JL Langer	not out	20	44	43	46.51
ML Hayden	not out	23	44	22	104.54
Extras	(lb 3)	3			
Total	**(0 wickets; 10.5 overs; 44 mins)**	**46 (4.24 runs per over)**			

Did not bat ✶RT Ponting, MEK Hussey, MJ Clarke, A Symonds, ✛AC Gilchrist, SK Warne, B Lee, SR Clark, GD McGrath

Bowling	O	M	R	W	Econ
JM Anderson	4	0	12	0	3.00
SJ Harmison	5	1	13	0	2.60
SI Mahmood	1.5	0	18	0	9.81

Toss England, who chose to bat first

Better than a poke in the eye with a burnt stick

THE ONE-DAYERS

THE desire to retain some space on our bodies that wasn't bitten to pieces by the species of superbug that had infested the bedding at Billabong Gardens, our hostel in Newtown, won out over the inclination to try to rely on a ticket tout for entry to the Twenty20 match against Australia and the first of the one-dayers at the MCG on the Friday, even though we had tickets for that. I was also guided by the urge to visit Tasmania, missed on my previous tour to Australia in 1994-5 even though England had played a tour match there, and to use the tickets for the two one-dayers at Bellerive Oval – tickets that, not surprisingly, had proved unpopular enough for me to book when I sat up all night in England on the internet.

So we got an early cab to Sydney airport and flew down to what must rank as the smallest international airport in the world at Hobart, a city bordered on one side by the mouth of the Derwent River and the other by Mount Wellington, nearly 4,000 feet of rock with a looming presence. The airport was not exactly teeming with options to get to the city centre about 16 kilometres away, but there was a shuttle bus which would drop you off at your hotel for a reasonable sum. We had booked at the last minute, giving us little choice in the accommodation department, ending up in Wrest

Point, a circular tower with an expensive revolving restaurant at the top that moved indiscernibly slowly. It was a few minutes on from the city and a mecca for the gambler – it was the first casino in Australia. We shared the bus with about 15 others, one a lone Pom down for the cricket, who got off at a rickety hostel in the city centre. It was raining when he jumped off, which delighted one of the Australians on board. "It's the only wash they get," she said, repeating the prejudice oft sounded by the Fanatics that we're all scruffy, unhygienic bastards. While her compatriots laughed, we sat grim and stony faced at the back.

We had five days before any more live cricket – the Australia game against New Zealand, which I was determined to attend so that I could actually enjoy seeing the Australian batsmen batter another bowling attack into submission and, two days after that, England also took on the Kiwis. To me this offered the best chance of witnessing an England win on Australian soil and one I didn't want to miss.

Mainland Australians, I had read, have an attitude to the islanders off their south coast as being in-bred, deformed and backward, and over-familiar with their livestock. The joke goes that you need to watch out for people with a scar on their shoulder – it's where their second head used to be before the surgery.

For John Shinnal, though, it was the whereabouts of his one and only head that caused concern. Shinnal was believed to be the first Aboriginal cricketer. From the Carlton area of Tasmania, he played with settlers in the early 1800s, long before that Aboriginal tour of England in 1868. Sadly, this member of the Moomaire Mener people, the original inhabitants of the area, died tragically young at the age of about 27, of unknown causes. An inquest into his death found little and ascribed his demise to "a visitation from God". However, when his autopsy was carried out, the resident medical officer removed his head without permission, trying to preserve it, it is believed, for scientific purposes – mainly to continue investigations, or lend support to, Darwin's theory of natural selection. He was buried in an Anglican churchyard, minus his head, which somehow turned up at the Royal College of Surgeons in Dublin, where it was housed in a jar and labelled as a "specimen of a rare species".

Tasmanians concerned with remembering the contribution of native peoples later took up his cause and after years of trying, managed to get his head repatriated: but it was not until 1992 that their efforts paid off.

This story, which I found strangely fascinating, was just one of those you can read about at the Tasmanian Cricket Museum at Bellerive Oval. The ground has always appeared among the most picturesque on the international circuit and like a few other English visitors, I had been lured there by snippets on Sky that indicated a cricket field on the edge of the sea. And, it is, almost literally, although what I had imagined as sea is actually part of the Derwent river. But as we approached from where we had been dropped off by Rod's water taxi, what you saw was a skinny crescent of beach that gave way to a piece of rough, grassy open space and, some 50 yards further inland, the back of the impressive Southern Stand, the most modern part of the construction completed in October 2001.

We found a way in, feeling ever so slightly like trespassers, and almost immediately stumbled upon a legend. We had seen him in many guises on this tour, most notably as a small plastic doll, who would offer up some interesting catchphrases and a cartoon character who would wander on to the replay screens at the various venues and mumble in his deep Tasmanian timbre: "We'll have those Ashes back now, thanks," but not until now, in the flesh. And where better to find him than on home ground. Yes, it was Boony, who was mumbling something incoherent into his mobile phone. I thought about trying to catch an impromptu exclusive interview with him, but, in my awe and intimidated by the dimensions of his moustache in close proximity, I simply asked him if he could point us the way to the museum. Later, I had my photograph taken with his statue, which depicts him flaying a boundary, no doubt off an England bowler, in typically robust style and pressed a button on an exhibit disguised as a drinks buggy that allowed me to listen in to his reaction on first being called up to the Australia squad. He was in an antiques shop when he got the news, it transpired.

Among the museum's other exhibits was an interactive bat, which you can use to test your reflexes against different bowlers, the fastest of them Shane Watson, who turned out for Tasmania before returning to his native Queensland, at an express 140kph. I was pleasantly surprised to find that I hadn't completely lost it when I managed to respond to his opening delivery in a frankly impressive 0.04 seconds. However, my pride was somewhat dented when Sue showed she could handle him in 0.01 seconds. This meant one of two things; either she had got his loosener, or she was England's missing link.

Just because we had the time to do some touristy things didn't mean that I wasn't still keen to keep one eye on England. The Twenty20 international had significance in that it marked the return to competitive action, and the captaincy, of Michael Vaughan. That we would hurry back to the hotel to watch after booking a trip to Bruny Island in the Hobart tourist information office. Even this I tried to fit around the cricket. England were due in Melbourne for the first one-day international on Friday, so I was keen to keep that day free. Unfortunately, the Bruny Island excursion was fully booked for the Thursday, so I had no choice but to reserve our places for a day later. Or risk the wrath of Sue.

She was astounded that I would want much more to do with the England cricket team, at least for a while, and when I looked at the schedule for the Bruny Island trip, which included a daring three-hour outing to the edge of the Southern Ocean in a 40-foot 'eco-cruiser' or, more simply, a bloody big inflatable speedboat, taking in views of ancient sea stacks, blowholes and seal colonies – the latter whiff I can tell you – I could see her point. However, I did manage to calculate that we'd be back in time for the second innings.

England's sizeable defeat in the shortest form of the game was straightforward; getting to Bruny, essentially two islands joined by a thin neck of land with water on both sides off the south-east coast of Tasmania, is not. It requires a coach trip to a peaceful harbour at Kettering – the peace was long in coming; it was once a violent outpost where local Aborigines were persecuted by whalers and seal hunters – a ferry crossing to Roberts Point on North Bruny, where you can pause to buy local cherries, and another coach journey to Adventure Bay in the south. There, after a coffee and bun in one of the low-rise holiday buildings along the front, you get trussed up in a waterproof coat about seven sizes too big for you, put on your life vest and step on to a boat manned by a couple of Australians you're not sure you want to entrust your life to.

They're tanned, bristly, but disappointingly, neither of them is called Bruce. They're Rob and Mark.

Before we knew it we were being whisked off into the ocean and driven at breakneck speed through gaps in rocks that the cruisers can only pass between by being revved up to full power and tipped onto one side. It's an interesting view whichever side of the boat you're on, if taking an intellectual perspective on your imminent death is possible. "Don't worry," said Rob, as a meaty swell threatened to unbalance our craft. "When we got the boat the two of us brought it back by sailing it across the Bass Strait."

Now we knew they were insane. They should have been wearing badges: "You don't have to be mad to work here, but if you have been sectioned at least once, it helps." Later, we reversed up close to some of the rugged cliff face that comprises most of the island's coast and soars up to 200 metres above sea level. These, we were assured, were some of the highest sea cliffs in Australia and keeping your back to the rock face and tilting your head back gave you the best perspective. Or made you dizzy.

A small boy was moved from the front of the craft, where every slight bounce was experienced as an enormous judder, and reseated at the back, where it was smoother and where, should he have decided to regurgitate his breakfast, the wind direction would ensure it did least harm to the other occupants.

We enjoyed a few minutes circling with some wild dolphins, which is when I discovered the limits to digital cameras, or mine, at least. For some reason, the shutter takes an age to react when pressed. Hence, what should be memorable pictures of porpoises pirouetting in a mid-air pas de deux end up being indistinct shots of the back ends of grey mammals disappearing under water.

As we set off for the seal colony, the storm clouds began to move in. We made it to the rocky outcrop on which the seals basked, and occasionally fought – although maybe that was just for the wildlife cameramen among us – and spotted one tiny penguin emerging from its nest higher up. Rob pointed out the Southern Ocean beyond, where the sky was a bleak, purply grey. And I thought about the only thing that I knew about the Southern Ocean: that it was a long way from anywhere, rough and extremely cold, and Tony Bullimore, the British sailor and adventurer – some, including the Australian Air Force, might have less polite names for him – had spent five days in it, under an upturned hull and with only a bar of chocolate for company. I hope it was Belgian.

It bucketed down on the way back, but the waterproofs did their thing, and we were greeted by bowls of piping pumpkin soup, another Australian culinary speciality, on our return. Then it was back off to Hobart, where we found a pub in time to see Andrew Flintoff putting in a useful turn with the lower order. Pietersen had gone for 85, but we didn't know he'd been clobbered in the ribs by McGrath – a blow that would put him out of the rest of the tour.

In the context of what I'd been fearing, 242 for eight wasn't too bad. It wasn't too good either – especially not for Australia, who knocked them off for the loss of only two wickets with nearly five overs remaining. Steve Harmison had announced his retirement from one-day internationals before the start of the Melbourne Test, but his ghost lived on in the form of Flintoff, whose first over cost 11, including two wides that went for four.

We wandered around Hobart the following day, via the hills of Battery Point, a prestigious suburb near our hotel, its extravagant houses and bungalows, most with beautifully-tended gardens, looking down over the waterfront. It adjoined Salamanca Place, a row of sandstone buildings once warehouses but now converted into craft shops, restaurants, bars, and the odd small theatre. We ambled from there to Shades Row, overlooked by the Hotel Grand Chancellor where Serena Williams, playing her first tennis tournament for months after injury, was said to be staying. Shades Row was in an area called Wapping, which, being a *Times* employee, interested me very much. It was, a sign said, a "place of dirt filth and rubbish, miserable noises, tumult and riots, drunkenness and obscenity". Not unlike the *Times* sports desk, then. Of course, it was referring to the 1800s because now it scrubbed up quite well. The Great Fire of 1890 had helped see to that, bringing this hidden community of tenements adjoining tanneries, slaughterhouses, gas works and open sewage pits to public notice and shaming the more affluent into improvements.

At the hotel that evening, the sports bar was packed as the domestic Twenty20 final between Victoria and Tasmania was broadcast from the MCG. We thought we'd meld in with the crowd and support the local team, but they lost by ten runs. Had they had two of their best players in action, they might have fared better, but they were needed for bigger things. Ricky Ponting would be making one of his rare appearances at his home ground in the first one-dayer against New Zealand the following day, while the selection of Ben Hilfenhaus, a promising fast bowler who'd dismissed Alastair Cook and Kevin Pietersen back in Canberra, had ratcheted the local interest up a few notches.

On a gloriously sunny morning, I am looking forward to some Australian carnage and when Ponting wins the toss, that's what we seemed destined to get, especially as Adam Gilchrist, restored to his limited-overs opening role, is finding the middle of his bat. He and Hayden smash 83 in the first 13 overs before Hayden gloves a pull down the leg-side. When Gilchrist, having hit a four and a six off Jeetan Patel, the off spinner brought on to take the pace off the ball, tries again and is controversially given out lbw, it sparks extended rumbles of displeasure among the home supporters, but nothing compared with the howls of despair when Ponting, on ten, drives a catch to short cover, who has only just been placed there by opposing captain Stephen Fleming. At 117 for three, the run-rate has been cut from 6.83 to 5.31 in a matter of ten overs. Nevertheless there is Andrew Symonds to come and this form of the game is his speciality. He has to wait until the last seven overs to really open up, though, with the help of Cameron White. A ball into the final over, from Shane Bond, they have added 77 in a murderous assault from 43 balls, when the New Zealand bowler, so talented but so hindered by injury over the years, hits back. First, White swings a catch to mid-wicket, then Symonds, stepping back to clout him through cover, edges thinly to McCullum. A slower ball to the incoming batsman Nathan Bracken beats the Australian all ends up and Bond's team-mates converge on him to celebrate the hat-trick. I tell Sue she has just witnessed an extraordinarily rare event, but her look tells me she doesn't feel overly privileged.

The New Zealand reply starts poorly. McCullum goes lbw to Hilfenhaus and Nathan Astle edges Bracken behind. It is seven for two – an unhealthy state of affairs, even against an attack lacking Brett Lee, Glenn McGrath and, of course, the retired Shane Warne. But Fleming and Ross Taylor, a player I know nothing about but soon realise can hit a meaty ball, consolidate before Peter Fulton, another cricketing mystery to me but from the same Land of the Giants inhabited by Jacob Oram, push on. At 161 for three from 30 overs, New Zealand are back in with a serious chance and, for the time being, the Bellerive Oval has lost its brash voice. But then something happens that is all too familiar to an England fan: there is a collapse and again it begs that question: is it Australian brilliance at work, their intimidatory powers or their opponents' ineptitude? Taylor is caught behind from the first ball of a new spell from the left-arm seamer Mitchell Johnson – great timing from his captain, you might say; then his replacement, Craig McMillan, is run out by a stunning throw from Michael Clarke. Ponting pulls Johnson straight out of the attack and restores Stuart Clark, who strikes second ball, an innocuous delivery punched off the back foot by Fulton parried by Symonds at short extra and taken at the second attempt. Even Cameron White, a very average leg-spinner, strikes first ball when he is recalled. When Patel drives Symonds down the ground to provide Hilfenhaus with the winning catch, New Zealand have lost seven wickets for 23 runs in 7.2 overs.

A few minutes later, sitting by the dock of the bay, wasting time, well, waiting until the little yellow water taxi arrived to return us to our accommodation across the Derwent river, we were joined by two New Zealand fans. "It could have been so much better," one moaned.

Welcome to the club, I thought, although I didn't say it out loud lest it should be regarded as sympathy and give them hope for the battle ahead, against England, 36 hours hence. It appeared now that the contests between our two also-rans would be the only thing to lend the Commonwealth Bank Tri-Series any spice. Although, judging by the Kiwi presence in the ground – seemingly one other man, who clapped long and enthusiastically whenever one of his bowlers delivered a dot ball – and the diminishing presence of England supporters, they would probably be played out in front of the proverbial man and his dog.

I may not have had the dog, but I was determined to be the proverbial man. If we could expose the New Zealanders' soft underbelly – the advance evidence made us look like the owners of a set of six-packs – I could yet experience a feeling so unfamiliar I'd forgotten what it was like: victory.

It was another cloud-free day, so Sue took advantage with some sun worship in the hotel garden, where she watched a series of overweight guests tear themselves away from the slot machines long enough to try to play tennis.

So I called Rod, the owner of the little yellow water taxi, and he soon appeared on the horizon from under the five-lane Tasman Bridge that crossed the bay near its mouth. Rod was an expert on the bridge, especially its tragic history on which he had a detailed file. In 1975, a section of the construction fell onto the *Lake Illawarra*, a ship carrying zinc, after it collided with the bridge in the dark. Seven crewmen perished as the vessel sank and five people died as their cars tumbled into the water. One of his tours would take you over the exact spot of the disaster, where 115ft below, the *Illawara* still lies, a massive slab of concrete on top of it.

Rod was a friendly guy and obviously a natural on the water – a notice inside his oddly-shaped contraption, which you entered through a hatch at the front, read "Born to Fish, Forced to Work," although it didn't seem a bad living. When up to full speed it was a bit unnerving: the back of the boat, which carried about ten people, sat deep in the water while the front pointed disconcertingly skywards. Spread the weight unevenly – five portly blokes on one side of the aisle, five slim girls on the other, and it listed scarily to the side. In such circumstances I would slide along the back row, trying to act as ballast.

I select a spot at the sparsely-populated ground at the front of the Southern Stand, just behind the bowler's arm, feeling strangely confident. This confidence is shattered within two balls, as Brendon McCullum flays Jon Lewis over cover and over the ropes. Six for nought. The fourth ball typifies England incompetence as it is steered aerially off leg stump towards long leg, where James Anderson runs in, is completely flummoxed by the spin as it bounces and watches perplexed as it reroutes around him and crosses the boundary. Now McCullum is all positivity and he steps down the wicket to the last ball of the over and flicks it down to Anderson again, for two. It's 12 for nought from one over. The first wicket, when it comes in the sixth over, is something of a relief; Anderson has McCullum caught at mid-off trying to slam it back over his head.

By the midway point, though, the Kiwis are down to four an over and four men have gone, including Nathan Astle, whose innings of 45 is ended by Paul Collingwood with the help of an enormous inside edge. Collingwood picks up another wicket, Flintoff gets rid of the giant Fulton, now known as "Two-metre Peter" and Monty Panesar's input has claimed another.

With ten overs remaining New Zealand have only three wickets in hand and need 48 just to reach 200. This though is not the thought occupying me most. For some time I have been watching a New Zealand supporter some yards to my right. He is tall, quite stocky, with bushy fair hair and a moustache and every time New Zealand find the middle of the bat, he stands up, waves a huge All Blacks flag in his right hand and a huge national flag in his left, while clutching to his stomach an enormous cuddly Kiwi soft toy.

This is no mean feat. He doesn't eat or drink throughout and his creaseless attire of matching khaki shirt and trousers gives him the look of a scout master in search of a jamboree. Not surprisingly, he's on his own. What's more, I subsequently see him everywhere, mostly at matches I'm not attending. I catch glimpses of him on television in Brisbane, Adelaide, Perth, then in New Zealand when Australia go there for the three matches in the Chappell-Hadlee Trophy; he also pops up at the World Cup months later.

I'm fascinated: who is this man and what is his story? Somebody must know. You can keep your fancy dress Saturdays, your men in drag, your Mexican waves and your attempts to create the longest snake of plastic beer glasses in living memory, this bloke is crazier than them all – barmier than the barmiest member of the Barmy Army.

New Zealand scratch together what I'm convinced is an inadequate 205 and Anderson, after his fielding mishap, has bowled well, picking up four for 42 in his ten overs. There are also two wickets apiece for Flintoff, who has spoken of his intention just to enjoy this series, and Collingwood.

It is great to see Vaughan back at the top of the innings, but this is an important match for both openers: Strauss, after a miserable Test series, is desperately in need of runs. But in the second over Vaughan pushes a single into the leg side and seems to be in trouble, physically. Not the knee, please, not the knee that has kept him out of cricket for two Test series. He stays on, however, and plants a knee, not sure whether it's the injured one, down the track and drives James Franklin through the covers with an elegance that can't be matched by anyone around the world. By the ninth over, however, Jamie Dalrymple has come out as a runner. If Vaughan's going to win this match off his own back, Dalrymple's going to have a lot of running to do. He isn't detained for long, though, as Vaughan, having added another couple of crisp fours, tries his other favourite shot, the pull, and slaps it straight to mid-wicket. By the end of 15 overs, England are 54 for one, comfortable if slow. The 18th over brings more woe for Strauss, however, as he gets an inside edge into his pad, a big one too, but is given out. Soon Jeetan Patel and Daniel Vettori, the experienced left-arm spinner, are in tandem and with the run-rate dropping to 3.39, it's time for that Ian Bell running madness to surface again. He pushes Vettori to point, sets off and Patel's superb direct throw catches Ed Joyce centimetres short.

I move seats, illogically really since my switch from behind the bowler's arm to side-on is hardly likely to force Collingwood and Bell into a rethink of their cautious strategy. At the end of the thirtieth over, England now need 5.4 an over. The spinners have bowled 11 overs between them for just 28 runs. And it's about to get worse as Collingwood's horrible swish off Patel gives a straightforward catch to mid-wicket.

At 98 for four, it's all about Flintoff now, and he starts in laissez-faire fashion by swatting Patel for four over mid-wicket and making it look easy. In fact, mid-wicket, which has proved the Lancastrian's most profitable area throughout the Test series, takes a bashing. Even without the best timing he sends Bond and Patel to the boundary there with sheer force of bat and will.

Patel hits back with a plumb lbw verdict against Bell and for the first time I'm beginning to think we're going to cock this up. English supporters are exchanging nervous glances. I think about jumping off the Tasman Bridge. Yet we still only need 51 off 60 balls, we have five wickets in hand and one of the most feared one-day destroyers at the crease (and I don't mean Paul Nixon). At the beginning of the 45th over, 39 now required after some tight dibbly-dobbers from Craig McMillan, Flintoff gives it the big heave, Ross Taylor gets underneath it at deep mid-wicket, but somehow it just has enough on it to escape the New Zealander's fingertips. The big man is having to take a few more quick singles than is ideal, but it's one of these, scampered off Vettori, that brings him his fifty. McMillan now proves expensive as Flintoff hits down the ground for a couple, gets two more to leg and then, sod it, flat bats across the line and the mid-wicket boundary opens itself up to receive his offering.

Four overs to go, Mark Gillespie returns, a man surprisingly quick for his size and build, 21 runs required. Surely we're safe now. But the fifth ball brings a drama wrapped up in a conundrum. Gillespie delivers it from round the wicket, a full toss that Flintoff aims to swat towards mid-wicket – where else – but he's got a top edge, Taylor's running round, he's underneath and he's caught it. Noooo! Heads in hands, New Zealanders celebrating, Flintoff going. But he isn't. He's standing there. The umpire at square leg is explaining to the bewildered fielders. He's got his arm out. Yes! It's a no-ball, over waist height. Good decision, ump.

Heart rates fall, but only momentarily, because, at the start of the next over, Nixon comes back for two from a mistimed stroke over cover. He's never going to get there. He's out! A mad second run, why didn't he just give Flintoff the strike? Second ball of the penultimate over, Dalrymple goes, caught brilliantly at point by Patel, for one. Five runs needed from ten balls but Jon Lewis can make no ground with the next three balls, one a swing and a miss, as Ian Botham would say. But he makes contact with the final ball, it pierces the infield and they take the run.

Four to win - just one boundary, one lucky swat, an inside edge - and the final over to be bowled by McMillan, yet we have the wrong man on strike. The wrong man slashes the first ball to point: no run. He thuds the second to mid-on and gets the single. Three needed from four. Flintoff picks the next up over the infield for two. Well, at least we've got the tie, I think, and I'll take that if I have to. The fourth ball is struck straight back to McMillan. It's with one ball to spare that we finally do it, Flintoff drives straight, takes the single and we've won. Let me spell that out for you. W-O-N. My, we were awful, but who cares?

The next day, we were scheduled to leave Tasmania. We had tickets for the Australian Open tennis in Melbourne, which would be a nice muscle relaxant after the tension of the cricket, especially because Tim Henman wasn't playing, but as we assembled at the airport, the sight of several English cricket journalists and broadcasters waiting for the following flight to Brisbane made me think again. Nasser Hussain and Mike Atherton were sitting only seats away from us in the departure lounge. I suddenly had this urge to switch flights and revisit the Gabba – Somewhere to Stay, the anarchists who don't do mornings and all – for surely this victory over New Zealand was just the start of things, the launchpad for a series of victories. Australia were next. I was on the whiskey, as ever before a flight, even an early morning one, but surely this wasn't having such an impact on my mental faculties so quickly.

Chemicals can be queer things, but I would need a few more if I was going to get this past Sue. Tennis was more her game and she was desperate to add the Australian Open to her grand-slam experiences of Wimbledon and Flushing Meadow. I slugged back another Johnnie Walker's miniature and began to speak. "Sue?" I said questioningly. "How about we give Melbourne a miss and…" I was cut off in my prime. "Will all passengers on Virgin Blue flight DJ367 to Melbourne please proceed to the gate?" the announcement boomed out. It was too late now. "Come on," said Sue, picking up her hand luggage.

Fate had intervened and, I was to discover, in a good way for once, although our first match at the Vodafone Arena, the equivalent of Wimbledon's Court No 1, seemed ready to stuff Australian sporting excellence down our throats again. Alicia Molik, from Adelaide, had been a quarter-finalist in 2005 and had reached a career-high of No 8 in the world later that year. An ear ailment had since forced her down the rankings, to the low hundreds but The Fanatics, who showed they didn't restrict themselves purely to cricket, were there in abundance, a lake of yellow and green on one side of the arena, and they weren't going to let the fact that Molik's opponent, Patty Schnyder, was the No 8 seed, get them down. "Let's go Molik, let's go," they chanted at regular intervals while between games one person from the group would seemingly take on a dare to do something solo and stupid, like run around the group, plop a yellow lampshade on their head and shout something incomprehensible, action that earned wholehearted applause from their comrades. And there wasn't just that to clap in the first set as Molik dismissed Schnyder 6-3. But from the second set onwards, things began to change and as the Swiss girl hit back, The Fanatics grew quieter, their games less free-spirited, their chants less audible. Molik won only two more games in the match and although I had nothing against her personally, I revelled in the disappointment of her compatriots on the sidelines. I hadn't seen them like this before.

Now, if England could just do something similar in Brisbane tomorrow.

We had tickets for the tennis again, but we weren't over-excited by the schedule: the best of an unappetising bunch of matches offered us a couple of Frenchmen playing each other. That was a dilemma: what do you do when you want both to lose? So we went to the Turf Bar on Queen Street, which had served as a Barmy Army haunt during the Test match. There were screens everywhere, so we could keep an eye on progress at the Aussie Open, while watching a rejuvenated England in Brisbane.

Michael Vaughan's problem had been diagnosed as a tear to a hamstring, so Flintoff had been reinstated as captain and Mal

Loye flown in from club cricket in New Zealand to sweep Australia's fast bowlers into the kind of oblivion he had done so often to English bowlers with his unorthodox style in domestic cricket.

It takes him only four overs to find his range. Brett Lee delivers a 150kph ball on middle stump and Loye is down on his front knee in an instant, heaving the ball over his left shoulder – and long leg – for six. The Australians in the pub rub their eyes in disbelief, but first impressions are that they quite enjoyed it. Two balls later, he stabs the ball over square leg for four more, again off his middle stump. Even better, though, is when McGrath comes into the attack. His first ball is dismissed over mid-wicket, his second, outside off stump in the McGrath corridor of uncertainty, treated with the total disdain of Loye's big sweep. McGrath is chuntering on the walk back to the end of his run, the little shake of the head that is usually the trademark of his displeasure visible.

But at 52 for nought after 11 overs, the inevitable happens. Loye edges a good one from Nathan Bracken and Hayden takes the slip catch. Still, Strauss is playing quite well. McGrath bowls the next over to him and the fourth ball, short of a length, he pulls. But it's not high enough to clear the infield, nor low enough to have mid-wicket stooping. In fact, it's just about the right height to be caught. "He's gone. Oh what a catch!" We hear it before we see it. The camera is not quick enough to pan out but Brad Hodge is getting up with the ball. The replay shows it wasn't close to him, but a spectacular dive has eaten up the air space and the unfortunate England opener has found another way to get out. Four overs later, Ed Joyce goes, an uncomfortable stay ending when he inside edges McGrath to Gilchrist. It's now a slightly uncomfortable 70 for three. Mitchell Johnson comes in to bowl the next over and I experience a sense of déjà vu. Bell guides it down towards gully and sets off, but Collingwood, who has only just taken up residence at the non-striker's end, is unsure. There's to-ing and fro-ing and the batsmen meet in the middle, there's more hesitation as Bell figures which way to run. But there's time to get back, just make up your mind man, because, although Cameron White has dived to his left to stop the ball in the gully, he's fielded it with his right hand; he's in no position to shy at the stumps from there. He doesn't need to though: from his prone position, he tries a back-handed flick at the wicket and, totally unexpectedly, it hits. Bell's headed back but is barely in the picture. It's Adelaide revisited. I do a Victor Meldrew.

"I don't fucking believe it."

It's 71 for four, but Collingwood is frozen to the spot now, a rabbit in McGrath's headlights, and edges the first ball he receives to Gilchrist.

Meldrew is lost for words. Well, ones that have more or fewer than four letters. Sue acts instinctively; she's seen it too many times in the past three months. She drags me off to the Vodafone Arena to watch two Frenchmen do battle. Only one of them loses. Life isn't fair.

Later, much, much later, we find that England made it to 155, thanks to Flintoff and Jamie Dalrymple, before Jon Lewis, with a fine spell of swing bowling, and James Anderson, had reduced Australia to 108 for six themselves. It's not a bad effort in the circumstances, I think, and it's only the stickability of Michael Hussey, supported by Brett Lee, that has seen Australia home. Then, though, I read something that brings my blood pressure back up to Gas Mark 9. Hussey had apparently admitted to James Anderson that he had edged a ball to Paul Nixon when he was on 19, but Daryl Harper, the umpire, had given him not out. "I'm not a walker. I take the good decisions with the bad ones," he is quoted as saying.

Hussey is the Australia hero again two nights later when they sneak past New Zealand after being 17 for three, and that's good news if we want to qualify for the best-of-three finals. As long as we just keep beating the Kiwis. But, chasing a little over 200 again at Adelaide, we don't. We capitulate horribly to be 120 all out and with 12 overs unused. And three days later, on Australia Day, we plumb new depths, reach a nadir – I don't know, I'm running out of clichés to describe it. It's bad though. The Australians may have woken up to the fact that we're a pretty damn demoralised cricket team by now, but the Adelaide public must feel they've been singled out to witness just how low we can go. We're all out for 110, the Aussies knock them off in 24 overs. And the one wicket we get, well, that's a run out. The game is done and dusted in little more than half its allotted running time. It's a day-night game in which they've not had to turn on the lights.

I long for a darkened room.

As the Commonwealth Bank roadshow moves on to Perth, where Australia beat New Zealand by the tightest of margins in a 670-run thriller and New Zealand beat us in less demanding circumstances, we get back on the road ourselves. We have tickets for two more one-dayers, England versus Australia at the Sydney Cricket Ground on February 2 and the second of the finals at the same venue on February 11. That gives us enough time to take what we judge to be the scenic route from Melbourne, so fill up the hired Hyundai to bursting point again and set off. Our first aim is Dandenong - about 30 miles south of Melbourne and not to be confused with the Dandenong Ranges, a set of mountains to the east - where Sue is rumoured to have a cousin that she's never met: Cousin Tony, the butcher. But our search for his shop, Corbett's Cuts, proved fruitless and we carried on along the Princes Highway dodging the logging lorries that made driving more work than play, which is probably how it should be.

It is certainly how it should be as far as the Australian road authorities are concerned: signs every couple of miles remind you of your mortality. *STOP, REVIVE, SURVIVE* they tell you, or *MICROSLEEPS KILL*, and, most disturbingly, should you feel compelled to drive up the wrong side of a dual carriageway, *WRONG WAY! GO BACK!* Just how many pissed up Australians have done this for such a warning to be necessary I don't know.

In fact, the Australian obsession with safety seems completely at odds with its evolution, as a land and as a people. It has many of the most dangerous creatures on earth – yet most of them, it seems, are operating Sydney's buses: a radio report informed us that the same 31 drivers were responsible for more than 1,000 accidents in the city. Some retraining might be called for.

And at the SCG, you can't stand up without being reminded of the hazards of sitting down again: the electronic scoreboard regularly flashes up prompts to inform you that you are in the precarious presence of flip-up seats. Even more alarming, notices at the front of the stands warn you of the risk of being hit by balls. What, at a cricket ground? How in the name of Dame Edna Everage did the Aussies tame this perilous place?

We motored on, remembering to stay awake and not go the wrong way along dual carriageways, passing possible places to stop for the night, then opting to push on further, almost certainly to Lakes Entrance, a popular tourist town and fishing port. Until Sue, delving deep into our guide book, spotted an attractive alternative. "The unhurried charm of Metung," said our *Lonely Planet*, "is contagious. This picturesque village on Bancroft Bay has a shoreline dotted with jetties and small wooden craft."

And a population of 519. That clinched it. We needed some real peace and we found it, at the end of a long, winding waterside road. In fact, as we arrived in the late afternoon sunshine, it was decidedly sleepy. We found some two-storey motel-style chalets at the end of the peninsula where we could drive no further and, after doing some quick financial calculations, I sent Sue into the small shop serving as a reception area to haggle over price. The owner of the resort, The Moorings, showed us three first-floor apartments, each better than the other in size and comfort and each with a view out over Lake King. We were tempted by the first until we saw the second and the second seemed perfect until we viewed the third. We settled on the second – the one-bedroom apartment – and while Sue unpacked her bag (we had almost immediately decided this was too good a place not to stay for an extra day) I tried to catch up on the news from the Waca with the rare luxuries of a comfy sofa, a widescreen TV and air-conditioning.

Later, we walked about 100 yards into the main part of the village and found Marrillee, a pleasant restaurant where you could dine al fresco – the other one, Mosaic, seemed to be up for sale and was closed – and then wandered back in the twilight to take some sunset snaps. Heading out to the edge of the lake was something of a minor mystical experience. The water was almost transcendentally calm, and black swans glided, as black swans should, smoothly across it. It was utterly quiet. We listened to it: the sound of silence.

"This is one of those moments," I said to Sue.

"One of what moments?"

"You know, one of those moments," I replied, but by talking about it I had broken the spell.

"You know," I continued as we walked back to sit on our surprisingly spacious balcony, "like Ferris Bueller says: 'Life moves pretty fast. If you don't stop and look around once in a while, you could miss it.'"

"Who's Ferris Bueller?" said Sue.

After a boat trip to Lakes Entrance, where we saw trawlers surfing in through the narrow mouth from which sand had been dredged to allow access to the inland waterways – no small act of skill – we continued our journey east, travelling more or less parallel to the Victorian south coast. Shortly after Cann River, a tiny town that provides access to Point Hicks, the first land on the east coast to be sighted by Europeans, we began to turn north, passing Genoa, the last village before you cross into New South Wales. Then it was onwards and upwards, incorporating a stop at Eden – claimed to be the halfway point between Melbourne and Sydney - because it sounded nice, and it was. We sat on a bench across the road from a beach and stared out at the sea, a beautiful panorama, augmented by the sight of the odd jogger and dog walker making use of it. I learned later that in the 1920s, a pod of killer whales, which as everyone knows are the largest species of the dolphin family, used to rat on their sea-going brethren, hunting whales and herding them into nearby Twofold Bay. While the whalers, on whose industry the town had been built, picked up the blubber, the killer whales fed on their lips and tongue. Mmm, nice.

We stopped overnight at Bateman's Bay, in a motel on the seafront. In the morning, as we prepared for the last leg of the journey I sat outside while Sue got ready and watched as a dolphin leaped out of the water maybe forty feet away and vanished as quickly as he'd appeared. I called Sue but she was too late and I'm not sure whether she believed me.

It was good to be back in Sydney; we had found a hotel in Randwick, not too far from the cricket ground and, peering from our 'balcony' – it had a door leading out on to it but was so small anyone trying to stand on it would have immediately toppled five floors to their death – we could see the Harbour Bridge to the left and the sea to the right. It was a room with a view. Sort of. The next day, match No 10 was upon us. Lose this and we could almost certainly say goodbye to our chances of making the final.

It is a steamy afternoon at the SCG as we take our position in Bay 22, in front of Yabba's Hill. "We'll have a bat," says Flintoff to Mark Nicholas as the replay screens broadcast the toss, and most of Australia groans. England's batting has been so bad in the preceding matches that no one is putting bets on having to use the floodlights. "The trouble with England," remarks an Australian in front of us, "is they get to 87 for one, then they're all out for 110." I think that is giving us more credit than we're due.

Both teams have made changes, some enforced, some not: Brett Lee is rested as Australia give Shaun Tait a chance to claim a World Cup place and Ponting sits this one out with a hip strain, making room for Brad Hodge. Ravi Bopara gets an international debut with Paul Collingwood ill, the erratic Sajid Mahmood comes in as James Anderson flies home with back trouble and England choose to push Ed Joyce up the order to open with Mal Loye, while Strauss drops down to No 5.

It's a predictably sluggish start and after receiving 14 balls, Loye has yet to entertain us with his slog sweep; he hasn't even hit a four. Joyce has found the ropes once but then gone into his shell and after 5.1 overs we are 17 for nought. Nathan Bracken bowls the second ball of his over to Joyce, who, sensing a little urgency is required, runs down the wicket, carving grotesquely towards wide third man. Tait moves round and takes up the perfect position as the ball sails towards him, but it plops into his hands and straight out again. It is an absolute dolly and an unbelievable let off. Can England take advantage? It seems so, for three balls later, Loye unfurls his trademark shot and it's a huge six, well beyond Tait. Bracken's next over costs 12 and England are on their way, 57 for nought from ten when McGrath finds his way into the attack. Fifth ball, he nobbles Loye. The Lancashire batsman thinks he's picked the right ball to sweep but top-edges the ball into the grille of his helmet. He's cut his chin and the physio runs on with an icepack, which he presses to the batsman's cheek. After a long delay, Loye decides he is fit to continue, McGrath decides to bounce him and the resultant hook ends up in the hands of deep square-leg.

England pass the 87 for one barrier in the eighteenth over and Joyce, now more settled, and Ian Bell are batting serenely. We pass 100, still for only one wicket, then 150. We are in uncharted territory. Joyce reaches his fifty, Bell joins him and it is 169 for one when McGrath comes back and removes the Warwickshire man with his first ball. Flintoff wants a piece of the run party, so comes in at No 4 but the score has advanced by only seven when he is lbw to the non-spinning leg-spinner Cameron White. The collapse is on again. But Strauss is rejuvenated at No 5, banging his first ball for four, and adding 46 with Joyce in quick time before failing badly with his attempt to scoop sweep Bracken.

Joyce gets to an excellent hundred, forgetting his early rush of blood, and Jamie Dalrymple and Liam Plunkett boost England's final total to 292 for seven. Unforeseen riches, but I still expect Australia to chase it down without too much ado.

Plunkett must be so pleased with reaching double figures that he starts the Australia innings with his tail up: from round the wicket, he delivers a full, pacy number which swings desperately late through Adam Gilchrist's defence and splatters his stumps. One ball, Australia nought for one. Hodge is in earlier than he would have expected and gets off the mark but Sajid Mahmood picks up where Plunkett leaves off and as the Victorian tries to leave his second delivery, it catches the bottom edge of his bat and cannons on to his wicket. It's 45 for three when Michael Clarke chases a wide one from Plunkett, can hardly lay a bat on it but does just enough to edge it through to Nixon.

However, Matthew Hayden and his partner in big-game brutality, Andrew Symonds, remain undisturbed and add a hasty 71 in just over eight overs. They are 116 for four at almost six an over when Hayden goes, flashing a Mahmood half-volley to Dalrymple at short extra cover.

If that's a huge boon, what comes next is even better, although I feel a lesser man for admitting it. Symonds has carved one through point a little earlier and seems to have done himself a mischief. He's flexing a bicep as if that's what's causing the pain and after a discussion with the physio, he retires hurt. Two things here: if he's going off, it must really smart something rotten, and this is a man who could probably beat us with one bicep anyway.

Nevertheless, the natives are restless, especially when Ravi Bopara, in his second over in international cricket, forces Michael Hussey to chop the ball on to the stumps. The non-walker has to go. Is this the sound of triumphalism you hear in my voice? Yes. It. Bloody. Well. Is.

The Australian crowd respond the only way they know how: they ignore what's going on on the pitch and try to start a Mexican Wave. This is a risky procedure because, officially, it's been banned. Cricket Australia has announced a zero-tolerance approach to the manoeuvre and the state police have promised to evict anyone spotted starting it. This is a strategy doomed to failure, as they haven't the manpower to enforce it, and one that is plain unjust, the cops plucking hapless individuals from the crowd at random. One Australian a few rows in front of us, whose capacity to get blindingly drunk on light beer has amazed the more sober in the vicinity, gets away with his shenanigans despite continuously getting up on to his seat, facing away from the cricket and conducting the countdown to the wave. Another nearby, though, is less fortunate and is dragged away shortly after starting to tuck into a hot pizza. It's a sad sight to behold, his pitiful attempts to bite another chunk from his deep-pan ham and pineapple as he is hauled away by a posse of blue uniforms just adding to the tragedy.

Earlier, in another of the bizarre rules forced on the unsuspecting public, Sue has gone to buy a beer and is ordered to remove her sunglasses to prove she is not intoxicated and a well-behaved England fan close to us returns from a similar foray empty-handed after being told he can't buy alcohol without a shirt on.

Still, let us not dwell on the negative, Australia have folded to 200 all out, Plunkett has taken three for 24 and we've beaten them by a massive 92 runs. You might want to read that sentence again. Now all we need is for Australia to maintain their winning run against New Zealand in match 11 and for us to beat the Kiwis in match 12. Not much to ask, is it?

As it happens, it isn't. Australia wrap up a five-wicket win in Melbourne and in Brisbane, in the winner-takes-all match, England contrive a 14-run victory as New Zealand, needing 88 to win off the last 16 overs with seven wickets in hand, totally lose their bearings. Michael Vaughan, back as captain and despite a first-ball duck, is instrumental in the victory, switching his bowlers superbly and inviting his opponents to self-destruct, which they do nicely amid Stephen Fleming's 106.

So, bizarrely and by a circuitous route, we're in the finals. We talk about flying up to Melbourne for the first, but by now we're nicely ensconced in a hotel opposite Bondi Beach. We enjoy simple pleasures, strolling to neighbouring beaches, sipping fruit smoothies – the Stress Buster, extra ginseng, was a favourite I recall – and reading by the rooftop pool. We even popped into the city for a walk round the Botanical Gardens. In a sense we were winding down – we were due to fly home on February 16 – but we were also gathering strength, building up as it were, to one last challenge.

It is an incongruous setting, sitting cross legged on the bed, the crashing surf of Bondi and the connected human activity going on outside the window, while our main concentration is on Channel 9 and events at the MCG – or simply the G, as I've recently found out it's known to locals. Vaughanie has aggravated his hammy and is to fly home, so it's all eyes on Flintoff again. For the first 30 overs, what we witness is not pretty, a second-innings partnership of 138 in 24 overs giving Australia the perfect launchpad for a 300-plus score. Double what you have after 30 overs, the pros say, so that means the hosts are on course to hit 340. But then Monty Panesar drops one short, Ponting rocks back and creams it and Paul Collingwood plucks it out of the air at short cover. It's a rare occasion when Ponting misses out like that. He could have hit it to any point of the MCG compass but his map-reading skills are askew. Within three overs, Matthew Hayden has gone too, Jamie Dalrymple, an off spinner who approaches the wicket as if he's rocking a cradle, luring him into a big shot to long-on. With Collingwood on fire in the field, effecting the run-outs of Michael Clarke and Brett Lee, Australia do a very passable impression of England, tumbling to 252 all out and committing the cardinal sin of failing to bat out their overs.

Now 252. That's do-able. But is it do-able by us? I'm desperate to see the start of the England reply, but Sue is in need of food, so we slip out for a quick meal at a nearby café. I gulp down a lasagne but Sue is lingering over a glass of wine. "Come on, get it down your neck," I prod. "They'll be about seven for three by the time we get back." I'm not far wrong: it's 15 for three. Mal Loye's gone for a duck, Ed Joyce has gone for six and Andrew Strauss has lasted two balls. Paul Collingwood scored an important hundred in the last match against New Zealand, so we can't expect him to do it again. But the artisan of this England side doesn't live by the law of averages and starts to craft something from the misshapen mess his side is in. In this he is joined by the more expressive Ian Bell, who is aided by a craven drop of a sitter by Glenn McGrath, celebrating his 37th birthday, at square leg when he only has 18. It would have been 33 for four and no way back. Even with this let-off England remain in consolidation mode, and after 18 overs are well behind the required rate, which has risen to 6.15 an over. As if sensing it's now or never, the pair begin to press. McGrath goes for eight and Shane Watson, surely the weak link in this attack, for 13. Collingwood's brave gamble, walking down the pitch to hammer a straight six off McGrath in the next over, pays off and the over costs 12. By halfway, England have reached 111, reduced the run rate required to 5.68, Collingwood has his fifty and Bell is not far behind. Seven overs later, Bell is lost, Brett Lee's inswinging yorker – reverse swing someone suggests – doing the necessary. We need more than six an over again and with Flintoff needing to atune, the rate rises to seven by the end of the 37th over. It's time for some humpty, as Ian Botham might say. Flintoff runs the equation through his mind as Brad Hogg turns to bowl: Left-arm spinner + a bit of additional flight + enormous bottom-handed biff = six wide of long-on. His calculation is premeditated but precise and he adds two more twos and Paul Collingwood a couple of singles to reduce the asking rate by half a run in the space of an over. With ten overs to go, we need 64 from 60 balls, so gettable I'm on the end of the bed now, fidgeting.

Collingwood brings up a brilliant hundred in the 45th over, the fact that he has hit only four fours and a six testament to his extraordinary work ethic and optimism but in the next he loses his partner. Only 31 is needed off 29 balls when Flintoff edges a pull off Watson through to the wicketkeeper. This is not an ideal position for Dalrymple and his run-out is the last thing we want. Nixon emerges from the pavilion. Not the Australians' favourite Englishman and now it's looking tough. Three overs, 25 runs, four wickets is what it has boiled down to, but Watson shows his nerves, a full toss and a slower ball enabling Collingwood to sweep successive boundaries. Singles off the next four balls leave England 12 short with two to go. McGrath comes back for a final fling and concedes four from four before Collingwood drills him down the ground for four more; stunning. Bracken bowls the last, Nixon, with his bottom-handed whip through mid-wicket grabs two and a chip to mid-on brings the scores level. We've got it now, it's in the bag. Collingwood, fittingly, scores the winning run and the cameras bring us pictures of pandemonium on the pitch and outside the England dressing-room.

I'm leaping around the room wishing I'd been there but happy that, whatever happens on Sunday, we can't lose the series then. When I calm down I start to consider the logistics: if we don't win on Sunday, it goes to a decider. In Adelaide. It will probably cost us another $500 between us to get down there and back. And it's Adelaide, a name to strike terror into the heart of any Englishman after the events of the past three months. How has a place of such beauty turned into a byword for disaster?

No, it's no good. It's Sydney or bust. If England can't do it on Sunday, they don't deserve my support in Adelaide.

We have to move hotels again in the day between the two finals, so it's off back to King's Cross after a morning sitting on the steps at Bondi watching the various life-saving clubs in the vicinity compete on the beach: sprints and relays on the sand, team surfboat races and kayaking are among the disciplines and the combative element of Australian sport is on display, no less among the veterans than in those at the peak of fitness. Everyone wants to win, so badly it almost hurts; no quarter is given. Perhaps that's endemic in Australian society. It takes me back to an extraordinary scene I witnessed while riding the bus to the SCG during the Test match. Two middle-aged but able-bodied women had settled into seats set aside for the elderly or infirm. I was at the back of the bus but I noticed a disturbance at the front after it stopped to pick up another passenger. This new passenger, it emerged, was blind, unable to find her way safely down a rocking bus without aid and had asked the other two to move. They had refused and it was left to an elderly man to give up his seat and head down towards me, muttering. They breed them hard here, I thought. With that kind of intransigence no wonder we couldn't win a Test match.

And so, it's down to the SCG one more time, a day-night

match, scorching again but with the threat of showers as the day wears on. Better bat first if we get the chance. We do, and get off to a reasonable start, 79 for two from 18 when Loye is run out, courtesy of more indecision from Bell, but soon it's 86 for three when Strauss fails again – he's one man who must be desperate to get home – and 112 for four at halfway when Bell is caught short of his ground, the third execrable run out of the tour involving he and Paul Collingwood, who really should get together in the dressing-room and discuss their differences. Still, it gives Collingwood the opportunity to be a hero again, and one he doesn't miss. His usual sensible batting rubs off on his captain and the pair have added 97 when Flintoff, on 42 from 50 balls, is brilliantly caught and bowled by Lee. Collingwood battles on to 70, with only two fours and Dalrymple completes a trio of ridiculous run-outs in a mix-up with Nixon.

We've made 246 for eight, 46 short of our total eight days ago and I can't see Australia having too much difficulty with that. And there's no miraculous start for England's bowlers this time, Plunkett and Mahmood conceding 25 from their first three overs. But with the first ball of the fourth Mahmood strikes, Hayden going to that loose drive to short extra again. The ball, though, is beginning to swing extravagantly and Plunkett is shaping it away, pitching it full, bringing Ponting forward, tempting the drive. We have a marvellous view of the movement from close to the sightscreen at the Randwick End and I get a sense, just a sense, that Plunkett's got him where he wants him. Sure enough, two balls into the fifth over, Ponting pushes too hard, it clips the edge in perfect accordance with the laws of physics, and Strauss rolls to his left to take a low catch.

But the clouds, big, black, bulky ones, are approaching from over the Messenger and Bill O'Reilly Stands. When the rain comes it's sudden and hard and, because everyone is trying to get out of the same exit at the same time, there is chaos. By the time we reach shelter we are soaked through. While Sue, prepared for all eventualities, nips off to the ladies' to change, I stand dripping miserably and peering up the steps to the blackened sky, against which, under the floodlights, the downpour seems to be setting in. Six overs doesn't constitute a match. This could be going to Adelaide after all.

Suddenly, I remember the grey sweatshirt I have in my bag, bought in desperation for a chilly trip to Phillip Island, south of Melbourne, where tiny penguins emerge from the sea en masse as darkness falls and return to feed their young after a day's fishing. I strip off my sopping shirt and put it on. It is to make me a marked man.

When the skies clear and the drying rope has been trailed round the outfield, play resumes. And how. It's Plunkett again, from round the wicket, and that late swing, in through the gate and Gilchrist's gone. Three balls later, he runs the ball away from Brad Hodge, who edges, and Collingwood of all people, at second slip, can't hang on. Hodge takes the run, exposing Michael Clarke and after a ball of watchful defence, Plunkett does it again, less movement, a thinner edge and Nixon throws it skyward. This is unbelievable, beyond wild dreams and I can't contain myself. I've had a bellyful of Australian gloating and now it's my turn. I jump to my feet, spin round and point at the Australians all around me. One, in his 50s, doesn't like it and signals for me to be reseated. It's 45 for four from eight overs. The eleventh, Plunkett's sixth, goes for 12 runs as Australia launch a counter-attack, Hodge smashing three fours, two that fizz through mid-wicket and another through the covers. The Durham fast bowler has picked up three crucial wickets but he's going at eight an over; that seems like the end of his spell as he is sent to long-off at the beginning of Flintoff's second over.

A group of Australians a few rows behind me are beginning to get mouthy. "Plunkett's a wanker," they chime up, almost insensible from the booze.

"What do you mean," I turn and shout back. "He's just got three wickets."

They seem taken aback by my intervention and change tack. "Flintoff's a wanker," they chant and with immaculate timing the England captain pushes one a little wider to Hussey, who, runless after ten balls, swings wildly and carves straight to the only slip.

I'm up again, pointing, clenching my fists, pumping them in the direction of the Neanderthals. This, they notice. I swear I can hear their brains ticking over as they think of a comeback. "Oh, grey shirt," one sings, finding nothing about me immediately arresting enough at which to direct their ire apart from my clothing.

But this opens up a germ of an idea in another and I have to admit it hits home. "Grey shirt, grey hair, grey man, grey country," he hollers and the Australians around me, not just his group, roll around in the aisles. That's harsh. The shirt, the man and the country I can take, but the hair? It's not like I'm completely grey. There's a bit around the edges I grant you, but Sue says it makes me look distinguished. Is she fibbing? Comments like that could give me a complex.

After 16.2 overs, the rain begins to fall again on my silvery locks and there's a further delay. This is not good. Adelaide is still lurking on the horizon. For goodness' sake, we only need to bowl another 3.4 overs for the game to count. The covers rumble on.

The resumption brings an updated Duckworth/Lewis ruling. Australia need another 147 runs from 24 overs, not out of the question, but there's still weather around. Watson spanks Panesar for a six over long-on and edges a four next ball at the start of the nineteenth over. By the time twentieth has been and gone Australia need another 109 from 13 overs. Adelaide is receding. Paul Collingwood replaces Panesar at the Paddington End and the last ball of his over confirms this. Watson slashes it uppishly towards backward point, it's travelling and it's way to his left. But this is going to be England's day, the players are beginning to believe it now and I'm sure Dalrymple, his thoughts processing at the speed of light, thinks; "Why not? I'll have a go." And off he flies, parallel to the turf, with the athleticism and extension of a high-jumper performing the Fosbury Flop. He cuts off the ball with his left hand, three or four feet from the ground, and it sticks. It is a breathtaking catch. The best I have ever seen, any time, any place, anywhere.

Australians are flocking to the exits, more so when Hogg and Hodge go, the latter a run short of a deserved fifty. Even my tormentors have disappeared, tiring of shouting "grey shirt" at my back and at 152 for eight, Australia still need 60 from 36 runs when the rain comes again.

We turn from our seats five rows back in Bay 26 and scarper for the cover of the overhanging Churchill Stand, eschewing celebration for shelter. I would have been happy to remain singing in the rain, revelling in the Australian spectators' unfamiliar experience of the shock of defeat but Sue was leading me towards the exit. As we leave the ground we hear the announcement that England have won the game by 34 runs, and with it the Commonwealth Bank series. As we reach the bus stop, Paul Nixon is probably throwing himself into a small group of England supporters, but this, if I remember correctly, is where we came in…

Commonwelath Bank Series - 2nd match

Australia v New Zealand

Played at Bellerive Oval, Hobart, on 14 January 2007 (50-over match)
Result Australia won by 105 runs

Australia innings (50 overs maximum)		R	M	B	SR
✝AC Gilchrist	lbw b Patel	61	78	58	105.17
ML Hayden	c ✝McCullum b Gillespie	27	58	39	69.23
✱RT Ponting	c Fleming b Gillespie	10	41	22	45.45
MJ Clarke	c Astle b Bond	33	58	52	63.46
A Symonds	c ✝McCullum b Bond	69	109	70	98.57
MEK Hussey	c sub (HJH Marshall) b McMillan	20	33	32	62.50
CL White	c McMillan b Bond	45	36	32	140.62
MG Johnson	not out	2	5	1	200.00
NW Bracken	b Bond	0	1	1	0.00
SR Clark	not out	1	1	1	100.00
Extras	(lb 7, w 6, nb 8)	21			
Total	**(8 wickets; 50 overs; 214 mins)**	289 (5.78 runs per over)			

Did not bat BW Hilfenhaus
Fall of wickets 1-83 (Hayden, 13.2 ov), 2-104 (Gilchrist, 16.5 ov), 3-117 (Ponting, 21.5 ov), 4-164 (Clarke, 31.4 ov), 5-196 (Hussey, 40.2 ov), 6-286 (White, 49.2 ov), 7-286 (Symonds, 49.3 ov), 8-286 (Bracken, 49.4 ov)

Bowling	O	M	R	W	Econ	
JEC Franklin	4	0	31	0	7.75	(2nb, 1w)
SE Bond	10	0	61	4	6.10	(2nb, 4w)
MR Gillespie	10	2	50	2	5.00	(2nb)
JS Patel	10	0	64	1	6.40	(1nb)
DL Vettori	10	1	48	0	4.80	(1nb, 1w)
NJ Astle	4	0	18	0	4.50	
CD McMillan	2	0	10	1	5.00	

New Zealand innings (target: 290 runs from 50 overs)		R	M	B	SR
✝BB McCullum	lbw b Hilfenhaus	5	15	16	31.25
NJ Astle	c ✝Gilchrist b Bracken	0	8	3	0.00
✱SP Fleming	c Hussey b Johnson	29	73	47	61.70
RL Taylor	c ✝Gilchrist b Johnson	84	114	82	102.43
PG Fulton	c Symonds b Clark	37	59	44	84.09
CD McMillan	run out (Clarke)	2	6	7	28.57
DL Vettori	c Hayden b Clark	1	14	5	20.00
JEC Franklin	c Clarke b White	6	18	13	46.15
SE Bond	b Symonds	2	5	5	40.00
MR Gillespie	not out	4	7	4	100.00
JS Patel	c Hilfenhaus b Symonds	4	4	5	80.00
Extras	(lb 3, w 7)	10			
Total	**(all out; 38.3 overs; 166 mins)**	184 (4.77 runs per over)			

Fall of wickets 1-5 (Astle, 2.2 ov), 2-7 (McCullum, 3.6 ov), 3-80 (Fleming, 19.3 ov), 4-161 (Taylor, 31.1 ov), 5-165 (McMillan, 32.4 ov), 6-166 (Fulton, 33.2 ov), 7-171 (Vettori, 35.3 ov), 8-175 (Bond, 36.5 ov), 9-175 (Franklin, 37.1 ov), 10-184 (Patel, 38.3 ov)

Bowling	O	M	R	W	Econ	
NW Bracken	7	0	25	1	3.57	
BW Hilfenhaus	7	1	26	1	3.71	(1w)
MG Johnson	7	0	27	2	3.85	(2w)
SR Clark	8	0	40	2	5.00	
A Symonds	6.3	0	41	2	6.30	(3w)
CL White	3	0	22	1	7.33	(1w)

Toss Australia, who chose to bat first

Commonwelath Bank Series - 3rd match

England v New Zealand

Played at Bellerive Oval, Hobart, on 16 January 2007 (50-over match)
Result England won by 3 wickets (with 1 ball remaining)

New Zealand innings (50 overs maximum)		R	M	B	SR
✠BB McCullum	c Vaughan b Anderson	16	28	15	106.66
NJ Astle	b Collingwood	45	106	63	71.42
✱SP Fleming	b Anderson	12	39	29	41.37
RL Taylor	c Vaughan b Anderson	1	5	7	14.28
PG Fulton	c Vaughan b Flintoff	27	65	52	51.92
CD McMillan	c & b Collingwood	22	59	40	55.00
DL Vettori	lbw b Panesar	11	21	17	64.70
JEC Franklin	c Collingwood b Flintoff	20	45	30	66.66
SE Bond	not out	22	57	37	59.45
MR Gillespie	b Anderson	10	15	10	100.00
Extras	(lb 9, w 10)	19			
Total	**(9 wickets; 50 overs; 221 mins)**	**205 (4.10 runs per over)**			

Did not bat JS Patel

Fall of wickets 1-26 (McCullum, 5.3 ov), 2-61 (Fleming, 13.6 ov), 3-67 (Taylor, 15.4 ov), 4-97 (Astle, 23.4 ov), 5-127 (Fulton, 32.1 ov), 6-144 (Vettori, 36.4 ov), 7-146 (McMillan, 37.2 ov), 8-185 (Franklin, 46.4 ov), 9-205 (Gillespie, 49.6 ov)

Bowling	O	M	R	W	Econ	
J Lewis	9	0	51	0	5.66	(1w)
JM Anderson	10	0	42	4	4.20	(3w)
A Flintoff	10	1	37	2	3.70	(2w)
MS Panesar	10	0	36	1	3.60	(1w)
PD Collingwood	10	1	25	2	2.50	
JWM Dalrymple	1	0	5	0	5.00	

England innings (target: 206 runs from 50 overs)		R	M	B	SR
AJ Strauss	lbw b Franklin	28	79	58	48.27
✱MP Vaughan	c Taylor b Franklin	17	49	29	58.62
IR Bell	lbw b Patel	45	112	72	62.50
EC Joyce	run out (Patel)	5	29	19	26.31
PD Collingwood	c Taylor b Patel	10	22	21	47.61
A Flintoff	not out	72	101	75	96.00
✠PA Nixon	run out (Vettori/ ✠McCullum)	15	57	22	68.18
JWM Dalrymple	c Patel b Gillespie	1	3	5	20.00
J Lewis	not out	2	9	6	33.33
Extras	(b 1, w 2, nb 8)	11			
Total	**(7 wickets; 49.5 overs; 224 mins)**	**206 (4.13 runs per over)**			

Did not bat MS Panesar, JM Anderson

Fall of wickets 1-39 (Vaughan, 11.5 ov), 2-62 (Strauss, 17.3 ov), 3-79 (Joyce, 23.5 ov), 4-98 (Collingwood, 30.2 ov), 5-138 (Bell, 36.5 ov), 6-198 (Nixon, 47.1 ov), 7-201 (Dalrymple, 48.2 ov)

Bowling	O	M	R	W	Econ	
JEC Franklin	9	1	34	2	3.77	
SE Bond	8	0	29	0	3.62	(2nb, 2w)
MR Gillespie	6	0	40	1	6.66	(5nb)
NJ Astle	2	0	4	0	2.00	
JS Patel	10	1	34	2	3.40	(1nb)
DL Vettori	10	0	42	0	4.20	
CD McMillan	4.5	0	22	0	4.55	

Toss New Zealand, who chose to bat first

Commonwealth Bank Series - 10th match

Australia v England

Played at Sydney Cricket Ground on 2 February 2007 - day/night (50-over match)
Result England won by 92 runs

England innings (50 overs maximum)		R	M	B	SR
EC Joyce	c Bracken b Tait	107	201	142	75.35
MB Loye	c Bracken b McGrath	29	52	33	87.87
IR Bell	c Gilchrist b McGrath	51	96	60	85.00
✳ A Flintoff	lbw b White	3	12	10	30.00
AJ Strauss	c Clark b Bracken	26	25	24	108.33
JWM Dalrymple	run out (Clarke/ ✟Gilchrist)	30	27	18	166.66
✟PA Nixon	c Hodge b Tait	4	3	2	200.00
RS Bopara	not out	7	14	5	140.00
LE Plunkett	not out	10	8	7	142.85
Extras	(lb 5, w 19, nb 1)	25			
Total	**(7 wickets; 50 overs; 219 mins)**	**292 (5.84 runs per over)**			

Did not bat SI Mahmood, MS Panesar
Fall of wickets 1-58 (Loye, 10.6 ov), 2-169 (Bell, 33.1 ov), 3-179 (Flintoff, 36.4 ov), 4-222 (Strauss, 42.3 ov), 5-256 (Joyce, 46.2 ov), 6-261 (Nixon, 46.6 ov), 7-274 (Dalrymple, 47.6 ov)

Bowling	O	M	R	W	Econ	
SW Tait	10	0	68	2	6.80	(5w)
NW Bracken	9	1	53	1	5.88	(2w)
SR Clark	10	0	55	0	5.50	(1w)
GD McGrath	10	0	51	2	5.10	(1nb, 2w)
MJ Clarke	4	0	18	0	4.50	
A Symonds	2	0	16	0	8.00	
CL White	5	1	26	1	5.20	(3w)

Australia innings (target: 293 runs from 50 overs)		R	M	B	SR
✳ ✟AC Gilchrist	b Plunkett	0	1	1	0.00
ML Hayden	c Dalrymple b Mahmood	51	103	62	82.25
BJ Hodge	b Mahmood	1	8	6	16.66
MJ Clarke	c ✟Nixon b Plunkett	18	47	29	62.06
A Symonds	retired hurt	39	64	35	111.42
MEK Hussey	b Bopara	6	20	14	42.85
CL White	c ✟Nixon b Flintoff	13	25	20	65.00
NW Bracken	b Panesar	21	34	26	80.76
SR Clark	not out	15	10	23	65.21
GD McGrath	lbw b Plunkett	1	10	7	14.28
SW Tait	run out (Bell)	11	6	10	110.00
Extras	(lb 8, w 16)	24			
Total	**(all out; 38.5 overs; 168 mins)**	**200 (5.15 runs per over)**			

Fall of wickets 1-0 (Gilchrist, 0.1 ov), 2-4 (Hodge, 1.2 ov), 3-45 (Clarke, 12.2 ov), 4-116 (Hayden, 20.4 ov), 4-130* (Symonds, retired not out), 5-137 (Hussey, 24.4 ov), 6-160 (White, 30.1 ov), 7-180 (Bracken, 33.6 ov), 8-187 (McGrath, 36.3 ov), 9-200 (Tait, 38.5 ov)

Bowling	O	M	R	W	Econ	
LE Plunkett	9.5	1	24	3	2.44	(6w)
SI Mahmood	7	0	38	2	5.42	(4w)
A Flintoff	8	0	47	1	5.87	(1w)
MS Panesar	10	0	64	1	6.40	
RS Bopara	4	0	19	1	4.75	(1w)

Toss England, who chose to bat first

Commonwealth Bank Series - 2nd Final

Australia v England

Played at Sydney Cricket Ground on 11 February 2007 - day/night (50-over match)
Result England won by 34 runs (D/L method)

England innings (50 overs maximum)		R	M	B	SR
EC Joyce	c Hodge b McGrath	15	37	27	55.55
MB Loye	run out (Hayden)	45	85	61	73.77
IR Bell	run out (Hussey)	26	84	45	57.77
AJ Strauss	c ✝Gilchrist b Bracken	6	6	5	120.00
PD Collingwood	c ✝ Gilchrist b Bracken	70	119	90	77.77
✳ A Flintoff	c & b Lee	42	71	50	84.00
JWM Dalrymple	run out (Hodge/ ✝Gilchrist)	5	21	10	50.00
✝PA Nixon	c Hodge b McGrath	6	13	7	85.71
LE Plunkett	not out	8	9	10	80.00
Extras	(b 5, lb 4, w 9, nb 5)	23			
Total	**(8 wickets; 50 overs; 226 mins)**	**246 (4.92 runs per over)**			

Did not bat SI Mahmood, MS Panesar
Fall of wickets 1-34 (Joyce, 8.1 ov), 2-79 (Loye, 18.3 ov), 3-86 (Strauss, 19.3 ov), 4-112 (Bell, 25.4 ov), 5-209 (Flintoff, 42.6 ov), 6-231 (Collingwood, 46.6 ov), 7-233 (Dalrymple, 47.3 ov), 8-246 (Nixon, 49.6 ov)

Bowling	O	M	R	W	Econ	
B Lee	10	0	53	1	5.30	(5nb, 2w)
NW Bracken	10	1	38	2	3.80	
GD McGrath	10	0	41	2	4.10	
SR Watson	8	0	46	0	5.75	(2w)
MEK Hussey	2	0	12	0	6.00	(2w)
GB Hogg	10	0	47	0	4.70	(3w)

Australia innings (target: 187 runs from 27 overs)		R	M	B	SR
✝AC Gilchrist	b Plunkett	20	36	17	117.64
ML Hayden	c Collingwood b Mahmood	5	16	9	55.55
✳RT Ponting	c Strauss b Plunkett	7	6	6	116.66
MJ Clarke	c ✝Nixon b Plunkett	0	17	9	0.00
BJ Hodge	c Bell b Dalrymple	49	85	46	106.52
MEK Hussey	c Strauss b Flintoff	0	18	10	0.00
SR Watson	c Dalrymple b Collingwood	37	37	44	84.09
GB Hogg	c Flintoff b Collingwood	10	17	14	71.42
B Lee	not out	10	15	7	142.85
NW Bracken	not out	3	5	3	100.00
Extras	(lb 2, w 6, nb 3)	11			
Total	**(8 wickets; 27 overs; 126 mins)**	**152 (5.62 runs per over)**			

Did not bat GD McGrath
Fall of wickets 1-25 (Hayden, 3.1 ov), 2-33 (Ponting, 4.2 ov), 3-39 (Gilchrist, 6.1 ov), 4-40 (Clarke, 6.6 ov), 5-63 (Hussey, 11.2 ov), 6-109 (Watson, 20.6 ov), 7-132 (Hogg, 24.4 ov), 8-139 (Hodge, 25.3 ov)

Bowling	O	M	R	W	Econ	
LE Plunkett	6	0	43	3	7.16	(2nb, 5w)
SI Mahmood	6	0	31	1	5.16	
A Flintoff	5	1	10	1	2.00	(1nb)
MS Panesar	2	0	15	0	7.50	
JWM Dalrymple	4	0	25	1	6.25	(1w)
PD Collingwood	4	0	26	2	6.50	

Toss England, who chose to bat first

Mad as a cut snake

ENGLAND, AFTERWARDS

FOUR weeks after returning to England after the ill-fated tour I was in hospital with a serious case of pneumonia. Coincidence? I think not. Cricket has always held sway over my emotions, a distinctly unhealthy state of affairs, and one that has no basis in rationality, yet that is how it is. The doctors may claim it was an infection, but in my mind it was psychosomatic, if somewhat delayed.

Another example. In 1974, aged 11, in the garden of the Sussex coastal bungalow that our family rented for two weeks every summer I was playing a 'Test match' against my elder brother, in which he had good-naturedly accepted his role as the Australians, in an era when they didn't always beat us. Bowling in the style of Tony Greig – his long, loping diagonal run-up could be completed by starting forward, and several yards to the right, of the jumper that marked the crease, running adjacent to the undergrowth encircling the playing area and then doubling back just before reaching the delivery stride – I induced an edge and my brother was caught behind by the hammock which served as Alan Knott and a small slip cordon.

I had barely finished my appeal when our dad called us in to watch the latest 20 minutes of live coverage on *Grandstand* of the real Test between England and Pakistan from the Oval.

As we were passing through the doorway he relayed the news that he had obviously got from Frank Bough that Knott had just got out. I never tired of watching Knottie, proudly regarding him as the best wicketkeeper in the world even when measured against the brilliance of Rod Marsh, and admiring the way his slight frame, propped in the crease in that slightly awkward open stance, defied the fastest, biggest and nastiest fast bowlers. But I was infuriated. My young mind, unsure where to direct its anger, picked on the nearest thing: my brother, who was following me into the front room, whom I turned to and kicked viciously on the shin.

The problem in Australia, obviously, was that I knew it was no longer acceptable to kick. I was 43 after all, and we all have to grow up some time. It meant that the anger, the frustration, the discontent and the disappointment had had nowhere to go until it metamorphosed into a big broiling bundle of bacteria, that finally found a home in my left lung.

I suppose I could have taken the advice of one correspondent who wrote on the blog after the Adelaide débacle. He proposed a five point plan for getting over the disappointment of England's defeat:

1 *Build a time machine*
2 *Travel back in time*
3 *Convince your great great grandfather to nick an apple*
4 *Dob him in to the constabulary and make sure he gets a free boat trip courtesy of the King*

5 Be reborn as an Australian and bask in the sunshine and glory of being a member of the world's number one sporting nation.

It was an option, but I thought, on reflection, I'd rather stay a whingeing Pom.

GLOSSARY OF AUSTRALIAN TERMS

If It Was Raining Palaces, I'd Get Hit by the Dunny Door
Always unlucky, even when things seem to be going well

She'll Be Right
Don't worry, everything will turn out fine

Done Like a Dinner
Get badly beaten in a fight, or sporting contest

Happy as a bastard on Father's Day
Obviously, not best pleased

The middle of the bloody day and not a bone in the truck
A lot of effort expended for little reward

Up and down like a bride's nightie
A period of changeable fortunes

As miserable as a bandicoot
Extremely pissed off, although there is no definitive zoological evidence to suggest bandicoots are any more miserable than other small furry marsupials

Walking the wallaby trail
The path to oblivion, often to the interior of Australia, taken by failures

Better than a poke in the eye with a burnt stick
Things have turned out better than expected, but in an unusual way

Mad as a cut snake
Angry, crazy, you name it: a cut snake is even more upset than a whole one